Understanding the Iglesia ni Cristo

What They Really Believe and
How They Can Be Reached

Anne C. Harper

Foreword by Dr. Joseph Shao

WIPF & STOCK · Eugene, Oregon

Wipf and Stock Publishers
199 W 8th Ave, Suite 3
Eugene, OR 97401

Understanding the Iglesia Ni Cristo
What They Really Believe and How They Can Be Reached
By Harper, Anne C.
Copyright©2014 APTS Press
ISBN 13: 978-1-5326-3399-7
Publication date 5/31/2017
Previously published by APTS Press, 2014

This edition is published by Wipf and Stock Publishers
under license from APTS Press.

Publisher's Preface

We are pleased to introduce this third volume of the APTS Press Monograph Series. As the author mentions in her preface, this book is an abridged edition of her doctoral dissertation, which she completed at the Asia Graduate School of Theology—Philippines (www.agstphil.org) in 2011. The purpose of this series is to give our readers broader access to academic scholarship that would otherwise be unavailable outside of the academic community. This is part of our ongoing commitment to discipleship through publishing.

The other two monographs in this series, *Theology in Context: A Case Study in the Philippines*, by Dr. Dave Johnson and *Leave a Legacy: Increasing Missionary Longevity*, by Dr. Russ Turney, are now available. For information on where to purchase these and other APTS Press books, please contact us through our website, www.apts.edu.

We hope you enjoy the book.

THE PUBLISHER

Author's Preface

I began my journey with the Iglesia ni Cristo in 1994 when we first arrived in Manila as academic missionaries to the Philippines. I immediately noticed their beautiful chapels throughout Metro Manila and asked about them. Other missionaries in our agency, Blair and Debbie Skinner, had collected some of the publications of the group and showed them to me.

The lifestyle and teachings of the group fascinated me. So for 20 years I have read their monthly publication, *Pasugo*, and any other publication with information about them, and interacted with numerous members and those who have left the group. In 2005 I began doctoral work and chose to focus my research on this church. Six years later I graduated after submitting "The Iglesia ni Cristo: A Case Study of a New Religious Movement and Exploration of Culturally Appropriate Outreach Methodologies" as my dissertation.

This monograph is an edited version of that dissertation for the Filipino evangelical audience. Sections dealing with culture and values, background information on New Religious Movements and a number of appendices have been deleted due to space limitations and the expected audience for this book.

My desire and, I believe, God's desire is to see members of the Iglesia ni Cristo discover the true Christ, both God and human, and experience the freedom of forgiven sins and the empowering of the Holy Spirit. I pray that those reading this book will catch God's heart and use their creativity in reaching out to these people so that we may rejoice with them in heaven. *"Because of our love for you we were ready to share with you not only the Good News from God but even our own lives. You were so dear to us!"*—1 Thess. 2:8 (GNT)

Anne C. Harper, D.Miss.
Quezon City
June 2014

Foreword

New religious movements normally either start out as a new movement to their followers or as a reaction to existing church beliefs. The intention of any new religious movement would be good, as viewed by its leaders and followers. For non-followers, they might have different opinions. As evangelicals, we normally approach any new religious movement by non-involvement or by being defensive with direct confrontation.

The Iglesia ni Cristo is a new religious movement that anyone who lives in the Philippines and anywhere beyond Asia with Filipino populations should understand. With its beautiful sanctuaries and its church buildings with similar edifices throughout the world, many will be attracted to the outward features of the church. The Iglesia ni Cristo has passed its test of continuity from her founder to her third-generation leader. With various labor disputes and complaints in the Philippines, many industries and chain stores are hiring this group's members because of their close-knit obedient relationships with church leaders. Even some evangelical churches have hired Iglesia ni Cristo members to work as janitors and drivers because of their faithful characters. By the command of their great leader, the Iglesia ni Cristo is quite strong in politics with solid bloc voting for selected candidates or a particular political party. With rewards given to this new religious movement, its members have become influential leaders in the marketplace, higher education, the judiciary, and even governance in the public arena.

This is an important and interesting book on the Iglesia ni Cristo. The author has done extensive research in the primary sources of this religious movement in the Philippines in her doctoral dissertation. She continues to teach a course on this and has benefited from interaction with the input of her students. It is a scholarly book with its comprehensive understanding of the movement and practical with its case studies. It is a balanced book, both for the novice, as well as those who care for the members of the Iglesia ni Cristo. In reading the book, the reader will be exposed to the formation and growth of the Iglesia ni Cristo. The belief system is presented in a readable manner. The church culture of the Iglesia ni Cristo is discussed with its intersection with existing Philippine culture.

Filipinos are now in at least 200 nations in the world. With globalization, this book will give you an understanding of a very special phenomenon in the Philippines. For missiological concern, by following the recommendations of the author, some churches may want to re-think their creative way of worship or even their solemn teaching of Bible.

We hope that this book will be a blessing to the critical thinker of theology, the fervent seeker of truth and the passionate Christian worker.

Dr. Joseph Shao
General Secretary, Asia Theological Association

Acknowledgments

I am deeply indebted to many people who assisted me during the course of this lengthy study, and it would be impossible to acknowledge and thank them all. However, a few names stand out.

First, I am grateful for my dissertation advisor, Dr. James Chancellor, *W. O. Carver Professor of Christian Missions and World Religions at the Southern Baptist Theological Seminary*, for bearing with me during delays caused by several continental moves and illnesses. His knowledge and guidance were invaluable in broadening my understanding of New Religious Movements and their members. Dr. J. Gordon Melton, Director of the Center for the Study of American Religion, graciously served as mentor for two of my D. Miss. research tutorials. I also thank Dr. Timoteo D. Gener, Professor of Theology at and President of Asian Theological Seminary, for serving as outside reader, and Dr. Larry Caldwell, Director of the Doctor of Missiology Program at Asia Graduate School of Theology-Philippines for encouraging me to pursue study of the Iglesia ni Cristo in doctoral work.

Editors Frank McNelis and Dave Johnson offered very helpful guidance in editing and reducing my original dissertation into a form suitable for this monograph.

I could not have accomplished this work without the indulgence of administrators and colleagues at Action International Ministries and Evangelical Theological Seminary, Osijek, Croatia, who encouraged me to pursue doctoral work and allowed me the necessary time to pursue this research.

John Morehead and colleagues serving with me on the Lausanne 2004 Forum Group Sixteen gave invaluable insights, feedback and discussion.

A number of Filipino colleagues assisted me in finding former members of the group to interview: Pastors Jun Divierte, Roberto de Fiesta, R.G. Foncardas, Fernando Lua, Leonardo Tan, and

Joselito Zafra. I am greatly appreciative of the former Iglesia ni Cristo members I interviewed for their candor and vulnerability. They helped me gain major insights for parts of this book. My students at several schools were invaluable in allowing me to test run some of my ideas, and they also assisted me with observations and gathering first-hand information.

Dr. Timothy C. Tennent, formerly Professor of Missions at Gordon-Conwell Theological Seminary and now President of Asbury Theological Seminary, spurred my interest in anthropological study of different cultures and gave helpful feedback on some of my earliest insights and writing about the Iglesia ni Cristo.

Action missionaries Blair and Debbie Skinner began the work of collecting materials published by the Iglesia ni Cristo back in the 1990s and graciously allowed me access to them. Their work on the teachings of the group served as a catalyst for me to initially begin studying the group.

Finally, I thank my family for their support and prayers. While growing up in the Philippines my daughters Ruth and Meg bore the embarrassment of a mother who was always stopping to talk to "strangers" about their experiences in the Iglesia ni Cristo. My husband has stood with me over the many years of study and research—cooking meals, doing housework, and being a sounding board for my observations and ideas. He lightened my work load, lifted my spirits in times of discouragement, and sharpened my thinking.

DEDICATION

To my husband George
with love and thankfulness for our journey together
over thirty-six years
in three continents
serving the Lord Jesus Christ.

Abbreviations

CEM	Chief Executive Minister of the Iglesia ni Cristo
CEM	College of Evangelical Ministry
CWS	Children's Worship Service
DEM	Deputy Executive Minister of the Iglesia ni Cristo
GEM	Grand Evangelical Mission
IEMELIF	Iglesia Evangelica Metodista en las Filipinas
INC	Iglesia ni Cristo
KKK	Kataastaasang Kagalanggalangang Katipunan Ng Mga Bayan (Highest and Most Respected Sons of the People)
NEU	New Era University
NRM	New Religious Movement
PNK	Pagsamba ng Kabataan ("Children's Worship Service")
SDA	Seventh-Day Adventist
WCG	The Worldwide Church of God, now called Grace Communion International

Contents

Chapter 1	Introduction	1
Chapter 2	Understanding the Iglesia ni Cristo as a New Religious Movement	5
Chapter 3	The Formation and Growth of the Iglesia ni Cristo	17
Chapter 4	The Belief System of the Iglesia ni Cristo	35
Chapter 5	The Influence of Filipino Cultural Values on the Beliefs of the Iglesia ni Cristo	63
Chapter 6	The Iglesia ni Cristo— A Distinct Culture: Part I	77
Chapter 7	The Iglesia ni Cristo— A Distinct Culture: Part II	105
Chapter 8	Missiological Research on Culturally Appropriate Strategies and Methodologies	129
Chapter 9	Case Studies	159
Chapter 10	Recommendations	181
Appendix A		195
Index		198
References Cited		200

Chapter I

INTRODUCTION

When my family and I arrived in the Philippines in 1994, we immediately noticed the beautiful Iglesia ni Cristo chapels which towered above the Manila landscape. When we asked about them, we were told three things repeatedly by missionaries and Filipino Evangelical Christians:

- That the Iglesia ni Cristo was a *cult* which *worshipped* its founder, Felix Manalo,
- That its members were primarily poor, and they were *forced* to give significant parts of their meager incomes to the group,
- That members wanted to be in their church buildings when Jesus returned and the rapture occurred because the *buildings would rise in the air* and be placed in the New Jerusalem.

I became curious. As we continued to live in the Philippines, several other discoveries and experiences spurred me to begin and then continue research on the Iglesia ni Cristo.

I discovered that the three pieces of information I had been told repeatedly about the group during our early weeks in the Philippines were not true yet widely believed by Evangelicals: the Iglesia ni Cristo does *not* worship Felix Manalo but does hold him in high regard. Church members are *not* forced to give large amounts of money. They are encouraged to give to the Lord and the church in similar ways as Evangelical churches. Also, the Iglesia ni Cristo does *not* currently teach that their chapels will rise in the air upon Christ's return.

As I read materials written by Evangelicals about the group, I saw that almost all were out of date and hostile, focusing on areas of disagreement rather than attempting to communicate and convert. The most recent academic work had been done in the late 1960s and early 1970s. That material is 45 to 55 years old now! There is nothing describing the group as it exists today a century since its beginnings in 1914.

I also had a number of experiences, which contributed to my desire to discover more about the Iglesia ni Cristo. We had a gardener for a number of years who worked for us once a week and on other days for other missionaries. He was a member of the Iglesia ni Cristo. No one had spoken with him about his faith or their faith because as a member of the Iglesia ni Cristo he was perceived as unreachable. At one of my mission's field conferences when a fellow missionary heard I was studying the Iglesia ni Cristo, he reacted with a 20-minute diatribe about not wasting energy on trying to reach members because they were horrible, Satan-controlled people and therefore "unreachable."

On one vacation, our family was driving up to Baguio. When we reached Tarlac, we'd been driving for 6 hours and hadn't seen another white person. We went into a McDonald's restaurant to have some food, and I saw two young men in white shirts with black badges who were obviously Mormon missionaries. I went over and greeted them. They were homesick, and so happy to see other Americans. When they discovered we were missionaries, they were shocked that we were speaking with them and friendly. Their experience with other missionaries had been bad—they had been treated with extreme dislike or else ignored by them.

My reaction to these discoveries and experiences was sorrow. How could members of the Iglesia ni Cristo or other New Religious Movements ever hear the Good News if they were perceived as unreachable and if what they were seeing and experiencing from Evangelicals was not the love of Christ but disdain and judgment?

My initial investigation of the group led me to believe that the Iglesia ni Cristo is hostile towards the Christian message because this has not been presented in a relational way. Attempts at communication have focused primarily on proclaiming "the truth," debunking false doctrine. Since Filipino culture is a relational culture, that form of the Christian message has not been well received.

Further, through my study and interaction with Iglesia ni Cristo members and former members, I've realized that the Iglesia ni Cristo, though strongly influenced by Philippine culture, has a distinct culture of its own. In order to effectively communicate with members, we need to understand their distinct worldview and values.

I hope that this book, which is an abridged version of my doctoral dissertation,[1] will enable that community to gain a better understanding of the group and therefore become better equipped to reach out to members of the Iglesia ni Cristo in contextual ways that can more readily be received and embraced.

The Iglesia ni Cristo has spread throughout the world, with congregations in forty-three U.S. states, six Canadian provinces and eighty-eight other foreign nations and territories. A realistic estimate of their number is about three million, though estimates have run as high as seven million. They are a significant unreached people group for which the evangelical community has no intentional evangelistic strategy. Evangelicals need to learn about the group and devise appropriate methods to reach them with the Gospel. Wouldn't the angels rejoice if many came into a saving

---

[1] Anne Catherine Harper, "The Iglesia ni Cristo: A Study of a New Religious Movement and Exploration of Culturally Appropriate Outreach Methodologies," dissertation presented to Asia Graduate School of Theology, 54 Scout Madrinan, South Triangle, Quezon City, Philippines on February 7, 2011.

knowledge of Christ as the group reaches its 100-year-old mark in 2014?

How can we help the evangelical community see the large people group of the Iglesia ni Cristo as unreached neighbors and not as cultists to be feared? Please read this book. Do not expect to find a point-by-point refutation of Iglesia ni Cristo teachings at odds with orthodox Christianity. Other books have already done this and some of them do it very well.[2] Instead, come expecting to learn about the history, worldview and activities of the Iglesia ni Cristo with the aim of understanding its members and discovering culturally-appropriate bridges for the Gospel to enter this group. Ask the Lord of the Harvest to bring you into contact and friendship with members of the Iglesia ni Cristo, and ask Him to enlarge your heart towards them. Pray. Ask others to join you in prayer that many would clearly hear and receive the Good News.

---

[2] I recommend Alex Wilson and Christine Tetley, *Witnessing to the Cults: A Practical Study Course for Christian Workers* (Parañaque City, Philippines: Church Strengthening Ministry of Foreign Mission Board, SBC, Inc., 1985) which is available from The Conservative Baptist Extension Seminary Training, PO Box 1882, Manila, Philippines, and Donald L. Platt, *Counterfeit?* (Manila, Philippines: OMF Literature, 1981).

CHAPTER 2

UNDERSTANDING THE IGLESIA NI CRISTO AS A NEW RELIGIOUS MOVEMENT

To fully understand the Iglesia ni Cristo, it is important to recognize that it is a New Religious Movement. New Religious Movement (NRM) is a sociological term. In times of social change, especially rapid social change, these movements often emerge around a prophetic or messianic figure. Often they are attempts at cultural continuity because a society is demoralized by the influx of new ideas or a different worldview or religion.[1] The groups meet emotional, social and adaptation needs in a variety of ways. They may offer a sense of identity and security, they may provide unity and confirmation of cultural values, or they may offer the answers people need in trying to understand their experiences during the cultural upheaval.[2]

Sociological and anthropological studies are particularly helpful in understanding the nature of these groups. Sociologists Rodney Stark and Williams Sims Bainbridge note that the rise of these movements is a "normal" response to social change.[3] Many NRMs have arisen over the course of history, but not all have survived and become institutionalized as the Iglesia ni Cristo has.

---

[1] Lorne L. Dawson, *Comprehending the Cults: The Sociology of New Religious Movements* (New York, NY: Oxford University Press, 1998), 65.
[2] John A. Saliba, *Understanding New Religious Movements* (Grand Rapids, MI: Eerdmans, 1995), 118-121.
[3] Rodney Stark and William Sims Bainbridge, *A Theory of Religion* (New Brunswick, NJ: Rutgers University Press, 1987), 155-193. Sociologist James A. Beckford, ed., *New Religious Movements and Rapid Social Change* (London: Sage Publications/UNESCO, 1986), vii, xii, agrees with this assessment.

The late 1800s and early 1900s saw much political and social upheaval in the Philippines. This was due to the rapid increase in the exchange of ideas from Europe, the quest for freedom and self-government, and the change from Spanish to American control over the islands. Sectarian movements arose such as the Anglipayan church, IEMELIF (*Iglesia Evangelica Metodista en las Filipinas*), which was a split from the Methodist church in the Philippines, and the Iglesia ni Cristo.

New Religious Movements often grow through population shifts.[4] The Filipino diaspora has enabled the rapid and pervasive spread of the Iglesia ni Cristo to North America and to all continents but Antarctica.

J. Gordon Melton offers an important observation about these groups. He describes them as being on the "fringes" and in the "contested places" of society. They differ significantly from the dominant or tradition religion of society from which they spring. They propose radical innovations to what are considered essential beliefs and practices, and they are so different that they are "unacceptably different" to people of their surrounding culture.[5] This is certainly true of the Iglesia ni Cristo. The group's teachings and lifestyle have put it at odds with much of "normal" Philippine Roman Catholic culture. They do not participate in barangay activities like fiestas because these center around worship and adoration of saints, veneration of the Virgin Mary or views of Christ, such as the Santo Niño, which they consider unbiblical. Members do not eat an important food, *dinuguan*, because it

---

[4]J. Gordon Melton, "Introduction: When Prophets Die: The Succession Crisis in New Religions," in *When Prophets Die: The Postcharismatic Fate of New Religious Movements*, ed. Timothy Miller (Albany, NY: State University of New York Press, 1991), 7-8.

[5]J. Gordon Melton, "Introducing and Defining the Concept of a New Religion," in *Teaching New Religious Movements*, ed. David G. Bromley (Oxford: Oxford University Press, 2007), 33, 35. Also J. Gordon Melton, "Towards a Definition of 'New Religion,'" *Nova Religio* 8, 1 (July 2004): 73, 75, 79.

contains blood. Members have a stronger allegiance to their church than to family members who are outside the church. They don't celebrate Christmas, which is a major season for Filipinos. All of these put the group and its members at odds with prevailing Philippine culture.

New Religious Movements are radically different from orthodox religions. They often combine bits and pieces from a variety of religious traditions.[6] The combination and influence of a number of Protestant denominations as well as Roman Catholicism is evident in the structure and teachings of the Iglesia ni Cristo. They are a reflection of Felix Manalo's spiritual journey through five denominations, which is discussed in more detail in the next chapter. For example, the influence of the Roman Catholic Church is seen in the style of authority invested in leadership, males only in leadership, Felix Manalo's infallibility, and the necessity of the church itself, baptism and Holy Communion (Santa Cena) for salvation. The idea that a holy God who cannot be approached directly comes from folk Catholicism. A number of Manalo's convictions come from his involvement with Mision Cristiana, the Christian Mission of the Disciples of Christ: baptism by immersion as essential for salvation, primitivism, the claim that the true church disappeared with the death of the apostles and has now reappeared, the importance of the name "Church of Christ," not celebrating Christmas, claiming to speak only where the Bible speaks and be silent where the Bible is silent, limited atonement only for members of the group, and stress on performance that is works, which are necessary for salvation. The importance of the Bible comes from general Protestantism. From Seventh Day Adventism Manalo learned the importance of the Bible and prophecy, the importance of the Sabbath, food restrictions,

---

[6]Irving Hexham and Karla Poewe see NRMS as global cultures. These groups choose strands from different religious traditions and weave them together to form a new religion. Irving Hexham and Karla Poewe, *New Religions as Global Cultures: Making the Human Sacred* (Boulder, CO: Westview Press, 1986), 37.

emphasis on the Second Coming of Christ and Felix Manalo as the final messenger as Ellen White's role as messenger to the Adventists.

New Religious Movements, in contrast to ethnic religions, actively and even aggressively attempt to gain new members from their surrounding cultures. This is certainly true of the Iglesia ni Cristo. Its monthly magazine, *Pasugo,* highlights its evangelistic activities throughout the world.

Sociologist James Beckworth notes some additional elements that New Religious Movements share: they allow people to be involved more fully in the performance of religious activities, and they encourage people to apply their spirituality to everyday life.[7] As described further in later chapters, these are characteristics of the Iglesia ni Cristo.

NRMs set clear boundaries between who is "in" and who is "out," and they perceive themselves as elite, special or chosen. Often their members are not tied to each other because of family, religious or cultural heritage, but because of shared commitment to the group, its beliefs and its cause. They readily oust those not following expectations/rules, and they demand total allegiance.[8] Those joining the Iglesia ni Cristo must undergo a lengthy process (described in more detail in a later chapter) and receive a new identity in the true church. They are the "flock" of Christ.

NRMs often share other elements in common, most notably a charismatic founder who has special status because of a sacred myth. These leaders may be prophets claiming revelations, which serve as legitimation for their authority and the formation of the movements. Often he or she assumes a new name, title or identity, which has spiritual meaning.[9] Hexham notes this is often iconic

---

[7]Beckford, *New Religious Movements and Rapid Social Change,* xii.
[8]Saliba, *Understanding New Religious Movements,* 114, 115. See also George D. Chryssides, *Exploring New Religions* (London: Cassell, 1999), 5.
[9]David G. Bromley. "Teaching New Religious Movements/Learning from New Religious Movements," in *Teaching New Religious Movements,* ed. David

leadership; that is, the person is seen as a real life, concrete "representation of the holy."[10] Felix Manalo has a special status as the Last Messenger of God based on Revelation 7.

The period following the death of this charismatic leader is a critical one. If adequate structures have been put in place and leadership trained, the transfer to this new administrative leadership is more likely to be successful. This results in the continuation of the movement, and most often, its institutionalization. Timothy Miller and J. Gordon Melton note that the New Religious Movements that do survive this transition will become stable institutions because power passes to new leadership.[11] The Iglesia ni Cristo has passed this test.

Another common characteristic is the role of salvation or restoration myths, which give a special status or role to the group. In movements rising out of the Christian tradition, such as the Iglesia ni Cristo, these myths most often claim to restore the church to its original, uncorrupted or true form. The group claims to be the reemergence of the true church. These stories may also offer the group's answers to the problems of the world.[12]

Susan Palmer and David Bromley point out that these myths are usually "oppositional" in character because they aggressively refute the myths, which legitimize the institution of the host culture: "In short, NRMs and their charismatic leaders pose a challenge to the status quo."[13] The Iglesia ni Cristo's restoration myth is an attack on the Roman Catholic Church and the Council

---

G. Bromley (Oxford: Oxford University Press, 2007), 13. See also Saliba, *Understanding*, 114.

[10]Hexham, *Global*, 57.

[11]Timothy Miller, ed., *When Prophets Die: The Postcharismatic Fate of New Religious Movements* (Albany, NY: State University of New York Press, 1991), vii, 8.

[12]Bromley, "Teaching," 13.

[13]Susan J. Palmer and David G. Bromley, "Deliberate Heresies: New Religious Myths and Rituals as Critiques," in *Teaching New Religious Movements*, ed. David G. Bromley (Oxford: Oxford University Press, 2007), 136.

of Nicea when the doctrine of the Trinity was clarified. The Council was the point, they claim, at which the true church disappeared. Now, through the message of the angel Felix Y. Manalo and the Iglesia ni Cristo, the one true Church of Christ has been restored.

Many New Religious Movements teach Scripture with a predetermined interpretation in order to give credence to their authority claims and "illuminate" the teachings of the group.[14] A proof-texting approach is also common. This is seen repeatedly in Iglesia ni Cristo teachings which often take Bible verses out of context, and also their reliance on multiple Bible translations in order to get just the "right" wording to prove their teaching.

Finally, a high level of tension with the surrounding culture is one of the most important features of a New Religious Movement and a key component in its continuing existence and success.

Why People Join NRMs

Why do people join New Religious Movements? The unspoken assumption of an apologetical approach is that they join because of a NRM's belief system. If we can only show them how false those beliefs are, it is assumed they will want to turn to the truth. In reality, most people do not join a NRM because of its belief system. They join for a myriad of reasons, which will be discussed below. Jan Karel van Baalen wrote as early as 1958 that "More and more I have come to the conclusion that we can learn from the cultists, not only noting what not to believe, but also bearing in mind that cults are the unpaid bills of the Church."[15]

What are those unpaid bills? Colin Snee, Provost of Southwark Cathedral in London argues from his experience and research that

---

[14] Colin Snee, "New Religious Movements and the Churches," in *New Religious Movements: Challenge and Response*, ed. Bryan Wilson and Jaime Cresswell (New York: Routledge, 1999), 175.

[15] Jan Karel Van Baalen, *The Chaos of the Cults: A Study of Present-Day Isms* (Grand Rapids, MI: Eerdmans, 1958), 14.

mainstream churches have failed those who join New Religious Movements in four ways: "teaching," "instruction," "commitment," and "acknowledgement of complexity."[16] Former college chaplain and longtime pastor Harold Busséll, notes that some contemporary New Religious Movements (such as Jim Jones's People's Temple) have been started by or have attracted primarily evangelical Christians. Why? Because the evangelical church has revered the "wrong" signs of spirituality, such as:

- Spiritual testimonies based on dramatic conversions, rather than the outworking of the gospel in people's lives (fruits of the Spirit, transformation into Christ's image);
- Leading ("the Lord led me"), teaching or phrasing which sounds spiritual, but is not biblical (in other words, it has not been evaluated against the whole of Scripture);
- The importance of being a New Testament church or an "ideal" Christian community;
- Acceptance of packaged and attractive preaching and answers to life's questions and problems without critical thinking, and allowing leaders to have inordinate authority and power in their lives;
- Legalism (for example, specific behavioral taboos, such as not drinking, smoking or attending dances as measures of spirituality);
- Focus on one aspect of Scripture such as biblical prophecy, spiritual experiences or doctrine without warmth and community.[17]

John Lofland and Rodney Stark extensively studied one New Religious Movement, the Unification Church, looking particularly at why and how people joined the group. From their research, they proposed a seven-step process now known as the Lofland-Stark

---

[16]Snee, "New Religious Movements and Churches," 171.
[17]Harold L. Busséll, *Unholy Devotion* (Grand Rapids, MI: Zondervan, 1983).

Model of Conversion. According to their model, movement from potential interest to full-fledged commitment and incorporation involves seven significant turning points or aspects:

[For] persons to convert to a cult they must:

(1) experience enduring, acutely felt tensions in their lives,
(2) within a religious problem-solving perspective (as opposed to a psychiatric or political problem-solving perspective),
(3) which leads them to think of themselves as religious seekers. With these three 'predisposing conditions' in place, the individuals must then
(4) encounter the cult to which they convert at a turning point in their lives,
(5) form an affective bond with one or more members of the cult,
(6) reduce or eliminate extra-cult attachments, and
(7) be exposed to intensive interaction with other converts.[18]

In this model, if one of the conditions fails to materialize conversion will not take place.[19]

A number of studies of other New Religious Movements have tested this model with mixed results.[20] However, Dawson concludes that the "research consistently [has] confirmed some of these 'conditions' and led to the formulation of systematic reasons why they may vary."[21]

---

[18]Dawson, *Comprehending*, 78.
[19]*Ibid.* "It is the cumulative effect of all these experiences. . . .that produces a true conversion. Each step is necessary, but only the whole process is sufficient to produce a true conversion."
[20]*Ibid.*, 78-80.
[21]*Ibid.*, 79.

Looking for common threads in specific case studies of New Religious Movements, sociologist Lorne Dawson proposes some "empirical insights" into how and why members join:

- Recruitment happens primarily through existing social networks and relationships;
- "Affective bonds," relationships with those already in the group, are an important factor leading to deeper involvement;
- "Intensive interaction" between recruits and group members is necessary for both recruiting and keeping membership;
- "Fewer and weaker extra-cult social ties," that is, social relationships and commitments outside the group, are not strong or are eliminated;
- "Fewer and weaker ideological alignments," that is, recruits do not have a strong faith commitment and belief system before joining;

Dawson believes that conversion is a rational choice. People join New Religious Movements for the same reasons other religious people follow their own faiths: "to live in a meaningful and orderly world."[22] Further, he argues that it "is their social circumstances, including the pervasive failure of conventional religions to keep a vibrant sense of the transcendent or supernatural alive in our societies," which results in the attractiveness of these groups.[23]

The work of Group Sixteen on "Religious and Non-Religious Spirituality in the West" from the Lausanne Forum in 2004 highlights this need for the transcendent:

- One way of looking at the New Spiritualties is to see them as an attempt to fill the world with a new sense of spiritual wonder, mystery and vitality. Many feel disillusioned with the heartbeat of

---

[22] *Ibid.*, 159.
[23] *Ibid.*, 160.

modernity-based ideas where the world is reduced to non-spiritual explanations.[24]

- A part of that mystery is the charismatic leader who often claims a special prophetic voice. In the first generation of a movement, Irving Hexham and Karla Poewe, a sociologist-anthropologist team, note the importance of a potential convert's interaction with the charismatic leader. These numinous experiences are often life-changing encounters in which they feel as though they are "participating in the divine."[25]

In addition to this need for transcendence, George Chryssides and Margaret Wilkins propose several other reasons why people join New Religious Movements:

- The need to belong
- The search for answers
- The search for wholeness
- The search for cultural identity
- The need to feel special
- The need for spiritual guidance
- The need for vision
- The need to be involved.[26]

---

[24]Philip Johnson, Anne C. Harper and John W. Morehead, eds, *Religious and Non-Religious Spirituality in the Western World ("New Age")*, Lausanne Occasional Papers, No. 45, General ed. David Clayton (Sydney: Lausanne Committee and Morling Press, 2004), 24.

[25]Hexham, *Global*, 55, 57.

[26]George W. Chryssides and Margaret Z. Wilkins, *A Reader in New Religious Movements* (London: Continuum, 2006), 339.

Summarizing Comments

The Iglesia Cristo is a New Religious Movement which started as a small seed in Manila, Philippines, and has grown to become an international movement with branches throughout the world. The challenge before us in the evangelical church is to apply the lens of New Religious Movement in studying the group, its members and their worldview so that we can communicate the whole gospel to them in a way they will understand and embrace. The chapters following will utilize missiological tools in analyzing the group and searching for appropriate strategies to reach them with the gospel.

CHAPTER 3

THE FORMATION AND GROWTH OF THE IGLESIA NI CRISTO

The Iglesia ni Cristo arose in the Philippines in the early 1900s. This chapter examines the formation and early growth of the group. We begin with a short note on the Philippine context into which Felix Y. Manalo, the man instrumental in forming this church, was born and raised.

The Environment

From 1565-1898, Spain had control of the Philippine islands and they brought with them a form of Spanish Catholicism that Peter Brown calls "the cult of the saints."[1] This led to a folk Catholicism in which Filipinos had absorbed the symbols of Roman Catholicism and maintained their animistic understanding of a high God far removed from people. As a result they could not have direct access to God, but needed the priests and other intermediaries such as the saints or the Virgin Mary to reach and contact God.

The late 1800s and early 1900s saw rapid changes in the Philippines. The political turnover from Spanish to American

---

[1] For a detailed description of the practices and beliefs of this "cult of the saints," see Peter Brown, *The Cult of the Saints: Its Rise and Function in Latin Christianity* (Chicago, IL: University of Chicago Press, 1982) and William A. Christian, Jr., *Local Religion in Sixteenth Century Spain* (Princeton, NJ: Princeton University Press, 1981). For a discussion of the "Filipinization" of Spanish Catholicism see John L. Phelan, *The Hispanization of the Philippines: Spanish Aims and Filipino Responses 1565-1700* (Madison, WI: The University of Wisconsin Press, 1959).

control in 1898 had a profound impact in a number of areas, which are important to understanding the formation of the Iglesia ni Cristo. The American occupation brought dynamic social change to the Philippines in many areas: political, economic, religious and educational. Church historian Arthur Tuggy points out that one of the most important contributions of the U.S. to the Philippines was an educational system that opened new opportunities to the masses.[2] Church Historian Anne Kwantes notes three important differences between the Spanish and American approaches to the Filipino people. The first was the American perspective on the separation of church and state. Missionaries bringing the Protestant gospel to the Philippines at this time believed and ministered from this perspective. The second was the desire to provide medical care to the common people, not just the upper classes. The third was the use of qualifications such as education and technological skill, rather than race or relationship, to choose leaders. This was a vast change from the Spanish way of structuring society and filling jobs.[3]

Prior to American control the Roman Catholic Church held a stranglehold not only on the religious life of Filipinos but their social life as well. American dominance opened the way for Protestant missionaries to come to the Philippines, and with them came a new source of religious authority: the Bible. Prior to American control, Bibles were not allowed in the Philippines. Also, these missionaries brought an understanding of God as accessible without the use of intermediaries.

Felix Y. Manalo was profoundly influenced by these Western missionaries and the forms of Christianity and the Bible which they brought.

---

[2]Arthur Tuggy, *The Philippine Church: Growth in a Changing Society* (Grand Rapids, MI: William B. Eerdmans Publishing Company, 1971), 85.

[3]Anne C. Kwantes, *Presbyterian Missionaries in the Philippines: Conduits of Social Change: (1989-1910)* (Quezon City, Philippines: New Day Publishers, 1989), 4-5.

Felix Y. Manalo

There are a number of sources of information about Felix Manalo's life. Most draw on the major study by Julita Reyes Sta. Romana published in 1955[4] and a series of journal articles in 1955 and 1961 by Joseph J. Kavanaugh.[5] The Iglesia has published material on the life of Felix Manalo, most notably a biography by Dolores G. Garcia in its fiftieth anniversary commemorative publication.[6] Manuel Alonzo, Jr.'s research was published by the University of Sto. Thomas in 1959.[7] Other major works include Arthur Leonard Tuggy's doctoral research published in 1976, offering additional information and clarifications,[8] and, from a Roman Catholic perspective, Fernando O. Elesterio's book,[9] which draws primarily on Sta. Romana's study. Material by Albert J. Sanders in Gerald Anderson's book looking at the church in the Philippines also draws on Sta. Romana's work.[10] Religious historian

---

[4] Julita Reyes Sta. Romana, "The Iglesia ni Cristo: A Study," *Journal of East Asiatic Studies*, 4, 3 (July 1955): 329-430.

[5] Joseph J. Kavanaugh, "The Iglesia ni Cristo," *Philippine Studies* 3, 1 (1955): 19-42; "The Stars that Fall—and Mr. Manalo," *Philippine Studies* 3, 3 (1955): 289-296; and "Survey," *Philippine Studies* 9, 4 (1961): 651-65.

[6] Dolores G. Garcia, "Felix Manalo: The Man and His Mission," in *50 Anibersaryo, 1914-1964*, Iglesia ni Cristo (Manila: Iglesia ni Cristo, July 1964), 179-183.

[7] Manuel Alonzo, Jr., *A Historico-Critical Study on the Iglesia ni Cristo* (Manila: UST Press, 1959).

[8] Arthur Leonard Tuggy, *The Iglesia ni Cristo: A Study in Independent Church Dynamics* (Quezon City: Conservative Baptist Publishing, Inc., 1976); also, A. Leonard Tuggy, "Iglesia ni Cristo: An Angel and His Church," in *Dynamic Religious Movements: Case Studies of Rapidly Growing Religious Movements Around the World*, ed. David J. Hesselgrave (Grand Rapids, MI: Baker Book House, 1978), 85-101; see also Hirofumi Ando, "A Study of the Iglesia ni Cristo: A Politico-Religious Sect in the Philippines," *Pacific Affairs* 42:334-345.

[9] Fernando O. Elesterio, *The Iglesia ni Cristo: Its Cristology and Ecclesiology* (Manila: Cardinal Bea Institute, Loyola School of Theology, Ateneo de Manila University, 1988).

[10] Albert J. Sanders, "An Appraisal of the Iglesia ni Cristo," in *Studies in Philippine Church History*, ed. Gerald H. Anderson, (Ithaca, NY: Cornell University Press, 1969), 350-36; Clymer, *Protestant Missionaries in the Philippines*. See also Bautista, "Colonization," 139-159.

Kenton Clymer examined denominational records and correspondence for his study of Protestantism in the Philippines during the early decades of the American occupation. That study sheds light on some areas which have been unclear, particularly Manalo's departure from the Seventh-Day Adventists.[11]

Manalo was born on May 10, 1886, in Tipas, Taguig, Rizal province, to the east of Manila. He was the first child of Mariano Ysagun, a fisherman and farmer, and Bonifacia Manalo, a devout Roman Catholic.[12] Both Sta. Romana and Alonzo indicate he was the first of two sons.[13] Kavanaugh and Garcia indicate he had a sister, Praxedes,[14] who was one year younger. His public education was only through the second or third grade.[15] When he was ten years old, his father died, and his mother became the sole breadwinner. Several years later while visiting his uncle, Father Mariano Borja, Felix found a Bible in the church. When his uncle came upon him reading it, he strongly chastised Felix. Discovering the Bible was the beginning of Felix's odyssey through several Protestant denominations and the founding of the Iglesia ni Cristo. Hungry for something the traditional Roman Catholic Church was not providing, he joined the initiation rites of the Mt. Banahaw Colorum sects. These were mysterious groups which met in mountain caves seeking to communicate directly with the Supreme Being. Felix soon discovered the voice was not that of God but merely another human being.[16]

In 1902, when Manalo was sixteen, he witnessed a debate between a Roman Catholic priest and a Protestant minister. The subject was whether worshipping images was scriptural. Given his

---

[11] Kenton J. Clymer, *Protestant Missionaries in the Philippines, 1898-1916: An Inquiry into the American Colonial Mentality* (Urbana, IL: University of Illinois Press, 1986).

[12] Sta. Romana, "Iglesia," 332.

[13] *Ibid.*; Alonzo, *Historico-Critical*, 5-6.

[14] Kavanaugh, "Iglesia," 21; Garcia, "Felix Manalo: The Man and His Mission," 180.

[15] Alonzo, *Historico-Critical*, 6.

[16] Garcia, "Felix Manalo: The Man and His Mission," 180.

upbringing in the Roman Catholic Church, he was surprised when the Protestant won the debate.[17] He began to investigate Protestantism, and in 1904, at age 18, he joined the Methodist Episcopal Church. After studying at the Methodist Theological Seminary he was named a pastor.[18] Shortly thereafter his mother became ill, and he returned to Rizal to be with her. He refused to allow last rites to be offered.[19] Following her death he took her name and used the first initial of his father's as his middle initial: Felix Y. Manalo.[20]

By 1905 Felix Manalo had returned to Manila to study at Ellinwood Bible Institute, the Presbyterian school. Some have noted this was because Ellinwood had better facilities than the Methodist school.[21] Following three-and-a-half years of study there, he decided to join the Mision Cristiana, the mission of the Disciples of Christ, and was baptized by immersion. At this point it should be noted that there is some confusion in the biographical works on Manalo. Garcia's biographical essay has Felix joining the Christian and Missionary Alliance (CMA) or the Churches of Christ (COC). However, the CMA was only working on the southernmost Philippine island of Mindanao, and the COC was not yet working in the Philippines. The Disciples were working on Luzon, and Manalo is noted in their denominational records.[22]

Designated an Evangelist by the Disciples, Felix studied another four years at Manila College of the Bible. It was there he came to know Disciples missionary Bruce Kershner, who was president and a professor at the school. Tuggy notes that Kershner

---

[17]Sta. Romana, "Iglesia," 332.
[18]Garcia, "Felix Manalo: The Man and His Mission," 180.
[19]Isabelo T. Crisostomo, "Remembering the Last Messenger of God, Felix Y. Manalo and the Iglesia ni
Cristo," *Pasugo Special Issue. 100th Birth Announcement of Felix Y. Manalo.* 38, 3, (May-June 1986): 5.
[20]Kavanaugh, "Iglesia," 21. "Manalo" means victory or triumph.
[21]Elesterio, *Iglesia*, 8-9; Garcia, "Felix Manalo: The Man and His Mission," 180.
[22]Tuggy, *Iglesia*, 27, 29, 30; Clymer, *Protestant*, 128.

was a significant person in Manalo's life, and they both had high opinions of each other.²³ During this time he married Tomasa Sereneo, and they had a son, Ricardo, who died young.²⁴ Sometime between 1911 and 1912 Felix attended a Bible study led by a Seventh-Day Adventist (SDA), intending to dispute the teachings. However, he was convinced by the missionary's arguments, converted and was baptized in the SDA church. Tuggy notes that some sources indicate Elder L.V. Finster personally converted him; though Elder Finster denies this.²⁵ He was, however, involved in training and discipling him. About this time Manalo's wife died of consumption. He became an instructor at the Bible Institute and was assigned to Malabon, Rizal, as a *mangagawa* ("worker").

In late 1912 Elder Finster was planning to go on furlough for a year. Manalo confided in him that he did not think he could work with Finster's replacement, Elbridge M. Adams, and submit to his authority. In early 1913 Manalo was accused of adultery and temporarily suspended.²⁶ He courted Honorata de Guzman and eloped with her on May 9. He was just shy of twenty-seven and Honorata was nineteen.²⁷ She was eventually to bear him two daughters and four sons.²⁸ He was again temporarily suspended, this time for eloping.²⁹ Clymer notes that elopement was not unusual during this time period; however, the mission did not approve of the marriage.³⁰ Despite this, Manalo and his wife moved to Malolos, Bulacan, where he was assigned as an Evangelist.³¹ In July of that year during the mission's annual training institute and conference, Manalo confessed to sins including working against

---

²³Tuggy, *Iglesia*, 28, 30.
²⁴Garcia, "Iglesia," 181.
²⁵Tuggy, *Iglesia*, 32.
²⁶Clymer, *Protestant*, 128.
²⁷Garcia, "Felix Manalo: The Man and His Mission," 181.
²⁸Alonzo, *Historico-Critical*, 8.
²⁹Tuggy, *Iglesia*, 34.
³⁰Clymer, *Protestant*, 128.
³¹Garcia, "Felix Manalo: The Man and His Mission," 181; Elesterio, *Iglesia*, 9.

Adams.[32] He also raised questions about SDA doctrine.[33] Mission administration required that he confess his sins publicly at the church in Malalos where he regularly preached. In Filipino culture this would have caused Manalo shame and loss of face, so it is not surprising that he avoided directly confessing sins and became defiant when pushed to be more specific. A week later he preached a sermon against the SDA doctrine of a Saturday Sabbath, and he left the SDA church.[34]

No longer in the ministry, Manalo returned to Manila and worked in a hat shop business he had previously started.[35] He began to associate with *mga pilosopo*, a derogatory name for freethinkers, agnostics and atheists. But when they deliberately misquoted the Bible he was offended and stopped meeting with them.[36] Manalo began his own intensive study of the Bible comparing Roman Catholic and Seventh-Day Adventist teachings.[37] He set "his goal [as] the end of religious disunity."[38] In November he closed himself in a room and asked his wife not to disturb him. After two days and three nights[39] his wife knocked on the door. At first annoyed, Manalo was surprised to discover how long he had been ensconced. He came out of the room convinced God had called him to start a new church, the Iglesia ni Cristo.[40]

---

[32]Clymer, *Protestant*, 128.
[33]Garcia, "Felix Manalo: The Man and His Mission," p. 181.
[34]Clymer, *Protestant*, 128.
[35]Sta. Romana, "Iglesia," 333.
[36]Garcia, "Felix Manalo: The Man and His Mission," 181; Tuggy, *Iglesia*, 34.
[37]Sta. Romana, "Iglesia," 333.
[38]Garcia, "Felix Manalo: The Man and His Mission," 181.
[39]*Ibid.,* 181; Tuggy, *Iglesia*, 41; and Elesterio, *Iglesia*, 41; all note two days and three nights. Sta. Romana says three days and three nights, "Iglesia," 333.
[40] Crisostomo, "Remembering," 7-8.

The Church's Early Years

Manalo began by preaching to four or five people in the workers' headquarters of the Atlantic Gulf and Pacific Company of Manila where old friends worked.[41] The first fourteen converts were baptized by immersion in the Pasig River.[42] He returned to Rizal province, preaching in Tipas. Garcia notes fierce persecution and few converts. However, the converted included several "Protestant ministers."[43] Manalo officially registered the Iglesia ni Cristo with the government on July 27, 1914.[44] This date was to hold special significance in later teaching about his special role as the "Last Messenger."

Seeing few converts, Manalo began to preach in Pulo, Rosario, and Pasig, then moved to Tondo, Manila, where small gatherings evolved into big assemblies with public debates. He was a charismatic preacher and effective debater, so these meetings began to attract more and more people. The first chapel was built in Tondo in 1915.[45]

As the movement grew in size, Manalo organized his first group of ministerial students, numbering thirteen. Some of these would become the "pillars of the church. . . .Some like Ora, Ponce and Basilico Santiago, would conspire to wreck it."[46]

Manalo's relationship with the Disciples must have remained strong due to his ties with Bruce Kershner: they honored him as an outstanding evangelist at a special ceremony on December 25, 1918. By 1919 the Iglesia ni Cristo had expanded into the Nueva Ecija and Pampanga provinces north of Manila, and in May the

---

[41]Garcia, "Felix Manalo: The Man and His Mission," 181. The Museum at the church's central complex has a series of well-done dioramas of this and other key events in Felix's ministry.
[42]Crisostomo, "Remembering," 8.
[43]Garcia, "Felix Manalo: The Man and His Mission," 181.
[44]Crisostomo, "Remembering," 9.
[45]Garcia, "Felix Manalo: The Man and His Mission," 181-182.
[46]Crisostomo, "Remembering," 9.

first ordination service for ministers was held.⁴⁷ Tuggy estimates the size of the Iglesia ni Cristo at that time as about 1,500. Felix Manalo traveled to the United States to study at the Pacific School of Religion in California.⁴⁸ On his return to Manila he discovered that rumors had been circulating about his moral integrity. He was confronted by some in leadership; Garcia's record of the incident is telling: "The evangelist maintained the invulnerability of the church doctrines, but he did not pretend to personal infallibility."⁴⁹ This led to the Ora rebellion in 1921, the first of several schisms in the group, which took a large portion the group's membership in one province.

The Iglesia ni Cristo survived the Ora schism, increasing in number where it already held a foothold and expanding into new provinces in Luzon farther north and south of Manila. By 1940 it had expanded into all of Luzon's provinces⁵⁰ and beyond Luzon into Mindoro Oriental and the Visayas Islands.⁵¹ A year later, in 1941, it had even reached Mindanao, the southernmost main island of the Philippines, when thirty church families moved into Cotabato as a group.⁵² The Iglesia ni Cristo now boasted 50,000 members.⁵³ World War II scattered people, including members of the Iglesia ni Cristo. This was used to the group's advantage following the War as Manalo enlisted them to evangelize in their home provinces.⁵⁴

---

⁴⁷*Ibid.*

⁴⁸Garcia claims he studied there for one year, but the school has no record of his attendance. Garcia, "Felix Manalo: The Man and His Mission," 181.

⁴⁹*Ibid.*, 182.

⁵⁰Tuggy, *Iglesia*, 61.

⁵¹Crisostomo, "Remembering," 10.

⁵²*Ibid.*

⁵³Robert R. Reed, "Migration as Mission: The Expansion of the Iglesia ni Cristo outside the Philippines," in *Patterns of Migration in Southeast Asia*, ed. Robert R. Reed (Berkeley, CA: University of California, 1990), 159; Sta. Romana, "Iglesia," 340. Note that Tuggy estimates a lower figure of 40,000 membership in 1944. Tuggy, *Iglesia*, 67-68.

⁵⁴*Ibid.*, 160.

The War impacted the group's growth for a time. The Japanese occupation was a devastating period for Filipinos and for the Iglesia ni Cristo in particular. The Japanese confiscated many properties, including those owned by Manalo and the church. The Iglesia claims that Manalo helped in the resistance movement by "serving as information officer and giving money, food and clothing" to the insurgents.[55] The church experienced little or no growth during this period.[56]

Immediately following the war the situation worsened as the *Hukbalahap*, the People's Army against Japan, popularly called the Huks, opposed Manalo because they thought he was an obstacle to their gaining control of the government. The kidnapping and martyrdom of church workers resulted.[57] But the Iglesia ni Cristo continued to grow, and by the late 1940s it had entered every major area of the Philippines; it was a national church.[58] With continued growth, by 1950 the church claimed two million members; however, Sta. Romana believes 100,000 is a better estimate.[59] Tuggy notes 75,000 in a report of Santiago, who left the movement,[60] and the *Philippines Free Press* notes "over a million" by that time.[61] Which number is correct? Probably not the claim of two million, but what is important to see is the explosive growth of the Iglesia ni Cristo during this postwar period. Philippine census[62] figures show those claiming Iglesia ni Cristo affiliation as:

---

[55]Crisostomo, "Remembering," 10.
[56]Elesterio, *Iglesia*, 18.
[57]See Ricardo V. Serrano, "Brothers of Faith and Courage," in Iglesia ni Cristo, *50th Anibersaryo 1914-1964* (Manila: Iglesia ni Cristo, July 1964), 184-186, for an example of the persecution workers faced.
[58]Tuggy, *Iglesia*, 72.
[59]Sta. Romana, *Iglesia*, 341.
[60]Tuggy, *Iglesia*, 79.
[61]Quijanode de Manila, "The Empire of the Iglesia," *Philippines Free Press*, April 27, 1963: 46.
[62] The accuracy of Philippine census figures is somewhat questionable. I would expect the published figures for those claiming Iglesia ni Cristo affiliation to be lower than the true numbers, since census figures in the Philippines can be manipulated in favor of a specific group.

1960—270,000
1970—475,407
1990—1,400,000
2000—1,804,000

This yields growth rates as follows:

1948 to 1960—9.8% per year over 12 years
1960 to 1970—5.8% per year over 10 years
1970 to 1990—5.6% per year over 20 years
1990 to 2000—2.6% per year over 10 years[63]

New Leadership and Expansion

In the early 1950s, Felix Manalo began to plan for his death and the succession of new leadership. He met together with all the division ministers and senior officials, and on January 23, 1953, they elected his son, Eraño Manalo, as his successor. Eraño Manalo took on more and more responsibility over the next decade, as Felix's health was increasingly frail due to a stomach ailment. In 1955 Felix Manalo traveled to the U.S for diagnosis and treatment and had surgery at Presbyterian Medical Center in New York City. However, by February 1963 he was gravely ill. He died at age seventy-seven on April 12, 1963, and Eraño Manalo took the reins of the Iglesia ni Cristo as Chief Executive Minister. He was thirty-eight years old.[64]

Eraño G. Manalo proved to be a capable administrator of the Iglesia ni Cristo, solidifying its organizational structure with strong leaders. He did not experience the defection of leadership his father saw at various points in his ministry. More than an able executive,

---

[63]Using an equation of $B(1+X)^{**} = E$, where ** means power of, X means growth rate and 100 x is the growth rate in percentages. Special thanks to David Bufford and Todd Moser, Massachusetts Institute of Technology graduates, who independently computed these rates for me for comparison. It should be pointed out that these figures represent the church only in the Philippines.

[64]Crisostomo, "Remembering," 23.

he was a warm pastor at heart and was widely loved by the members of his flock. From the outset of his new leadership he set out to visit all the local congregations under his care, and he regularly visited throughout the Philippines and overseas.[65] Born in 1925, "Ka Erdy" ("Brother Erdy"), as he was popularly called, died in August 2009 at the age of eighty-four. His birth anniversary on January 2 continues to be celebrated annually by the Iglesia ni Cristo. He was married to Cristina Villanueva and had six children: three boys and three girls.[66]

This Executive Minister did much more than strengthen the church's structure. Under his guidance the Iglesia ni Cristo's expansion exploded over thirty years. Since 1990 that growth seems to have slowed, but the movement still continues to see new recruits join at a good rate. The church has grown from around 270,000 when Eraño Manalo came into leadership to at least 2,700,000 in 2007.[67]

This growth was spurred by many new initiatives, including the use of radio and television and the founding of a hospital, a university, and a ministerial school. Outreach efforts creatively

---

[65]Adriel O. Meimban, "The 73rd Year of the Iglesia ni Cristo," *Pasugo* 39, 4 (July-August 1987): 12.

[66]Joel V. San Pedro, "The Church of Christ Triumphant," *Pasugo* 50, 8 (August 1998): 28; Crisostomo, "Remembering," 20; Leslie Ann G. Aquino, "Our Brother Eraño G. Manalo Has Been Laid to Rest—INC," *Manila Bulletin*, September 1, 2009, http://www.mb.com.ph/articles/218672/inc-s-era-o-manalo-passes-away (accessed September 2, 2009).

[67]The 2000 Philippine Census reports 1,804,357 claiming affiliation with the Iglesia ni Cristo. National Statistics Office, Republic of the Philippines, "Philippine Census 2000," http://www.census.gov.ph/census2000/p000000html (accessed May 12, 2010). This represents 2.36% of the population. Overseas workers (OCWs) number 1,016,000. A high percentage of OFWs come from the poorer and less educated classes as does the membership of the Iglesia ni Cristo. So it would be a conservative estimate to assume a similar percentage of affiliates among OFWs as that of the general population. Taking that conservative estimate adds an additional 239,776. Extrapolating the growth rate of 1990-2000 at 2.6% brings the total to 2,446,472. While the church claims 25% of its membership is non-Filipino, group pictures of members in the *Pasugo* indicate this figure may be inflated. Ten percent seems a safe estimate based on those photographs. This brings the 2007 total to 2,718,302.

moved from debating to door-to-door, leafleting and community services, such as cleanup days, planting trees and medical/dental help to the poor. Most importantly, the church moved beyond its Filipino confines to new places abroad beginning with a "Mission to the West" in 1968 when the Iglesia ni Cristo registered with the state government in Hawaii. This movement into the West was celebrated with great fanfare, as were efforts in the mid-1990s with the establishment of official groups in Rome (the seat of the "Great Apostasy"), Jerusalem (the birthplace of the church), and Greece (focus of the Gentile mission).[68] Today the church claims a membership that is twenty-five percent non-Filipino. Since actual membership figures are not published by the group, it is not possible to verify this number. However, pictures in *Pasugo*, the church's monthly magazine, and testimonies of converts, clearly show the church is adding a substantial number of non-Filipinos to its ranks, often through those who have moved overseas and chosen to marry foreigners. The Iglesia ni Cristo does not allow its members to marry outside the church, so those wishing to marry a church member must convert.

Those desiring to enter the ministry must travel to the Philippines for the five-year ministerial program at their seminary, the College of Evangelical Ministry (CEM). Roman Catholics and Protestants have always established training schools for ministers in the countries to which they have expanded. The fact that the Iglesia ni Cristo does not do this shows not only the continued importance of Filipino culture to the group but also its hierarchical structure. The church is strongly authoritarian, with centralized control. Weekly sermon outlines are disseminated from the Central Headquarters, and the same sermon will be preached in all chapels throughout the Philippines on a given Sunday. It is not clear if this

---

[68]For a discussion of how the Iglesia ni Cristo views these three events as the fulfillment of prophecy see, Anne C. Harper, "A Filipino Church at Eighty Years: The Iglesia ni Cristo at the Turn of the Century," in *Chapters in Philippine Church History*, ed. Anne C. Kwantes (Manila: OMF Literature, Inc., 2001), 429-462.

is also true for meetings outside the Philippines. Preaching and services are held in the vernacular of the area in which a congregation is situated—Tagalog or English in Manila and Central Luzon, Cebuano in the central Visayas islands and Mindanao, Ilocano in northern Luzon, and so on.

The rapid growth of the Iglesia ni Cristo necessitated the addition of able leaders to its hierarchical structure. Eraño Manalo made wise decisions as new departments and divisions have been added to his organization.

Further, the church gained political influence through bloc voting in Philippine elections. Today candidates for political office are not shy about courting Iglesia ni Cristo endorsement, and key government appointments for Iglesia members are the reward from those elected with the help of the group.[69] While tensions still remain with the surrounding Filipino culture, increasingly the Iglesia ni Cristo has become a respected member of Philippine society. Since the church does not allow its members to unionize and the members are known for their integrity, wealthy Chinese businessmen seek to employ them. When the church has been maligned publicly, it has required public apologies—keeping and saving face in a society which in the past viewed them askance.[70]

The Iglesia ni Cristo that exists today rests firmly on the foundations so carefully laid by Felix Y. Manalo and his son Eraño Manalo. It has grown not just in breadth, numerically, but in depth, deepening its reach into the surrounding culture as

---

[69]For example, see http://www.mb.com.ph/issues/2004/05/07/MAIN 200405078946_.html (accessed May 7, 2004).

[70]See, for example, Christina Mendez, "President Apologizes to INC for Task Force Fiasco, " *Philippine Star*, February 2, 2004, Metro: 1,4, and http://www.manilatimes.net/national/2003/may/11/metro/20030511met1.html (accessed May 7, 2004), and Marichu Villanueva and Christian Mendez, "President Apologizes to INC for Task Force Fiasco," *Philippine Star*, February 2, 1999, 4. For a suit the church filed against *Ang Dating Daan*'s Elias Soriano for libel, see *The Sunday Times*, "INC Files Libel Charges against Ang Dating Daan's Eli Soriano," http://manilatimes.net/national/may/2003/may/11/metro/20030511met1.html (accessed April 28, 2004).

modernization has continued in the Philippines. Eraño Manalo was not merely satisfied with what was, but looked to what would be— even after his death. He carefully groomed his son, Eduardo V. Manalo, to take the reins of the church following his death. Eduardo served as Deputy Executive Minister for over a decade before assuming the mantle of Chief Executive Minister in late 2009. The future of the church seems secure as it works to keep newer generations of children actively involved and reaches out to attract new converts. It is unlikely to fade into obscurity.

Reasons for the Iglesia ni Cristo's Growth

A number of researchers have discussed reasons why the Iglesia ni Cristo has grown and continues to expand:[71]

- It has dynamic and well-trained leadership.
- It is indigenous in nature.
- Every member is actively involved and organized for community, nurture and outreach.
- It is free of external control and self-supporting.
- It emphasizes stewardship, encouraging three kinds of giving on a regular basis: weekly, for special offerings and a year-end Thanksgiving offering.
- It is regularly in the public eye through its beautiful and clean chapels, community involvement and political sponsorship of candidates.

---

[71]See Alonzo, "Historico-Critical," 15; Albert J. Sanders, "Iglesia ni Cristo: Factors Contributing to Its Growth and Its Future," *The South East Asia Journal of Theology* 4, 1 (July 1962): 50-56; Arthur Leonard Tuggy and Ralph Toliver, *Seeing the Church in the Philippines* (Manila: OMF Publishers, 1972), 140-141; Ricardo Peña, *Major Religions in the Philippines*, (Pasig: Alliance Publishers, 1985), 124-125; Tuggy, "Iglesia ni Cristo: An Angel and His Church," 94-101; Robert Reed, "Migration," 163-171; and Robert R. Reed, "The Iglesia ni Cristo, 1914-2000 from Obscure Philippine Faith to Global Belief System," *Bijdragen tot de Taal-, Land- en Volkenkunde. Journal of the Humanities and Social Sciences of Southeast Asia and Oceania* 157, 3 (2001): 579.

- It assists members in need in a variety of ways.
- It evangelizes in a situation where both Roman Catholics and Protestants are often untaught regarding their church doctrines, offering biblical certainty for its teaching.
- It publishes an attractive monthly magazine, *Pasugo*, and utilizes radio and television effectively. Recently it has also expanded its postings on the Internet and begun to use it effectively for communicating church teachings and activities.

Summarizing Comments

The Iglesia ni Cristo appeared during a period of rapid social change in Philippine history. At the turn of the century there were strong movements to gain political independence from the Spaniards and then from the Americans. Paradoxically, the Americans, and especially the Protestant missionaries, brought increasing secularization to the Philippines. First Filipino culture was freed from the dominance of the Roman Catholic Church as the object and source of all social, economic and political activity, and then Protestants espoused the separation of church and state. So religion, even Protestantism, was no longer the focal point of life. People could gain the benefits of employment and wealth without relying on religious institutions or personnel.

In the midst of these dramatic changes, there was a seeking for continuity and unity which first reared its nationalist head in politics, but later also in the religious sphere as schisms occurred within the ranks of the newly Protestant Filipinos. They sought their "own" churches, sometimes keeping the doctrines of their Protestant mentors as in the Iglesia Evangelica Metodista en las Islas Filipinas and others, or as in the Iglesia ni Cristo, rejecting a packaged Western religion and choosing elements that fit the Filipino mindset.

As the Iglesia ni Cristo sought to expand, it experienced persecution and tensions, sometimes intense, with its surrounding society. However, by its indoctrination and culture the movement provided the unity and security that its members were seeking in the midst of radical social change. At the same time, it confirmed certain cultural values, such as the "big man" in charge as a reflection of the father's role in Filipino society[72] and use of the vernacular language.

Felix Manalo assured that the Iglesia ni Cristo would survive beyond his death by organizing structures and preparing leadership to take the reins upon his death. Having successfully weathered the transition of the death of its founder, Eraño Manalo continued aggressive evangelism while at the same time remaining fluid enough to develop institutional structures which would enable the rapidly growing movement to survive and thrive. Eraño Manalo, in turn, prepared his son Eduardo to follow as a capable leader. These were not small feats, for they have assured the continued success and expansion of this new religious movement so that it has taken its place in the world, not just the Philippine archipelago.

---

[72] For the "big man" value see Leonardo N. Mercado, "Retrospect: Some Comments on Filipino Religious Psychology," in *Filipino Religious Psychology*, ed. Leonardo N. Mercado (Tacloban City: Divine Word University Publications, 1997), 186.

Chapter 4

THE BELIEF SYSTEM OF THE IGLESIA NI CRISTO

Only primary sources written by the Iglesia ni Cristo are used as the basis for describing its teachings in this chapter. While the church has been publishing materials since the 1940s, for this book, which examines the church as it exists today, only more contemporary resources are cited. The primary publication utilized is *Mga Leksiyong Ministeryal* ("Doctrinal Lessons for Ministers") authored by the Chief Executive Minister, Eraño Manalo. All those desiring to become members of the Iglesia ni Cristo attend a series of twenty-four weekly doctrinal lessons,[1] which provide basic information on the group's beliefs. This material is usually only available to the ministers teaching the doctrinal lessons; it is not distributed. Information in articles from *Pasugo* ("God's Message"), the monthly publication of the Iglesia ni Cristo, and the church's hymnal augment the doctrinal lessons.

Authority

The first doctrinal lesson addresses the basis for the church's teaching and claims to authority: the Holy Scriptures. In fact, all the group's teachings are buttressed by quotations from the Bible. For the Iglesia ni Cristo, only the Bible is the written word of God.[2] Other religions may claim other bases for their beliefs, but

---

[1]The number of lessons has varied over the years. Current practice is twenty-four lessons in the Philippines, and in overseas locations an additional three lessons on the church's history are added.

[2]Eraño Manalo, *Mga Leksiyong Ministeryal* ("Doctrinal Lessons for Ministers"), trans. V. Santiago, (Quezon City: Iglesia ni Cristo, 1989) Lesson 1: 1.

the Bible makes this claim, and it is "God-breathed" based on 2 Timothy 3:16-17.[3] The Bible is described as "holy."[4]

The Bible is true because its prophecies have come to pass; examples given include the Second World War, and the famines and troubles, which followed the war.[5]

Most importantly:

> The Bible teaches the way of salvation so that we may have eternal life. . . We do not add anything to it so that we don't fall into the wrong faith (I Corinthians 4:6). . . Those who add to the Bible will be punished and not saved (Revelation 22:18-19).[6]

In an article discussing science and the Bible, *Pasugo* author Dennis Lovendino writes that the Bible is more reliable than science, and "[T]he words of God can withstand all scrutiny; they are error-proof and are surely bound to happen."[7]

In summary, the Iglesia ni Cristo holds an unshaken faith that the Bible is without error and true in all aspects, not just in matters of religion.

Interpreting the Bible

While the Bible is the source of truth, not just anyone can interpret or teach it. As an Iglesia ni Cristo hymn teaches,

And the teachings of God

---

[3] *Ibid.*, Lesson 1: 1-2.
[4] Iglesia ni Cristo, *Ang Bagong Himnario ng Iglesia ni Cristo* ("New Hymns of the Iglesia ni Cristo"), trans. V. Santiago, (Quezon City: Iglesia ni Cristo, 1981), Hymn 91.
[5] Manalo, *Mga Leksiyong Ministeryal*, Lesson 1: 2.
[6] *Ibid.*, Lesson 1: 3.
[7] Dennis C. Lovendino, "Science vs. the Bible?" *Pasugo* 54, 1 (January 2002): 6-8.

To the Messenger only were given
He is the only one who has the right to teach the truth[8]

The only ones given that authority by God are Felix Y. Manalo, who was a Messenger from God, and the Iglesia ni Cristo's ministers because they "hold the seal" prophesied in Revelation 7:2-3.[9]

The messenger is the only one who has the authority to preach the "pure Gospel."[10] This is because parts of the Bible are not only "mysterious" but "hidden, providing a double level of inscrutability."[11] This "hidden mystery" means that not just anyone can understand the Bible or teach from it. The group believes that many claiming to be Christians use the wrong translation or give verses a wrong interpretation. Because they are not ministers in the Iglesia ni Cristo they really cannot understand the Bible, and so are false teachers.[12] Further, parts of the Bible are "incomprehensible," readers cannot "rely solely on context." They need the Holy Spirit.[13] Because of this, members of the group are not encouraged to read the Bible for themselves.

God

The Iglesia ni Cristo teaches that the Father is the One who created all things, and he is the only true God. They specifically teach there is no such thing as the Trinity.[14] Jesus "speaks about the

---

[8]Iglesia ni Cristo, *Ang Bagong Himnario*, Hymn 91.
[9]Manalo, *Mga Leksiyong Ministeryal*, Lesson 8: 34.
[10]*Ibid.,* Lesson 8: 34.
[11]Rommel V. San Pedro, "The Stewards of God's Mysteries," *Pasugo* 53, 4 (April 2001): 10.
[12]Manalo, *Mga Leksiyong Ministeryal*, Lesson 13, 47-48; Iglesia ni Cristo, *Ang Bagong Himnario*, Hymns 30, 35, and Lloyd I. Castro, "Those Given to Know the Mystery of God," *Pasugo* 53, 5 (May 2001): 6.
[13]Rommel V. San Pedro, "Scripture Twisting to Their Own Destruction," *Pasugo* 53, 11 (November 2001): 7.
[14]Manalo, *Mga Leksiyong Ministeryal*, Lesson 2: 4, and Rommel V. San Pedro, "The Father Alone Is God," *Pasugo* 53, 6 (June 2001): 8.

Father" and "the Apostles introduce Him."[15] All things come from the Father,[16] who is invisible, and his state is spirit having no "flesh or bones."[17] Therefore, no one should make images of him to worship.[18] Further, the making of images is expressly forbidden in the Bible and is idolatry.[19]

There is a dichotomy in God's awesome holiness, which separates him from humankind, and his involvement with and concern for people. On the one hand, God's great power is seen in his creation,[20] he is omnipresent,[21] he is holy,[22] and he is in heaven.[23] On the other hand, God cares about us: He created man,[24] forgives sins,[25] helps in afflictions and life,[26] gives peace,[27] hears and receives,[28] and is full of love.[29]

Humanity

Humans are an evil race and we are sinners.[30]
Since Adam, man has rejected the law of God in
various ways. He let the law of sin reign over him.

---

[15]Manalo, *Mga Leksiyong Ministeryal*, Lesson 2: 4.
[16]*Ibid.*, Lesson 2: 5.
[17]Manalo, *Mga Leksiyong Ministeryal*, Lesson 2:5; Dennis C. Lovendino, "Worshiping the Creature Rather Than the Creator," *Pasugo* 54, 8 (August 2002): 6.
[18]Lovendino, "Worshiping the Creature," 6; Manalo, *Mga Leksiyong Ministeryal*, Lesson 24: 115, and Iglesia ni Cristo, *Ang Bagong Himnario*, Hymn 294.
[19]Manalo, *Mga Leksiyong Ministeryal*, Lesson: 4: 5.
[20]*Ibid.*, Lesson 2: 6.
[21]Editor, Letters to, "God Is Everywhere," *Pasugo* 54, 6 (June 2002): 2.
[22]Iglesia ni Cristo, *Ang Bagong Himnario*, Hymn 34.
[23]*Ibid.*, Hymn 294.
[24]Manalo, *Mga Leksiyong Ministeryal*, Lesson 2: 6.
[25]Iglesia ni Cristo, *Ang Bagong Himnario*, Hymns 2, 8, 14, 25, 358.
[26]*Ibid.*, Hymn 15.
[27]*Ibid.*, Hymn 20.
[28]*Ibid.*
[29]*Ibid.*, Hymns 34, 262, 294.
[30]*Ibid.*, Hymns 38, 39.

Man is, by nature, weak and as such he has easily been enslaved by sin.[31]

Because we sin, we are enemies of God. Our sins separate us from God and this leads to death.[32] The church does not teach there is original sin in man's nature, but that all sin. Infants do not sin,[33] but it is unclear at what age people begin to sin. Our good works are not enough to provide salvation.[34]

Satan

The world is deceived by Satan, also called the serpent or the devil.[35] He turns people from the truth by blinding them.[36] His desire is to destroy people and steal them.[37] His false prophets and preachers can perform false miracles and wonders.[38] Members of the Iglesia ni Cristo are sent to do battle with the Satan.[39]

Salvation

All humans are in need of salvation. Because of their sins, they are separated from God and face the judgment of death.[40] Only a few will be saved.[41] Salvation means that one is given life without

---

[31] *Pasugo*. "Not Good Enough," *Pasugo* 53, 1 (January 2001): centerfold pamphlet.
[32] Feljun Fuentes, "His Enemies No More," *Pasugo* 55, 6 (June 2003): 4.
[33] Editor, Letters to, "Are Infants Baptized in the Church?" *Pasugo* 55, 1 (January 2003): 2.
[34] *Pasugo*, "Not Good Enough."
[35] San Pedro, "Scripture Twisting to Their Own Destruction," 12; and Tomas C. Catañgay, "Salvation Is God's Gift," *Pasugo* 53, 3 (March 2001): 5.
[36] Gary P. Barrientos, "To the Law and the Testimony," *Pasugo* 54, 3 (March 2002): 6.
[37] Iglesia ni Cristo, *Ang Bagong Himnario*, Hymns 333, 366.
[38] Catañgay, "Salvation Is God's Gift," 5.
[39] Noel I. Ilan, "Keeping the Spiritual Fervor," *Pasugo* 53, 4 (April 2001): 7.
[40] Manalo, *Mga Leksiyong Ministeryal*, Lesson 4: 13, 14
[41] *Pasugo*, "Not a Numbers Game," *Pasugo* 54, 3 (March 2002): centerfold pamphlet.

end,[42] and one is saved from punishment.[43] Iglesia ni Cristo members often sing:

> I am saved, I am saved!
> I am saved from the punishments
> If only I'm true, until the end
> On Christ's Day I will be saved. . . .
> A true denial of ourselves
> To responsibility we must be faithful
> And when His Day will come
> I am still the elected one
> I am as well the elected.[44]

The way of salvation is only through membership in the Church of Christ, the Iglesia ni Cristo[45] because Christ founded only one true church.[46] One "enters" through Christ and becomes part of "one flock."[47] The true church must be named with Christ's name, and this is the only church saved through his blood.[48] It is also the only church whose worship and acts of service are accepted by God[49] and which has received his love.[50]

---

[42]Iglesia ni Cristo, *Ang Bagong Himnario*, Hymn 74.
[43]*Ibid.*, Hymn 117.
[44]*Ibid.*, Hymn 56.
[45]Dexter T. Manglicmot, "Why We Need the Church of Christ," *Pasugo* 55, 3 (March 2003): 8; Marlex C. Cantor, "Enhancing Spiritual Life," *Pasugo* 53, 6 (June 2001): 4; and Manalo, *Mga Leksiyong Ministeryal*, Lesson 4:15.
[46]Manalo: *Mga Leksiyong Ministeryal*, Lesson 3: 8.
[47]*Ibid.*, Lesson 4: 13.
[48]Editor. "Letters to the Editor: Is He Unfair?" *Pasugo* 55, 9 (September 2003): 2; Manalo, *Mga Leksiyong Ministeryal*, Lesson 3: 11; Lesson 4: 13; *Pasugo*, "Not Good Enough;" and Editor, "Editorial: The Work of Salvation," *Pasugo* 55, 3 (March 2003): 3.
[49]Manalo, *Mga Leksiyong Ministeryal*, Lesson 3: 11.
[50]Wilfredo B. Santos, "For Whom Is God's Salvation," *Pasugo* 54, 1 (January 2002): 10.

"The Church is essential not because it will save you, but because it is the one that Christ will save."[51] Salvation is in Christ Jesus,[52] but calling on the name of Jesus will not save a person.[53] Further,

> It is not enough for people to know and believe in Christ. More importantly, they must also be recognized by Christ as his own sheep and must be called by the name given to Him by God. . . . Christ's sheep are called by the name "Church of Christ."[54]

Man is called to serve God, but the only acceptable service is through the Iglesia ni Cristo.[55] Love for God must be expressed through works.[56] Faith alone is insufficient for salvation; works are also required.[57] Works done outside the church are not acceptable to God.[58] It is not enough merely to join the church, one must change his or her life and behavior, following the "changes He [Christ Our Savior] established" and "put on a new life."[59] This includes not keeping bad company, not drinking alcoholic beverages, not taking illegal drugs or engaging in sex outside of marriage.[60]

---

[51] Manalo, *Mga Leksiyong Ministeryal*, Lesson 4: 13, 16; see also Ruben D. Aromin, "No Other Way," *Pasugo* 54, 12 (December 2002): 6.
[52] Editor. "Editorial: The Work of Salvation," 3.
[53] Joel V. San Pedro, "The 'Jesus' that Does Not Save," *Pasugo* 53, 7 (July 2001): 23.
[54] Tomas Cantañgay, "I Know My Sheep and Am Known by My Own," *Pasugo* 53, 10 (October 2001): 4.
[55] Manalo, *Mga Leksiyong Ministeryal*, Lesson 3: 9, 10.
[56] *Ibid.*, Lesson 3: 10.
[57] *Pasugo*, "Have You Ever Asked Why #4?" *Pasugo* 55, 5 (May 2003): centerfold pamphlet; Manalo, *Mga Leksiyong Ministeryal*, Lesson 3: 10; Lesson 4: 15; and Iglesia ni Cristo, *Ang Bagong Himnario*, Hymn 6.
[58] *Pasugo*, "Not Good Enough;" and Manalo, *Mga Leksiyong Ministeryal*, Lesson 3: 10.
[59] Manalo, *Mga Leksiyong Ministeryal*, Lesson 14: 52.
[60] Catañgay, "Salvation Is God's Gift," 4; Editor, Letters to, "On Smoking and Drinking Alcoholic Beverages," *Pasugo* 52, 9 (September 2000): 2.

The work that is required is doing the will of the Father. What is the Father's will? That all come together in Christ through the Iglesia ni Cristo.[61] One must join[62] and be registered in the Iglesia ni Cristo in order to be saved,[63] and one must remain a member of the church to be assured of receiving salvation.[64] Those who are expelled from the group will lose their salvation.[65] Baptism in the church is essential for salvation and is a requirement for joining.[66]

Jesus Christ

The Iglesia ni Cristo describes Jesus Christ using a variety of terms indicating his role. He is the Savior,[67] the Redeemer of men,[68] the Mediator,[69] the Guide,[70] the head of the church[71] and the Messenger of God.[72] An Iglesia ni Cristo hymn describes his suffering to save the church:

> Christ experienced great sorrow and intense affliction
> In order to save his church, there at the judgment,
> He was crowned with the crown of thorns
> He was beaten and mocked
> And most of all he was in pain
> And nobody loved him.[73]

---

[61] Manalo, *Mga Leksiyong*, Lesson 3: 11.
[62] *Pasugo*, "Attaining Salvation and Eternal Life," *Pasugo* 54, 7 (July 2002): centerfold pamphlet.
[63] Manalo, *Mga Leksiyong Ministeryal*, Lesson 21: 91.
[64] *Ibid.*, Lesson 21: 88.
[65] *Ibid.*, Lesson 21: 92.
[66] *Ibid.*, Lesson 19: 77.
[67] *Ibid.*, Lesson 4: 13; Lesson 11: 42.
[68] *Ibid.*, Lesson 11: 42.
[69] *Ibid.*
[70] Iglesia ni Cristo, *Ang Bagong Himnario*, Hymn 87.
[71] Manalo, *Mga Leksiyong Ministeryal*, Lesson 4: 13, 15; Lesson 11: 42, and Iglesia ni Cristo, *Ang Bagong Himnario*, Hymn 293.
[72] Iglesia ni Cristo, *Ang Bangong Himnario*, Hymn 293.
[73] *Ibid.*, Hymn 65.

The church describes his attributes, but distinguishes these from his nature.[74] He is described as holy because God made him holy; they stress that he was not holy because of his own power.[75] God "sanctified him to be without sin."[76] While he did not commit any sins,[77] he became sin for us.[78] He is called "Son of God," and "Lord" as attributes, but "these do not show His nature."[79] Christ did not have inherent Lordship; it was given to him.[80] God is the One who made him Lord.[81]

It is God who has put Christ above all creation[82] and made his body the church.[83] It is God who commands humankind to worship him.[84] Christ's nature is human.[85] It was God who worked through him doing miracles.[86] Christ is still human in nature in heaven.[87]

The church teaches emphatically that belief in a dual nature (true God and true man) is false. There is no hypostatic union.[88] They distinguish between Christ as "God's Son" and his being a

---

[74] Manalo, *Mga Leksiyong Ministeryal*, Lesson 11: 41, 43.

[75] *Ibid.*, Lesson 4: 14.

[76] Editor. "Letters to the Editor: Christ Is Not Man," *Pasugo* 54, 4 (April 2002): 2.

[77] Lloyd I. Castro, "Salvation, Justice, and the Church," *Pasugo* 54, 4 (April 2002): 8.

[78] Manalo, *Mga Leksiyong Ministeryal*, Lesson 4: 14.

[79] *Ibid.*, Lesson 11: 41.

[80] San Pedro, "The Father Alone Is God," 8; and Catañgay, "I Know My Sheep and Am Known by My Own," 4.

[81] Manalo, *Mga Leksiyong Ministeryal*, Lesson 11: 41.

[82] *Ibid.*, Lesson 11: 42.

[83] *Ibid.*, Lesson 4: 14.

[84] *Ibid.*, Lesson 11: 42.

[85] *Ibid.*, Lesson 11: 41, 43.

[86] *Ibid.*, Lesson 12: 45, 46.

[87] Editor, "Letters to the Editor: Christ Is Not Man?" 2; and San Pedro, "The Father Alone Is God," 9.

[88] Editor, "Letters to the Editor: Jesus Christ and the Prince of Tyre," *Pasugo* 55, 8 (August 2003): 2.

"Son of God."[89] It is an incorrect Bible translation that calls Christ God's Son.[90]

They argue against Christ having a divine nature in a number of ways. The doctrine did not originate with the Apostles' teaching but at the Council of Nicea.[91] God has no beginning, but Christ has a beginning since he comes from God.[92] Christ did not have pre-existence.[93] He was only in God's mind and did not come into being until he was born of a woman.[94] The apostles taught that Christ was conceived and born of a woman.[95] Therefore, he cannot be God. Further, Christ died, but God is immortal.[96] Christ became tired, but God does not become tired.[97] Christ did not have the power to resurrect himself, God raised him.[98] Christ's lordship is different from God's because it "is not inherent, but was given through an act of God."[99] They claim that "Christ who is God over all" is an incorrect translation of Romans 9:5. Rather, it is God who is over all.[100]

What is Christ's role and work? He forgives and cleanses the Church of Christ from sin through his blood.[101] He builds[102] and

---

[89]Manalo, *Mga Leksiyong Ministeryal*, Lesson 11: 41, 42.

[90]*Ibid.*, Lesson 11: 42.

[91]Noel I. Ilan, "The Origin of the Doctrine of Christ's Alleged Deity," *Pasugo* 53, 12 (December 2001): 4.

[92]Manalo, *Mga Leksiyong Ministeryal*, Lesson 12: 45.

[93]Editor, "Letters to the Editor: Are Christ and Jehovah One God?" *Pasugo* 54, 12 (December 2002): 2.

[94]Manalo, *Mga Leksiyong Ministeryal*, Lesson 13: 48.

[95]Ilan, "The Origin of the Doctrine of Christ's Alleged Divinity," 4.

[96]Manalo, *Mga Leksiyong Ministeryal*, Lesson 12: 45; and Editor, "Jesus Christ and the Prince of Tyre," 2.

[97]Manalo, *Mga Leksiyong Ministeryal*, Lesson 12: 45.

[98]*Ibid.*, Lesson 12: 45.

[99]San Pedro, "The Father Alone Is God," 8, 9.

[100]Rommel V. San Pedro, "Refuting Christ's Alleged Deity in Romans 9:5," *Pasugo* 53, 7 (July 2001): 24-25.

[101]*Pasugo*, "Serving God in Truth," *Pasugo* 53, 10 (October 2001): centerfold pamphlet; and Iglesia ni Cristo, *Ang Bagong Himnario*, Hymns 18, 22, 40, 42, 93.

[102]Iglesia ni Cristo, *Ang Bagong Himnario*, Hymn 283.

redeems his church,[103] and serves as its head.[104] Through his death he paid for the church's sins.[105] He is "with" members of the Iglesia ni Cristo and watches over them.[106] He strengthens and guides his people.[107] He erases their troubles and takes care of them.[108] He is a companion in their struggles.[109] He protects them[110] and is a shelter.[111] He is "in" them,[112] and through him his people are "in God."[113] However, "[T]o have a true personal relationship with Christ is to join His Church."[114] Christ is the one to imitate in fulfilling required duties.[115]

In Christ "Real life"—life without end—is obtained.[116] Christ will come to earth again,[117] and he will take his church to a place where there is no suffering.[118]

God's Messenger in the Last Days

A central and foundational belief of the Iglesia ni Cristo is that Felix Y. Manalo is the "Messenger of God in the Last Days."[119] He is called "The Last Messenger" because "his work is God's last work of salvation."[120]

---

[103] *Ibid.*, Hymn 42, 141.
[104] *Ibid.*, Hymn 285.
[105] *Ibid.*, Hymn 66.
[106] *Ibid.*, Hymns 19, 285.
[107] *Ibid.*, Hymn 21.
[108] *Ibid.*, Hymn 22.
[109] *Ibid.*, Hymn 28.
[110] *Ibid.*, Hymn 293.
[111] *Ibid.*, Hymn 28.
[112] *Ibid.*, Hymns 42, 337.
[113] *Ibid.*, Hymn 337.
[114] *Pasugo*, "Not Good Enough."
[115] Iglesia ni Cristo, *Ang Bagong Himnario*, Hymn 27.
[116] *Ibid.*, Hymn 309.
[117] *Ibid.*, Hymn 9.
[118] *Ibid.*, Hymn 341.
[119] Manalo, *Mga Leksiyong Ministeryal*, Lesson 7: 31; Lesson 8: 32, and Iglesia ni Cristo, *Ang Bagong Himnario*, Hymn 3.
[120] Feljun B. Fuentes, "Why We Call Him 'The Last Messenger,'" *Pasugo* 55, 5 (May 2003): 4.

There are three dispensations of time: the era of the Patriarchs from creation to Moses' birth, the era of the Prophets from Moses' birth to Jesus' birth, and the Christian era from the birth of Jesus to the Day of Judgment.[121] The Christian Era has had four messengers: Christ, the Apostle Paul, Martin Luther and Felix Y. Manalo, each of whom had a specific work.[122] Christ brought in the Jewish converts, Paul converted the Gentiles, Luther denounced the papacy as the harlot in Revelation, and Manalo warned of the coming Judgment Day.[123]

The church strongly refutes that Manalo founded the Iglesia ni Cristo, because Christ is the one who founded the church called by his name.[124] Manalo's mission was to preach the gospel in the last dispensation of the church.[125] He was to "resurrect" the Church of Christ which had disappeared through false teaching and to bring people to Christ.[126] His role was to "deliver people from the slavery of unrighteous acts and false religion."[127]

Manalo's "appointment" as messenger was prophesied in Scripture,[128] and there is power in his preaching.[129] "Those who receive and accept the messenger receive Christ and God. Those who renounce the messenger renounce Christ and God."[130] It is through Manalo's "leadership" that the Iglesia ni Cristo is "called and sealed."[131]

Because of Felix Manalo's pivotal role in the formation of the Iglesia ni Cristo, those who have benefited from his preaching are

---

[121] *Ibid.*, 4.
[122] *Ibid.*, 5.
[123] *Ibid.*, 4-5.
[124] Manalo, *Mga Leksiyong Ministeryal*, Lesson 8: 32.
[125] *Ibid.*
[126] Fuentes, "Why We Call Him 'The Last Messenger,'" 4; and Manalo, *Mga Leksiyong*, Lesson 8: 32.
[127] Joel V. San Pedro, "Remembering God's Promises," *Pasugo* 53, 11 (November 2001): 4.
[128] Manalo, *Mga Leksiyong Ministeryal*, Lesson 8: 32.
[129] Iglesia ni Cristo, *Ang Bagong Himnario*, Hymn 4.
[130] Manalo, *Mga Leksiyong Ministeryal*, Lesson 8:35.
[131] Iglesia ni Cristo, *Ang Bagong Himnario*, Hymn 3.

urged to remember him "every time [they] reflect on [their] divine calling" and are encouraged to follow his example.[132] The church teaches against worshiping Manalo or any image of him, but remembers him on the anniversary of his birth based on Hebrews 13:7.[133]

Ecclesiology

The true church was founded by Christ in the first century.[134] It started as a small "flock," but expanded during the Apostles' leadership. Persecution occurred, and this flock was scattered.[135] As a result the church grew in size and reached the Gentiles. The name of the church that Christ founded is important: it is the Church of Christ.[136] Only the church called by Christ's name is the true church.

Apostasy

After the Apostles' time, false prophets appeared who misled the church.[137] This happened during the first century.[138] The Apostasy was made by Catholic priests who introduced a false faith in the Roman Catholic Church. This is a different church from the Church of Christ.[139] In fact, the Iglesia ni Cristo believes that Catholic priests are demons[140] and that the sign of the cross Catholics make on their foreheads using their right hands is proof the Roman Catholic Church is the anti-Christ.[141]

---

[132]Editor, "Editorial: Sent to Preach," *Pasugo* 55, 5 (May 2003): 3, 9.
[133]Editor, "Editorial: Lest We Forget Him," *Pasugo* 54, 5 (May 2002): 3.
[134]Manalo, *Mga Leksiyong Ministeryal*, Lesson 5: 17.
[135]*Ibid.,* Lesson 5: 17.
[136]*Ibid.,* Lesson 5: 17-18.
[137]*Ibid.,* Lesson 5: 17; Lesson 24: 117.
[138]Rommel V. San Pedro, "Is There Such a Thing as God's Chosen People?" *Pasugo* 54, 7 (July 2002): 11.
[139]Manalo, *Mga Leksiyong Ministeryal*, Lesson 5:17; Lesson 24: 117.
[140]*Ibid.,* Lesson 5: 18.
[141]*Ibid.,* Lesson 4: 19.

Also noted as the Apostasy is the use of images in worship; this idolatry is attributed to the time of Constantine when images of the saints and Mary were produced as objects of worship.[142] When the Roman Catholic Church executed people this was the proof of its apostasy.[143] Further, false teachings arose out of the man-made Councils of Nicaea and Constantinople: the teaching that Christ is true God,[144] and the teaching that the Holy Spirit is God.[145] The group also believes that the hypostatic union was a doctrine invented at Chalcedon.[146]

The Iglesia ni Cristo Is the Only True Church

An Iglesia ni Cristo hymn declares:

Only the Iglesia ni Cristo
That has the truth. . . .
We are the instruments,
The prophesied church.[147]

The Iglesia ni Cristo teaches that it is the only true church and the continuation of the church founded by Christ Himself. The true church is called by Christ's name: the Church of Christ, or Iglesia ni Cristo in Tagalog.[148] This continuation of the true church follows a gap of hundreds of years following the Apostasy.[149]

---

[142]Lovendino, "Worshiping the Creature rather than the Creator," 8.

[143]Manalo, *Mga Leksiyong Ministeryal*, Lesson 5: 20.

[144]Ilan, "The Origin of the Doctrine of Christ's Alleged Deity," 4-5; Editor, "Letters to the Editor," "The Name of the True Church," *Pasugo* 53, 3 (March 2001): 2; and Manalo, *Mga Leksiyong Ministeryal*, Lesson 11: 24.

[145]Manalo, *Mga Leksiyong Ministeryal*, Lesson 13: 51.

[146]Editor, "Jesus Christ and the Prince of Tyre," 2.

[147]Iglesia ni Cristo, *Ang Bagong Himnario*, Hymn 55.

[148]Editor, "The Name of the True Church," 2; and San Pedro, "Is There Such a Thing as God's Chosen People?" 11.

[149]Lloyd I. Castro, "God's Planting and Its Right to Serve," *Pasugo* 53, 7 (July 2001): 26-27; and Catañgay, "I Know My Sheep and Am Known by My Own," 5.

The emergence of the Iglesia ni Cristo was prophesied in the Bible, and those prophecies have been fulfilled.[150] The church was to come from a far land (Acts 2:39) and specifically from the Far East (Isaiah 43:5).[151] Christ prophesied in Matthew 24 that the end was near when wars appeared. The Iglesia ni Cristo believes this was the First World War which "erupted in 1914." Because the Iglesia ni Cristo was also registered with the Philippine government in 1914, it is the fulfillment of this prophecy.[152] Further, Jesus prophesied that he would bring other sheep into his "one flock" (John 10:16). To the Iglesia ni Cristo "one flock" means the church called by Christ's name, the Church of Christ or the Iglesia ni Cristo.[153] Christ is the founder of their church, and he is the one who owns it.[154] The church is synonymous with his kingdom.[155] Names used to describe the church include: one fold, one flock and one new man.[156]

Christ made the whole church his body.[157] "As a whole, it has become one new creation in Christ."[158] Those belonging to the church are children of God and his heirs (Isaiah 43:6).[159]

God's plan is that all should be gathered in the church in order to be cleansed, recognized as his own and gain entrance into

---

[150]Iglesia ni Cristo, *Ang Bagong Himnario*, Hymn 55; see San Pedro, "Is There Such a Thing as God's Chosen People?," 10-12, for more fulfilled prophecies.
[151]Iglesia ni Cristo, *Ang Bagong Himnario*, Hymn 289; and Manalo, *Mga Leksiyong Ministeryal*, Lesson 7: 28.
[152]Manalo, *Mga Leksiyong Ministeryal*, Lesson 7: 20.
[153]*Ibid.*, Lesson 7: 28.
[154]*Ibid.*, Lesson 7: 28, 31.
[155]Iglesia ni Cristo, *Ang Bagong Himnario*, Hymn 94.
[156]Rommel V. San Pedro, "Will Jesus Christ Save You?" *Pasugo* 55, 7 (July 2003): 27; and Celajes, "The People of God in these Last Days," 28.
[157]Manalo, *Mga Leksiyong Ministeryal*, Lesson 4: 14.
[158]*Ibid.*, Lesson 4: 15.
[159]*Ibid.*, Lesson 7: 31.

heaven.[160] The Iglesia ni Cristo as the only true church is the only way to be reconciled with God.[161]

Election, Sealing and Free Will

God only listens to the prayers of the elect.[162] The Father chooses those who will serve him.[163] Jesus also calls and chooses.[164] All the "rights, blessings and promises enjoyed by Israel and the first century church" now belong to those in the Church of Christ, the Iglesia ni Cristo.[165] The elect have a seal put on them by God.[166] The seal is the Holy Spirit, and the sealing "is done by means of preaching the gospel. . ."[167] Those who believe Manalo's and the church's teachings are the ones who are sealed.[168]

Three groups of people have been chosen and comprise the Church of Christ. The "first fruits" are the Jewish converts converted through Jesus. The second group are the Gentiles converted through Paul. The last group are the members of the Iglesia ni Cristo converted through Felix Y. Manalo.[169] One hymn teaches that infants who are elected and die will be saved.[170] The assumption is these are infants of Iglesia ni Cristo members.

---

[160]*Pasugo*. "What We Should Know and Understand," *Pasugo* 54, (August 2002): centerfold pamphlet; Abner M. Celajes, "The People of God in these Last Days," *Pasugo* 53, 2 (February 2001): 28; and *Pasugo*, "Serving God in Truth."

[161]Celajes, "The People of God in these Last Days," 28.

[162]San Pedro, "Is There Such a Thing as God's Chosen People?" 10.

[163]Iglesia ni Cristo, *Ang Bagong Himnario*, Hymn 27; and Castro, "God's Planting and Its Right to Serve," 26.

[164]*Ibid.*, Hymns 332, 342.

[165]Castro. "God's Planting and Its Right to Serve," 27.

[166]Iglesia ni Cristo, *Ang Bagong Himnario*, Hymn 289.

[167]Ruben D. Aromin, "The Wonder of God's Words," *Pasugo* 55, 10 (October 2003): 12.

[168]Gary P. Barrientos, "The Angel Who Ascended from the East," *Pasugo* 5, 53 (May 2001): 9.

[169]Fuentes, "Why We Call Him the Last Messenger," 4-5.

[170]Iglesia ni Cristo, *Ang Bagong Himnario*, Hymn 251.

While the church teaches that its members are chosen by God, they dispute the idea of predestination. God gives people "alternatives to make choices."[171] Humans have free will and are given the freedom of choice.[172] We can choose between right and wrong, and between life and death.[173]

The Holy Spirit

The Holy Spirit is not God, but is sent by God and Christ.[174] Christ, the Apostles and the Messenger had the Holy Spirit in them.[175] Members of the Iglesia ni Cristo receive the Holy Spirit as a seal through the teaching of Felix Manalo.[176] The Spirit lives "within" believers so that their spiritual life will be strong.[177] The Spirit teaches[178] and is sent to strengthen believers during worship services.[179] Christ joins the worship services through the Spirit.[180]

Church Administration and Governance

Pasugo articles promote and describe the role of the church's administration every year, usually in January. One such article teaches:

> Though Brother Felix Y. Manalo was laid to rest after almost 50 years of shepherding the Church of Christ, his

---

[171] *Pasugo*, "The Choices We Have to Make," *Pasugo* 54, 9 (September 2002): centerfold pamphlet.
[172] Noel I. Ilan, "The Freedom that the Bible Teaches," *Pasugo* 54, 10 (October 2002): 8.
[173] Ilan, "The Freedom," 8; and *Pasugo*, "The Choices We Have to Make," centerfold pamphlet.
[174] Manalo, *Mga Leksiyong Ministeryal*, Lesson 13: 51.
[175] Aromin, "The Wonder of God's Words," 5, 12.
[176] Reubin D. Aromin, "The Heirs of God," *Pasugo* 5, 45 (April 2003): 17; Noel I. Ilan, "The Gift of Understanding the Words of God," *Pasugo* 54, 1 (January 2002): 9; and Barrientos, "The Angel Who Ascended from the East," 9.
[177] Manalo, *Mga Leksiyong Ministeryal*, Lesson 15: 59.
[178] *Ibid.*
[179] Cantor, "Enhancing Spiritual Life," 5.
[180] Manalo, *Mga Leksiyong Ministeryal*, Lesson 15:59.

divine work and election continue through the present Central Administration.[181]

God gives the church board the authority "to make decisions in matters pertaining to service to God" such as assigning days of worship.[182] These leaders are to take care of church members and to direct their service to God.[183]

The Iglesia ni Cristo taught that the previous Chief Executive Minister, Eraño Manalo, was given "general authority."[184] Based on I Thessalonians 5:12-13, special respect was shown to this leader. On his birthday members were encouraged to thank God and pray for him.[185]

Church members are to submit to leadership and those appointed by them.[186] They are to be "registered" and under local authorities in the church.[187] "Assistant authority" is given to the ministers and workers in the local units. The church's ministers have the authority to preach the Word of God.[188] Each local chapel is "administered by a board of officers headed by a minister or worker."[189] The board consists of five head deacons, association presidents and the local secretary.[190]

Christ's words in Matthew 18:18, that whatever is bound on earth is bound in heaven, is proof of the Administration's authority.[191] Any regulations the Administration presents are to make sure that church members are "bound and remain obedient

---

[181] Fuentes, "Why We Call Him the Last Messenger," 5.
[182] Manalo, *Mga Leksiyong Ministeryal*, Lesson 21: 87.
[183] *Ibid.*, Lesson 21: 88.
[184] *Ibid.*, Lesson 21: 89.
[185] Editor, "Editorial: Onward to Spiritual Maturity and Perfect Unity," *Pasugo* 55, 1 (January 2003): 3.
[186] Manalo, *Mga Leksiyong Ministeryal*, Lesson 21: 88.
[187] *Ibid.*, Lesson 21: 87.
[188] Manalo, *Mga Leksiyong Ministeryal*, Lesson 21: 88.
[189] *Ibid.*, Lesson 24: 107.
[190] *Ibid.*
[191] *Ibid.*, Lesson 21: 89-90.

to the gospel."¹⁹² Rejecting the church's Administration or not submitting to its authority is "rejecting God and Christ because God placed the Administration in the Church."¹⁹³

Church Membership and Duties

One joins the church by "faith in God and Christ and recognition of the Church and the messenger of God."¹⁹⁴ But to remain in the church one must follow all of its regulations in order to prove that you are a true believer.¹⁹⁵ Further, salvation is dependent on remaining faithful in fulfilling duties. As one hymn encourages,

> If Christ will come
> I wish I will be caught,
> Doing my responsibility,
> And a faithful elect¹⁹⁶

It is not sufficient to simply join the Iglesia ni Cristo, one must have a changed life. Specifically this means not drinking alcoholic beverages, taking illegal drugs, cursing, dancing, playing cards, or gambling. Adultery, divorce, living together, cheating, or doing anything illegal or dishonesty in business are also prohibited.¹⁹⁷

---

¹⁹²Manalo, *Mga Leksiyong Ministeryal*, Lesson 21: 90.
¹⁹³Noel I. Ilan, "Who Are Guilty of Rejecting God?" *Pasugo* 53, 7 (July 2001): 30.
¹⁹⁴Manalo, *Mga Leksiyong Ministeryal*, Lesson 10: 39.
¹⁹⁵*Ibid.*, Lesson 10: 39, 40.
¹⁹⁶Iglesia ni Cristo, *Ang Bagong Himnario*, Hymn 62.
¹⁹⁷Manalo, *Mga Leksiyong Ministeryal*, Lesson 14: 53, Lesson 24: 120.

Baptism

Baptism is required in the church. It is "essential for becoming a disciple of Christ and for acquiring eternal salvation."[198] It is for the forgiveness of sin.[199]

In baptism one joins Christ's death. Because the act symbolizes burial it must be by immersion under water.[200] The old life and sins are buried in the water, and the event is the beginning of a new life and entrance into the Iglesia ni Cristo.[201] Baptism follows teaching and testings (doctrinal lessons and a probationary period of six months).[202]

Baptism from other churches is not accepted because those baptizing were not authorized to do so.[203] Infants are not baptized because they cannot believe and they have not "transgressed the law."[204]

Worship

Members are required to attend two worship services weekly. These are always on Sundays, and usually on Thursdays. Attendance is a "duty" to God.[205] Neglecting worship is "rejecting

---

[198] Manalo, *Mga Leksiyong Ministeryal*, Lesson 19: 77.
[199] *Pasugo*, "Frequently Asked Questions," *Pasugo* 55, 4 (April 2003): 9; and Manalo, *Mga Leksiyong Ministeryal*, Lesson 19: 78.
[200] Manalo, *Mga Leksiyong Ministeryal*, Lesson 19: 78-9.
[201] Iglesia ni Cristo, *Mga Bagong Himnario*, Hymns 212-214, 216-218, 220.
[202] Manalo, *Mga Leksiyong Ministeryal*, Lesson 19: 79-80.
[203] *Ibid.*, Lesson 19: 77.
[204] Editor, Letters to, "Are Infants Baptized in the Church?" 2; and Manalo, *Mga Leksiyong Ministeryal*, Lesson 19: 80.
[205] Tomas C. Catañgay, "Is Serving God a Waste of Time?" *Pasugo* 53, 1 (January 2001: 26, and Manalo, *Mga Leksiyong Ministeryal*, Lesson 15: 54, 55. In countries other than the Philippines the weekday worship is sometimes scheduled for days other than Thursday, see Iglesia ni Cristo, *Mga Bagong Himnario*, Hymn 264.

or turning [one's] back on the Lord."[206] Not attending worship services means, "there no longer remains any sacrifice to take away . . . sins."[207] The member not fulfilling this duty will be punished in the lake of fire.[208]

Further, attendance is a requirement for spiritual growth.[209] Worship must take place in Iglesia ni Cristo chapels because they are the equivalent to God's temple mentioned in Psalm 5:7.[210]

Attendance at Other Events

Members are required to attend weekly prayer meetings.[211] At these meetings they receive instructions from the church administration about other local (congregational) activities they must attend such as special meetings.[212]

Offerings

Tithing is not mandated in the church.[213] However everyone is to give regularly[214] because God commanded giving contributions, thanksgiving gifts, and offerings (*pag-aabuloy, pagpapasalamat, paghahandog*).[215] The church's anniversary and year end are celebrated with special thank offerings, the latter being prepared all year and done by weekly saving.[216] All contributions are to be done cheerfully and not grudgingly. They should be carefully prepared

---

[206]Ilan, "Who Are Guilty of Rejecting God," 30.
[207]Jose P. Salazar, "The Worthy and Acceptable Worship Service," *Pasugo* 55, 9 (September 2003): 2; and Iglesia ni Cristo, *Mga Bagong Himnario*, Hymn 54.
[208]Manalo, *Mga Leksiyong Ministeryal*, Lesson 15: 57.
[209]Cantor, "Enhancing Spiritual Life," 5.
[210]Manalo, Mga *Leksiyong Ministeryal*, Lesson 15: 55.
[211]*Ibid.*, Lesson 24: 105.
[212]*Ibid.*, Lesson 24: 105, 108.
[213]Editor, Letters to, "On the Giving of Tithes," *Pasugo* 54, 7 (July 2002): 2.
[214]*Ibid.*
[215]Manalo, *Mga Leksiyong*, Lesson 16: 62, 65, 66; and Iglesia ni Cristo, *Ang Bagong Himnario*, Hymns 81, 187, 264, 431-432.
[216]Manalo, *Mga Leksiyong Ministeryal*, Lesson 16: 66; Lesson 24: 122.

and set apart from your salary.[217] These are investments for gaining eternal life.[218]

Giving is therefore a duty of church members,[219] and not giving is a sin.[220] Further, by giving members share in teaching and spreading the gospel.[221]

Prayer

Christ commands prayer, so it is a duty to have prayer times.[222] Members are to pray every time they eat, after they arrive at work or school, before sleeping and when waking up.[223] Repetitive and nonsense prayers are forbidden.[224] Prayer is to God and to be done in Christ's name.[225] Prayer may also be to Jesus.[226] Not praying is a sin.[227]

Mission

It is the duty of church members to "go into mission or share the faith."[228] This involves inviting family and friends to teachings and sharing the faith on "the other side of the sea."[229] What this means in practice is described more fully later in the book.

---

[217] *Ibid.*, Lesson 16: 63, 64

[218] *Ibid.*, Lesson 16: 62, 67.

[219] Catañgay, " Is Serving God a Waste of Time?" 26; Manalo, *Mga Leksiyong Ministeryal*, Lesson 16: 62, 63; and Iglesia ni Cristo, *Ang Bagong Himnario*, Hymns 63, 17, 368.

[220] Manalo, *Mga Leksiyong Ministeryal*, Lesson 16: 62, 63.

[221] *Ibid.*, Lesson 16: 63; and Iglesia ni Cristo, *Ang Bagong Himnario*, Hymn 107.

[222] Feljun B. Fuentes, "Learning How to Pray," *Pasugo* 55, 2 (February 2003): 4; and Manalo, *Mga Leksiyong Ministeryal*. Lesson 20: 84-85.

[223] Manalo, *Mga Leksiyong Ministeryal*, Lesson 20: 85-86.

[224] Manalo, *Mga Leksiyong Ministeryal*, Lesson 20: 87.

[225] *Ibid.*, Lesson 20: 87.

[226] Iglesia ni Cristo, *Ang Bagong Himnario*, Hymn 18.

[227] Fuentes, "Learning How to Pray," 5.

[228] Lloyd I. Castro, "Can Faith without Works Save?" *Pasugo* 53, 2 (February 2001): 9; and Manalo, *Mga Leksiyong Ministeryal*, Lesson 20: 82.

[229] Iglesia ni Cristo, *Ang Bagong Himnario*, Hymn 17.

Brotherhood

God commands members to love each other as brothers.[230] This means that members must make amends if they wrong another member and forgive other members who sin against them.[231] They are to help others unless they are idle and not wanting to work.[232] They are not to take another member or the church administration to court, to cheat, or borrow money or an item and not return it.[233] They are to call each other brother and sister.[234]

Unity

Christ and the Apostles taught that the church should be one. "Therefore unity in the church must be maintained at all times."[235] This includes voting and church activities.[236] Casting votes is making a judgment, and church unity is destroyed if members take sides. Using the Jerusalem Council in Acts 15 as justification, the church teaches that the one assigned to make judgments is the General Authority (the Chief Executive Minister).[237]

---

[230] Manalo, *Mga Leksiyong Ministeryal*, Lesson 17: 67; and Reuben D. Aromin, "True Brothers and Sisters," *Pasugo* 58, 11 (November 2006): 11-13.
[231] Manalo, *Mga Leksiyong Ministeryal*, Lesson 17: 68.
[232] *Ibid.*, Lesson 17: 69.
[233] *Ibid.*, Lesson 17: 70.
[234] *Ibid.*, Lesson 17: 68-69.
[235] Manalo, *Mga Leksiyong Ministeryal*, Lesson 22: 95-97; and Iglesia ni Cristo, *Ang Bagong Himnario*, Hymn 224.
[236] Manalo, *Mga Leksiyong Ministeryal*, Lesson 22: 94.
[237] *Ibid.*, Lesson 22: 98-99.

Eating Blood

God prohibits eating blood so church members are forbidden to eat blood or any food mixed with blood.[238] This prohibition has been in all eras: the Patriarchs (Genesis 9:1-4), the Prophets (Deuteronomy 12: 22-23) and Christians (Acts 21: 25).[239]

Marriage

Marrying an unbeliever or non-member is prohibited and considered a serious sin.[240] So is elopement, because it shows disrespect to parents,[241] and so is divorce. Marriage is for life.[242]

Eschatology

The Iglesia ni Cristo has clear teaching on the afterlife, the end times and Christ's judgment.

Persecution

Christ and his disciples experienced persecution. Because of Christ's name, members of his church will also experience persecution and suffering. Triumph and perseverance through it "is the basis of inheritance of heaven's kingdom" and makes one worthy.[243] Suffering is the result of sin. Trials members face include "temptations, persecutions, poverty, false faith taught by false

---

[238]*Pasugo*, "Frequently Asked Questions," 9; and Manalo, *Mga Leksiyong Ministeryal*, Lesson 18: 73, Lesson 24: 123.

[239]*Pasugo*, "Frequently Asked Questions," 25.

[240]*Ibid.*, 10; and Manalo, *Mga Leksiyong Ministeryal*, Lesson 18: 76, Lesson 18: 73.

[241]Manalo, *Mga Leksiyong Ministeryal*, Lesson 18: 73, 76; Lesson 24: 123.

[242]Editor, "Editorial: To Have and to Hold," *Pasugo* 53, 5 (May 2001): 3.

[243]Aromin, "The Heirs of God," 17; Manalo, *Mga Leksiyong Ministeryal*, Lesson 9: 36-38 and Iglesia ni Cristo, *Ang Bagong Himnario*, Hymns 47, 49, 50.

teachers."[244] Some of these come so that "the works of God might be made manifest." Members should remain faithful to God drawing strength from the true faith and knowing their suffering is not in vain.[245] It is a privilege to suffer for the Savior's sake.[246]

Death, Judgment, Resurrection, the Second Coming

God has appointed death to mankind because man has committed sins. Jesus Christ conquered death by bringing life and immortality. Those in the Iglesia ni Cristo benefit from his saving grace.[247]

When a person dies, his/her body and soul both die and go into the grave. They remain there until Christ's second coming.[248] Wars, famines, and earthquakes are the signs that the end of the world is near.[249] Christ will come again and that day is the last day[250] and Judgment Day.[251] Then the entire world will be consumed by fire.[252] At Christ's return, those who were members of the Iglesia ni Cristo who remained faithful will be the first raised from the dead.[253] This is the first resurrection. Those in the Iglesia ni Cristo who are still alive will join those who are resurrected in

---

[244]Editor, "Editorial: Blessed Are Those Who Persevere," *Pasugo* 54, 11 (November 2002): 3, 11.

[245]Feljun Fuentes, "In the Face of Suffering," *Pasugo* 54, 11 (November 2002): 4.

[246]Fuentes, "In the Face of Suffering," 5.

[247]*Pasugo*, "Victory Over Death," *Pasugo* 53, 11 (November 2001): centerfold pamphlet.

[248]Steven V. Kroll, "What the Bible Teaches about Death," *Pasugo* 54, 11 (November 2002): 8.

[249]Manalo, *Mga Leksiyong Ministeryal*, Lesson 23: 10; and Iglesia ni Cristo, *Ang Bagong Himnario*, Hymn 327.

[250]Iglesia ni Cristo, *Ang Bagong Himnario*, Hymn 29.

[251]Manalo, *Mga Leksiyong Ministeryal*, Lesson 23:100, Lesson 6: 26; and Iglesia ni Cristo, *Ang Bagong Himnario*, Hymn 300.

[252]*Pasugo*, "Before Time Runs Out," *Pasugo* 52, 2 (June 2002): centerfold pamphlet.

[253]Kroll, "What the Bible Teaches about Death," 8; Editor, Letters to, "Not a Stubborn Fact," *Pasugo* 53, 6 (June 2001): 2; Manalo, *Mga Leksiyong Ministeryal*, Lesson 23: 102; and Iglesia ni Cristo, *Ang Bagong Himnario*, Hymn 110.

the clouds to meet Christ.²⁵⁴ They will not physically die.²⁵⁵ Both alive and previously dead Iglesia ni Cristo members who have been raised will never die.²⁵⁶ Those not in Christ will be judged.²⁵⁷ Their mortal bodies will be replaced with incorruptible ones.²⁵⁸ They will live in the Holy City or Holy Country forever.²⁵⁹

Not all the dead are raised in the first resurrection.²⁶⁰ After 1,000 years a second resurrection occurs.²⁶¹ This is for those who are outside the church. The wicked will be completely destroyed.²⁶² This is called the Second Death.²⁶³ They will be thrown into the lake of fire. So, there are two deaths for these people: "cessation of breath" or physical death and eternal death in the lake of fire.²⁶⁴ This is also called the eternal punishment.²⁶⁵

Reward: The Holy Land

Iglesia ni Cristo members are focused towards a future reward. For example, this hymn describes the experience they anticipate:

[T]here is a Holy Country/Land;
O, There is no crying at that Holy Country;
There everyone is happy;
Everyone is singing. . . .

---

²⁵⁴Kroll, "What the Bible Teaches about Death," 24.
²⁵⁵Editor, Letters to, "Not a Stubborn Fact," 2.
²⁵⁶*Pasugo*, "Attaining Salvation."
²⁵⁷Iglesia ni Cristo, *Ang Bagong Himnario*, Hymn 222.
²⁵⁸Noel I. Ilan, "Overpowering Death," *Pasugo* 53, 3 (March 2001): 9.
²⁵⁹Manalo, *Mga Lekisong Ministeryal*, Lesson 23: 100; and Iglesia ni Cristo, *Ang Bngong Himnario*, Hymn 104.
²⁶⁰Kroll, "What the Bible Teaches about Salvation," 24.
²⁶¹Manalo, *Mga Leksiyong Ministeryal*, Lesson 23: 102.
²⁶²*Ibid.*, Lesson 23: 101.
²⁶³*Ibid.*, Lesson 4: 14; Lesson 20: 84.
²⁶⁴Editor, Letters to, "Not a Stubborn Fact," 2; and Iglesia ni Cristo, *Ang Bagong Himnario*, Hymn 279.
²⁶⁵*Pasugo*, "Frequently Asked Questions," 10; *Pasugo*, "Victory over Death;" and Kroll, "What the Bible Teaches about Salvation," 24-5.

I will reside there
. . .[T]here is a new earth and heaven[266]

God will create an eternal new heaven and earth which the Iglesia ni Cristo will inherit. This is called the Holy City or New Jerusalem.[267] God and Jesus Christ will live there with them[268] as well as the Messenger, Felix Y. Manalo[269] There will be no death, and life will be eternal.[270] The people will no longer experience of worry, pain, sorrows,[271] persecution,[272] tears, hunger, or grief.[273]

---

[266] Iglesia ni Cristo, *Ang Bagong Himnario*, Hymns 11, 12.
[267] Johnny J. Martin, "God's Promise of Eternal Blessing," *Pasugo* 54, 2 (February 2002): 4; Iglesia ni Cristo, *Ang Bagong Himnario*, Hymns 11, 111; and Ramon C. Centeno, "To Dwell in the New Jerusalem," *Pasugo* 55, 6 (June 2003): 8-9.
[268] Martin, "God's Promise of Eternal Blessing," 4, and Iglesia ni Cristo, *Ang Bagong Himnario*, Hymns 29, 92.
[269] Iglesia ni Cristo, *Ang Bagong Himnario*, Hymn 60.
[270] Editor, Letters to, "Not a Stubborn Fact," 2; and Iglesia ni Cristo, *Ang Bagong Himnario*, Hymns 47, 58-59, 349, 354.
[271] *Pasugo*, "The Life Worth Living;" *Pasugo* 53, 12 (December 2001): centerfold pamphlet.
[272] Iglesia ni Cristo, *Ang Bagong Himnario*, Hymn 60.
[273] *Ibid.*, Hymn 23.

CHAPTER 5

THE INFLUENCE OF FILIPINO CULTURAL VALUES ON THE BELIEFS OF THE IGLESIA NI CRISTO

Filipino values have a clear influence on the worldview of the Iglesia ni Cristo. Non-Filipinos looking at the group may not understand some of the intrinsic beliefs and relational patterns which spring from Philippine culture. The first of these are kinship values.

Group-Based Thinking/Kinship

Filipinos approach the world together, not as individuals. Their approach to the world and life is not based on thinking of themselves alone. They are part of several in-groups, which must be considered because others in the group will be impacted by a member's actions, words and decisions. The result is that the in-group determines what is right or wrong for its individual members,[1] and the anticipation of what the in-group will think or say has a profound influence on how a Filipino acts.

A hymn made popular during the People Power Revolution says:

> *Walang sinuman and nabubuhay para sa sarili lamang,*
> *Walang sinuman and namamatay para sa sarili lamang,*
> *Tayong lahat ay may pananagutan sa isa't isa.*
> (No one lives for himself alone,

---

[1]Vitaliano R. Gorospe, *Christian Renewal of Filipino Values* (Quezon City: Ateneo de Manila University, 1966), 24.

No one dies for himself alone,
Each is responsible for everyone else.)[2]

Professor of indigenous Philippine psychology Virgilio Enriquez points out that the Tagalog word for self, *kapwa*, really means a unity of self and others. In English, the concepts of self and others are in contrast to each other, but in the Filipino worldview, they are integrated because the Filipino identity is shared with others.[3] Individualism and self-consideration are frowned upon. *Kanya-kanya* (to each his/her own) is discouraged.[4]

This shared sense of self means that group loyalty is an overarching or metavalue for the Filipino affecting all areas of life: family, behavior in and outside the group, planning, economics, politics, religion, and much, much more. No man or woman lives for himself or herself alone. Life is intertwined with others in such a way that survival is next to impossible outside a group. Further, no "normal" person would want to go his or her own way without the involvement and support of others.

The shared concept of self and group-based thinking of the Filipino starts with and radiates from the central kinship group. The kinship system provides the building blocks of Filipino life and culture. According to noted Filipino anthropologist F. Landa Jocano, it is the means by which "local authority, rights and obligations, and modes of interaction are expressed, defined,

---

[2]Manual B. Dy, Jr., "Outline of a Project of Pilipino Ethics," in *Values in Philippine Culture and Education*, Cultural Heritage and Contemporary Change Series III, Asia, vol. 7, ed. Manual B. Dy, Jr. (Washington, D.C.: Office of Research and Publications and The Council for Research in Values and Philosophy, 1994), 19.

[3]Virgilio Enriquez, *From Colonial to Liberation Psychology: The Philippine Experience* (Manila: De La Salle University Press, 1994), 45.

[4]F. Landa Jocano. *Filipino Value System: A Collective Definition* (Manila: Punlad Research House, Inc. 1997), 9.

ordered and systematized."⁵ Further, the system gives people their sense of place in life by assigning status and roles.

People are identified as having *magkakamag-anak* (kinship) on the basis of their birth, who they or their close relatives marry, adoption and formalized kinship rituals (*compadrazgo*).⁶ Kinship groups are not static, but are continually evolving from several sources: consanguinity (blood relatives), affinial (marriage), *compadrazgo* (alliance) and *barkada* (peer group).

Social activities are centered in the family, and the family also plays a central role in business and economic affairs.⁷ Wealth is used for pleasurable activities that others can also enjoy.⁸ The town fiesta and family celebrations are some tangible examples. When a Filipino is celebrating a birthday, he or she spends funds so that others can celebrate with him or her.

This family identity reaches further. Filipino society holds parents responsible for the actions of their children even when they are adults. This is one reason that individual religious conversion out of the Iglesia ni Cristo is so difficult.

From earliest childhood Filipinos learn that their priority is the family. They are taught that elders are to be revered and older siblings respected. Every individual born into a family group has a position which affects or determines his or her relationship with others in the group for his or her entire life.⁹ For instance, the sibling group relationship is lifelong and takes precedence over other obligations. An older sister is called *ate* and an older brother *kuya* in Tagalog. These are titles of respect that in turn carry the responsibility to care for and look out for younger siblings.

---

⁵F. Landa Jocano, "Filipino Social Structure and Value System," in *Filipino Cultural Heritage: Filipino Social Structure and Value Orientation*, ed. F. Landa Jocano (Manila: the Philippine Women's University, 1966), 3.

⁶F. Landa Jocano, *Filipino Social Organization: Traditional Kinship and Family Organization* (Manila: Punlad Research House, 1988), 11-14.

⁷Jocano, "Filipino Social Structure and Value System," 14, 15.

⁸Guthrie, "The Philippine Temperament," 54.

⁹Jocano, "Filipino Social Structure and Value System," 2-3.

Fulfilling kinship responsibilities takes precedence over individual desires.[10] Not fulfilling a familial responsibility brings severe social disapproval and even ostracizing.[11]

These values of kinship and group-based thinking have an overarching influence on the beliefs of the Iglesia ni Cristo. Relationship to the church and other members is everything. One is either inside or outside (insider-outsider category) the group, a believer or a non-believer. Only those inside may partake of its benefits, and *tayo tayo*, the group comes first before outsiders are considered.

Individualism and self-consideration (*kanya-kanya*) are actively discouraged. Fulfilling church responsibilities such as worship attendance and not marrying outsiders come before individual desires as would regular kinship responsibilities. This is evident in the teaching on giving to the church as well. One's resources are not for oneself alone, but for the good of the group.

The teaching on unity further illustrates the precedence group must take over individual desires and wishes. Members are to vote as directed by the church administration and to follow the directions of local leaders. Social disruption is a sin, which may result in expulsion from the group.

Membership in the Iglesia ni Cristo is a substitute for traditional extended kinship. The teachings on Brotherhood illustrate this. Members call each other *Kuya* (Brother) and *Ate* (Sister) offering the same respect as to family members. There is a sense of place in life by assigning status and roles, especially at the local (congregational) level. Members are expected to give aid to other members in need. They are taught to be in harmony with each other, forgiving where offense has occurred and making

---

[10]We often saw this with our seminary students who, because of the physical needs of their close kin, had to get jobs to earn money to assist their families. Some even needed to drop out of school for a period of time.

[11]Mary R. Hollnsteiner, *The Dynamics of Power in a Philippine Municipality* (Manila: Bookmark, 1971), 67-68.

amends where they have trespassed against another. Major decisions are made by the group's authorities as a parent or grandparent might in the traditional Filipino family group. These decisions include who to support (such in voting), how resources are spent (such as building new chapels), use of time and resources for regular and special church activities, and sometimes, where to work.

As in the general Philippine culture, baptism is a means of extending kinship. However, it is not through the use of godparents, but through baptism itself that the kinship group grows. Baptism is the rite by which members enter the group. Marriage also serves to extend the kinship group. Because believers cannot marry unbelievers, there is great pressure to "convert" unbelievers with whom members are romantically involved.

Those of lower status seek alliance with the Iglesia ni Cristo to have greater voice. Membership makes those lower on the status ladder be perceived as higher than they are. There is security through interdependence in the group.

Harmony/*Pakikisama*

Because of the importance of relations within the kinship group and the need to not offend in Philippine culture, harmony is sought in almost all situations. A popular Tagalog saying is:

Ang marahang pangungusap Sa puso'y makalulunas.
(A gentle manner of speaking soothes the heart.)[12]

Pakikisama is the Tagalog word for expressing the value of smooth interpersonal relationships. A literal translation might be

---

[12] A Philippine proverb; Frank Lynch, "Social Acceptance," in *Four Readings in Filipino Values*, ed. Frank Lynch (Quezon City: Ateneo de Manila University Press, 1964), 11.

"being along with," though "being with" has also been suggested.[13] It is a highly desired characteristic in Filipino culture and reflects a person's "community orientation, community thinking and community action."[14]

Pakikisama affects conversation, actions and decision-making. Since Filipinos place a high value on good relations, they will avoid confrontation and direct communication. They do not want to offend. As a result, they may agree with what someone says and not voice their concerns. *Siguro nga* ("I guess so" or "Could be") will be used to avoid disagreement.

Rolando Gripaldo and Leonardo Mercado both posit that the value of harmony extends beyond relations with people to include God and nature as well.[15] In Filipino folk Catholicism offerings and prayers are made to saints and the Virgin Mary to serve as intermediaries with God. Good relations are desired with these intermediaries and with God Himself.

Harmony is an important teaching within the Iglesia ni Cristo. Good relations are actively sought, and those creating disharmony through bad relations may be expelled from the church thereby losing their salvation. So, the incentive for smooth relations is high.

On a different level, harmony is sought with the Father. Because of sin, humans are out of relationship with God. The intermediary, Christ, came to renew that relationship through his

---

[13]Dante Luis P. Leoncini, "A Conceptual Analysis of *Pakikisama* [Getting Along Well with People]," *Filipino Cultural Traits*, Claro R. Ceniza Lectures, Cultural Heritage and Contemporary Change Series, IIID, Southeast Asia, vol. 4, ed. Rolando M. Gripaldo (Washington, D.C.: The Council for Research in Values and Philosophy, 2005), 163.

[14]*Ibid.*, 173.

[15]Rolando M. Gripaldo, "Introduction," in *Filipino Cultural Traits*, Claro R. Ceniza Lectures, Cultural Heritage and Contemporary Change Series IIID, Southeast Asia, vol. 4, ed. Rolando M. Gripaldo Washington, D.C.: The Council for Research in Values and Philosophy, 2005), 2. Leonardo Mercado, *Elements of Filipino Philosophy,* (Manila: Divine Word Publications, 1976), 159-164.

blood. Christ is a go-between to bring about good relations and harmony with God.

Respect and Place in Society/*Galing* and *Pakikipagkapwa*

Filipino culture is hierarchical and stratified. Seniority is an important element of the cultural framework. Each person has a place or space in society and expects to be respected and treated appropriately. This begins within the kinship group. As a person is born into a group and grows up, standards (*asal*) of behavior are internalized. This means that a Filipino learns how to speak and act with others of different position and also how to interpret their words and actions.[16]

Each generation has a structure within, but is also part of a larger societal structure both of which provide social control.[17] Within the generation each member has a place and role and should function accordingly. An older brother or sister will look out for a younger sibling, and, in turn, expect to be treated with greater respect. In like fashion, older generations expect to be treated with greater respect by later generations. For example, it would be a sign of extreme disrespect to disagree with an elder in public.[18] Melba Maggay calls this a "formal sense of place" which shows itself through a careful interplay of actions and

---

[16] Jocano, *Filipino Value System*, 52.

[17] For example, for a lengthy description of barrio fiestas and the role of each level of society, see Frank Lynch, "Town Fiesta: An Anthropologist's View," in *Philippine Society and the Individual: Selected Essays of Frank Lynch, 1949-1976*, eds. Aram A. Yenogyan and Perla Q. Makil (Ann Arbor, MI: Center for South and Southeast Asian Studies, The University of Michigan, 1984), 208-233.

[18] Andres and Alada-Andres, *Making Filipino Values Work for You*, 38; Frank Eggan, "Philippine Social Structure," in *Six Perspectives on the Philippines*, ed. George M. Guthrie (Manila: Bookmark, 1971), 9; Jocano, "Filipino Social Organization," 34-36, and Jocano, "Filipino Social Structure," 8.

communication patterns not only in the family but in the culture at large.[19]

The Filipino has a strong sensitivity to authority. Authority comes from status and age. Status may be associated with wealth and power, religious roles such as the priesthood, political positions, ancestry, or skin color (lighter color is considered of higher class). One does not usually make a decision alone, but seeks the advice of someone older or in authority. Seeking advice is another form of showing respect, and the giving of advice is a means of asserting control.[20] According to Gorospe, approval by those in authority is important and affects a person's sense of security.[21]

As Filipino culture is hierarchical and stratified, so is the Iglesia ni Cristo. The highest place is given to Felix Manalo who, though dead, is still honored on his birthday each year. Next was his son, Eraño Manalo, who was the Chief Executive Minister until his death in 2009. Now his son Eduardo Manalo is CEM followed by the church's central administration. Then there are divisional and local ministers and workers followed by deacons and deaconesses at the local level who hold weekly prayer meetings for an assigned group of members. As in general culture, authority comes with status and age, and communication is from the top down. Those in

---

[19] Melba Padilla Maggay, *Understanding Ambiguity,* in *Filipino Communication Patterns* (Quezon City: Institute for Studies in Asian Church and Culture, 2000), 31-32.

[20] Jocano, *Working with Filipinos,* 54; Cristina J. Montiel, "Filipino Culture, Religious Symbols and Liberation Policies," in *Values in Philippine Culture and Education,* Cultural Heritage and Contemporary Change Series III, Asia, vol. 7, ed. Manual B. Dy, Jr (Washington, D.C.: Office of Research and Publications and the Council for Research in Values and Philosophy, 1994), 105; and Guthrie, "The Philippine Temperament," 74

[21] Gorsope, *Christian Renewal of Filipino Values,* 45. Giving way to another is also a way of showing respect. We often saw this in faculty meetings, when Westerners would directly voice the path they felt the school should take. While Filipino faculty might feel differently, because of the perceived higher place of Westerners, the direction westerners preferred would be followed.

a higher position are treated with respect and obeyed. One gives way to those in authority.

Client-Patron Relationships

Client-patron relationships are an important part of Filipino culture. This is a reciprocal relationship where one of lower status and economic means seeks the assistance of someone in power and/or with more economic resources. In Philippine culture someone perceived to have the power, influence or the economic resources to assist others should do so.

In community life, a patron may offer loans with or without the expectation of repayment. Gifts of food or money during times of medical need and at important times such as marriages, baptisms or the death of a family member may be requested directly from a patron, or the patron may offer them without a request. Influence or help with getting a job or in dealing problems involving the government are also important services of the patron. In return for these gifts and assistance, the client is expected to show loyalty. For instance, when the patron requests that the client vote for his candidate or asks for assistance with a large project, clients are expected to do their part in grateful response for all the help they have received.[22]

In the Iglesia ni Cristo, the church is the patron; members are the clients receiving benefits, and they are expected to support the desires of the church/church administration. The church offers protection and assistance in return for work and loyalty.

---

[22]Frank Lynch, "Big and Little People: Social Class in the Philippines," in *Philippine Society and the Individual: Selected Essays of Frank Lynch, 1949-1976*, eds. Aram A. Yengoyan and Perlam Q. Makil (Ann Arbor, MI: Center for South and Southeast Asian Studies, The University of Michigan, 1984), 94-95, 98.

Debt of Gratitude and Reciprocity/*Utang na Loob*

Utang na Loob has been interpreted in a variety of ways: Debt of good will,[23] debt of gratitude, inside or interior debt,[24] debt of prime obligation,[25] indebtedness.[26] A literal translation of *utang* is "debt" and *loob* is "inside."[27] It is a sense of owing something to another because of a favor granted. It is not enough to merely repay a loan or a favor exactly, because the granting of the loan or favor was itself a gift of goodwill. The receiver therefore should, in turn, have goodwill towards the giver. As Filipinos say,

Ang utang na loob ay hindi mababayaran ng salapi.
(A debt of volition cannot be paid with money.)[28]

The lender has not just given goods, money or influence, he or she has given a perceived part of himself or herself. So, this incurs a "soul debt" which remains even after the original debt is repaid.[29]

Iglesia ni Cristo members have a debt to the Messenger and the church that they can never repay. They are under internal

---

[23] Leonardo D. de Castro, "Debts of Good Will and Interpersonal Justice." Paper presented at the Twentieth World Congress of Philosophy, Boston, MA, August 10-15, 1988 (accessed on http://www.bu.edu/scp/MainAsia.htm, April 7, 2008).

[24] Francis Dancel, "*Utang na Loob* [Debt of Good Will]: A Philosophical Analysis," in *Filipino Cultural Traits*, Claro R. Ceniza Lectures, Cultural Heritage and Contemporary Change Series IIID, Southeast Asia, vol. 4, ed. Roland M. Gripaldo (Washington, D.C.: The Council for Research in Values and Philosophy, 2005), 100f.

[25] Charles Kaut, "*Utang na Loob:* A System of Contractual Obligation among Tagalogs," in *Filipino Cultural Heritage: Filipino Social Structure and Value Education*, ed. F. Landa Jocano (Manila: The Philippine Women's University, 1966), 41.

[26] Ermita S. Quito, "The Ambivalence of Filipino Traits and Values," in *Values in Philippine Culture and Education*, Cultural Heritage and Contemporary Change Series III, Asia, vol. 7, ed. Manual B. Dy, Jr. (Washington, D.C.: Office of Research and Publications and the Council for Research in Values and Philosophy, 1964), 52.

[27] Dancel, "*Utang na Loob* ," 112; see also, Kaut, "*Utang na Loob*," 42-43.

[28] Kaut, "*Utang na Loob*: A System of Contractual Obligation among Tagalogs," 47.

[29] Dancel, "*Utang na Loob*," 113-118.

obligation to show gratitude to the church by giving to its support and mission and by obeying required duties such as worship attendance. This obligation to duty and works is continually emphasized. Salvation cannot be obtained without it. One should perform duties gladly and joyfully not under compulsion. Those who are grateful and loyal show their identity as Iglesia ni Cristo members.

Shame/*Hiya*

Hiya is an important concept in understanding a Filipino's world view. A popular Filipino saying is,

Di baling saktan mo ako, huwag mo lang akong hiyain.
(I would not mind if you hurt me physically, just
don't shame me.)[30]

Hija is a part of the Filipino ego and involves the sense of oneself as seen by others.

Missiologist and theologian Timothy Tennent describes shame as "represent[ing] a loss of face."[31] Sociologist David Ho describes face as an Eastern concept.[32] One can give face to another, or save the face of another or oneself. Giving face means to give the honor and respect due to a person for his age or social status, and saving face is not allowing oneself or another to be embarrassed by avoiding inappropriate words or actions. These are public and external values as opposed to internal and private ones.[33]

Jaime Bulatao sees *hiya* as much more than an emotion: it is a "sensitivity to rebuke" that inhibits actions, which would be socially frowned upon. It is not a concept concerned with the individual

---

[30]Jocano, "Filipino Social Structure and Value System," 23.

[31]Timothy C. Tennent, *Theology in the Context of World Christianity: How the Global Church Is Influencing the Way We Think about and Discuss Theology* (Grand Rapids, MI: Zondervan, 2007), 79.

[32]David Y. F. Ho, "On the Concept of Face," *American Journal of Sociology* 81 (1976): 867.

[33]Tennent, *Theology in the Context of World Christianity*, 94.

alone because it involves an individual's group as well.[34] Everyone is dependent on his/her group so that conscience is really an "external norm of conduct." *Hiya* means that an individual must conform to group expectations.[35] Therefore, Jocano defines *hiya* as a norm governing behavior, which is often mistaken for a value. "As a norm (*hiya*) prescribes how we behave in relation to each other in a specific situation, condition, or circumstance so that we do not offend or hurt feelings."[36]

Iglesia ni Cristo church members who do not comply with duties or who bring disunity are expelled. This may be because they bring shame to the group. Their actions reflect not only on themselves but on the perceptions of outsiders to the group. The Iglesia ni Cristo presents itself in a manner which shows order, beauty and consistency. Its publication, *Pasugo*, is well-written and illustrated. The group's chapels are beautifully designed, constructed and well-maintained—always clean, landscaped and appearing freshly painted. However, there is no overt teaching in the *Pasugo* or doctrinal lessons about bringing shame to the church.

Patience, Resiliency, Perseverence/*Bahala Na*

Filipino values educator and management expert Tomas Andres describes Filipinos as *kapalaran*-oriented (destiny-oriented). This is the value of hope that "God intervenes in the destiny of man."[37] In fact, the belief is that everyone must suffer hardship before gaining happiness.[38]

---

[34]Jaime Bulatao, "The 'HIYA' System in Filipino Culture," in *Filipino Cultural Heritage: Filipino Social Structure and Value Orientation,* ed. F. Landa Jocano, (Manila: The Philippine Women's University, 1966), 28.
[35]*Ibid.,* 30-33.
[36]Jocano, *Filipino Value System,* 71-7; and Jocano, *Working with Filipinos,* 68. In addition to calling *hiya* a behavioral norm, he describes it in terms of behavior: "The notion of *hiya* includes being polite, bashful, tender, compassionate, and considerate." F. Landa Jocano, *Filipino Value System,* 73.
[37]Andres, *Making Filipino Values Work for You,* 34.
[38]Bulatao, "The Manileño's Mainsprings," 79.

Guthrie calls this an "optimistic fatalism."[39] The Filipino expects that the will of God controls things and that he/she ultimately has no control over what happens. Favorable events are blessings coming from God, while unfavorable ones are merely misfortunes or the result of "cursing." All in all, whatever happens is fate.[40]

Bahala na is a common expression which means "leave it to God." Enriquez believes this best expresses the value. It influences behavior by: 1) stimulating inaction (no action); 2) helping people forget troubles; 3) encouraging perseverance and working hard; 4) giving *lakas ng loob* (courage) to continue through difficult situations; 5) stimulating creativity; and 6) enabling people to cope with uncertainty.[41] Professor of philosophy Joseph Tiangco describes this value as *katatagang-loob*, a "spirit of undying resiliency" shown in "acts of self-endurance and self-durability amidst challenges and adversity."[42]

The Iglesia ni Cristo teaches its members not just to endure hardship, sufferings and persecution but to expect these things. Those who persevere will receive a reward; they are to trust in God. This fits with the value of the general population, which expects that everyone will suffer hardship before gaining happiness. God is in control of their lives. *Lakas na loob* (courage) to continue through difficult situations is encouraged because there is the reward for those who endure: living forever without pain and suffering in the Holy Land with God, Christ and the Messenger.

---

[39] George M. Guthrie, "The Philippine Temperament," in *Six Perspectives on the Philippines*, ed. George M. Guthrie (Manila: Bookmark, 1971), 68.
[40] Eggan, "Philippine Social Structure," 68.
[41] Enriquez, *From Colonial to Liberation Psychology,* 73-74.
[42] Joseph Anthony Narciso Z. Tiangco, "Understanding the Filipino Philosophy of Resilience: *Katatagang-Loob* [Emotional Strenght {sic}/Resiliency] and Its Phenomenological Considerations," in *Filipino Cultural Traits*, Carlo R. Ceniza Lectures, Cultural Heritage and Contemporary Change Series, Southeast Asia, vol. 4, ed. Rolando M. Gripaldo (Washington, D.C.: The Council for Research in Values and Philosophy, 2005), 61-62.

Summarizing Comments

The beliefs of the Iglesia ni Cristo reflect the influence of Filipino values strongly. This is most obvious in its teachings on the nature of the church and unity, which reflect group identity and kinship values. It is also evident in the hierarchical structure and authority of the group, the duties it requires as *utang na loob*, its expectation of suffering and hardship, and its hope of God's giving a final reward to those who remain faithful.

All of these, but in particular, the group's emphasis on kinship structure, ties and obligations, should be considered in approaching members with the gospel and in attempts to draw people out of the group.

While the Iglesia ni Cristo developed in a Filipino cultural environment, it is also a distinct culture. The next chapter will discuss this distinctiveness.

CHAPTER 6

THE IGLESIA NI CRISTO—A DISTINCT CULTURE
PART I

Apologist Philip Johnson believes that New Religious Movements are distinct cultures and that "devotees of New Religious Movements. . . inhabit their cultures."[1]

Introduction

In recent years, a new approach to reaching those involved in New Religious Movements has emerged. This new paradigm has enabled some evangelicals to move beyond a solely apologetic approach and understanding of these groups to seeing them as distinct cultures, which need to be explored via a variety of missiological tools. The works of Irving Hexham, John Morehead, Philip Johnson, and Ken Mulholland as well as the Lausanne Forum 2004 Group Sixteen on *Religious and Non-Religious Spirituality in the Western World* have spearheaded this approach.[2] This chapter will draw on this perspective in further examination of the Iglesia ni Cristo.

---

[1] Philip S. Johnson, "Apologetics, Missions and New Religious Movements: A Holistic Approach," *Sacred Tribes Journal* 1, 1 (Fall 2002): 155, http://sacredtribesjournal.org (accessed September 10, 2009).

[2] For example, see Hexham, *Encountering New Religious Movements*; Johnson, *Religious and Non-Religious Spirituality in the Western World*; Johnson, "Apologetics, Missions," 153-162, http://www.sacredtribes journal.org; Smulo, "Missional Apologetics;" John Morehead's blog with links to a number of his papers http://johnmorehead.blogspot.com/ (accessed September 10, 2009); and Salt Lake Theological Seminary, *Bridges: Helping Mormons Discover God's Grace*. DVD (Salt Lake City: Salt Lake Theological Seminary, 2003).

The Iglesia ni Cristo has a distinct culture, which separates it from "normal" Philippine culture as well as the cultures to which it has emigrated. In the previous chapters, we examined the belief system of the group and how Filipino culture and values have influenced and are reflected in that belief system and worldview. This chapter examines the distinctiveness of Iglesia ni Cristo culture and discusses what it is like to be a member of the group. Drawing on the author's and her students' observations[3] and conversations with members and ex-members as well as five years' issues of *Pasugo*, a description of Iglesia ni Cristo life is presented.[4]

This chapter discusses the group's customs and distinct cultural markers, such as buildings, activities, rites and vocabulary, its structure and relationships, members' values and goals, and how all of these reflect their understanding of the world and life.

Worship Services: A Central Foundation

"Now my entire life revolves around my duty of attending the worship service," reflected one member of the group.[5] For Iglesia ni Cristo members the center of life is required attendance at worship services in special buildings called chapels. These services are a stark contrast to the worship activities of Roman Catholics and Protestants in the Philippines.

---

[3]Seminary students taking New Religious Movements courses taught by the author at Asian Theological Seminary in 2002 and 2004 were asked to attend an Iglesia ni Cristo worship service at a location of their choice and to talk with several members of the Iglesia ni Cristo and report on their findings.

[4]*Pasugo*, 51-56 (1999-2004). It is important to note here the work of Julita Reyes-Sta. Romana footnoted previously "The Iglesia Ni Kristo: A Study." Her extensive study of the practices of the group has never been duplicated. However, since this work is more than 50 years old, the author has not utilized it in the preparation of this paper. The aim of this paper is to examine the culture of the group as it exists today. See also Julita Reyes-Sta. Romana, "The Iglesia ni Cristo," *The Sower* 1 (3):36-42.

[5]David Melville-Laborde, "I Found the True Meaning of Happiness," *Pasugo* 54, 7 (July 2002): 31.

Group members attend worship services twice weekly, once on Sunday and once during the week as decreed by the Church Administration.[6] The services take place in special houses of worship because these chapels are considered to be "God's house."[7] For those living outside the Philippines this will often mean extensive travel to attend a service at an authorized chapel.[8] In earlier years, this activity may have required a long walk to attend services in the Philippines or even dangerous travel during the rainy season.[9]

Attendance is so important that even when one family learned a fire was destroying the building where their business was housed they continued to the worship service rather than trying to save their business.[10] Members are taught that missing a worship service is departing from the faith and makes them "adversaries" of God.[11] Because these services are so highly valued, attendance at them is taken. When members enter the chapel reception area, there are cabinets with nametags. A member will turn his or her tag over to

---

[6]Bienvenido C. Santiago, "Editorial: Called to Declare Praises for God," *Pasugo* 56, 8 (August 2004): 2; Editor, "Letters," *Pasugo* 55, 12 (December 2003): 7; and Manalo, *Mga Leksiyong Ministeryal*, Lesson 15: 55.

[7]For further discussion of this see the section on Houses of Worship later in this chapter; Arthur W. Jones, II, "No Longer Confused," *Pasugo* 56, 8 (August 2004): 17. Nang Khan Khual also notes this understanding from a discussion with an Evangelical Worker in "My Observations on a Regular Worship Service of the Iglesia ni Christo [sic]," Graduate research paper for a course on New Religious Movements taught by the Anne C. Harper and Michael McDowell at Asian Theological Seminary, Quezon City, 2002, 5.

[8]One convert describes traveling 200 miles to attend worship services. See Benjamin S. Sledge, "My Guide to Eternal Life," *Pasugo* 53, 3 (March 2001): 12. Another describes driving twelve hours every Sunday from Tennessee to Chicago. See Ray Burrows, "I Run This Race to Victory," *Pasugo* 53, 5 (May 2001): 27.

[9]Marie F. Ruiz, "Highway Hills: Rising above the Odds," *Pasugo*, 51, 1 (January 1999): 24.

[10]Marie F. Ruiz, "Cradle of Love," *Pasugo* 53, 5 (May 2001): 30-32.

[11]Feljun B. Fuentes, "Editorial: Seeking God in His Temple," *Pasugo*, 51, 3 (March 1999): 5. The Doctrinal Lessons teach that those who miss worship will be punished in the lake of fire; Manalo, *Mga Leksiyong Ministeryal*, Lesson 15: 57.

indicate they have attended a service.[12] If they are visiting a chapel, which is not the one at which they are registered, they will ask for a form to give to their home chapel as proof of meeting this requirement.[13] If a member misses a service, an officer will visit during the week to check on them, or else they will be asked why they missed worship at the small weekly prayer group to which they are assigned.[14]

The purpose of worship is to:

Reverently approach the holy presence of God to acknowledge His greatness and blessings. . . to be with God's people to express [their] love to God in prayer and praises, in singing psalms and spiritual songs, in listening and responding to His holy words preached. . .

---

[12]I observed this while attending a worship service in the San Jose, CA, chapel on July 5, 2009. See also Charles Ang, "Iglesia ni Cristo," graduate paper for New Religious Movements course taught by Anne Harper and Michael McDowell at Asian Theological Seminary, 2004, 3; Hyoung Beck (Peter) Kim, "Ethnographic Research Paper," graduate paper for New Religious Movements course taught by Anne Harper and Michael McDowell at Asian Theological Seminary, Quezon City, 2004, 5; Lal Uk, "A Research Paper on Iglesia ni Cristo Worship Service," graduate paper for New Religious Movements course taught by Anne Harper and Michael McDowell at Asian Theological Seminary, Quezon City, 2002, 4; Khual, "My Observation," 1; he also notes on p. 5 that the Minister told him the biggest sin is people who come and turn their card over and then return home; Lailo N. Reototar, "Light Has Shone on Me at Last," *Pasugo* 53, 6 (June 2001): 11.

[13]Larni E. Zuñiga, "Ethnographic Research Paper," graduate paper for New Religious Movements course taught by Anne Harper and Michael McDowell at Asian Theological Seminary, Quezon City, 2002, 2; Reototar, "Light Has Shone on Me at Last," 11; Eraño Manalo, *Mga Leksiyong Ministeryal*, Lesson 24: 113.

[14]David F. Dawes, "Iglesia ni Cristo: 'True Church' Denies Christ's Deity," *Christian Info News*, August 1997, quoting district secretary Rod Bruno: "Every week there are 'committee prayer' meetings in various homes. Group leaders will ask members why they did not attend services, but it's not to harass them, it's to offer them help. It's like a concerned parent taking care of children." www.canadianchristianity.com/cgi-bin/bc.cgi?bc/eccn/0897/iglesia, (accessed April 15, 2009); and Reototar, "Light Has Shone on Me at Last," 10.

and in making offerings; it is His command to give thanks during the worship service inside the house.[15]

Members do not go to worship services solely because it is a required duty. They desire the opportunity to commune with God in Iglesia ni Cristo chapels that they perceive as holy.[16] They seek guidance in life, and the teaching that happens during worship services provides an important part of what they perceive to be God's direction.[17]

Those attending services are required to dress in an appropriate manner, in "holy array."[18] For women, this means a skirt or modest dress, not pants.[19] For men this means clean formal shirts (at least a collared polo shirt, not a tee-shirt).[20] It also means proper shoes: no *chinelas* (flip-flops). Women serving in the front of the chapel in the choir or as the organist must have hair of a certain length and "look like a girl."[21]

Of extreme importance is worshipping God in an orderly and proper manner. This means seriousness and orderliness with no one talking.[22] Members are taught to highly value the solemnity of

---

[15] Santiago, "Called to Declare Praises to God," 2.

[16] Adriel O. Meimban, "The Spiritual Graces Received during the Worship Service," *Pasugo* 56, 10 (October 2004): 8, and Feljun B. Fuentes, "Editorial: Let Us Sing Praises to the Lord," *Pasugo* 51, 4 (April 1999): 3.

[17] *Pasugo*, "Frequently Asked Questions," 9.

[18] Benildo C. Santiago, "The Proper Way of Worshipping God," *Pasugo* 53, 7 (July 2003): 9.

[19] VJ, interview by author, Antipolo, Rizal, May 20, 2004; and Marlex C. Cantor, "Worshipping God in the Proper and Orderly Way," *Pasugo* 54, 5 (May 2002): 9.

[20] Santiago, "The Proper Way of Worshiping God," 9; Cantor, "Worshiping God in the Proper and Orderly Way," 9; Iglesia ni Cristo, "Worshipping God in an Acceptable Manner"; and Zuñiga, "Ethnographic," 7.

[21] VJ, interview, May 20, 2004.

[22] Jones, "No Longer Confused," 16; Iglesia ni Cristo, "The Iglesia ni Cristo and the Bible: Worshipping God in an Acceptable Manner," video internet file http://www.iglesianicristo.ws, (accessed April 6, 2009); Kim, "Ethnographic," 2.

services.[23] Observers have noted that no one smiles, and everyone looks serious during these times.[24]

Men and women enter the sanctuary on the left and right, respectively, and then sit separately, men on the left and women on the right.[25] Worshippers do not choose their seats, but fill in the pews from the front to the back in order as the ushers direct them.[26] In every third or fourth pew, an end-seat is left vacant for a deacon or deaconess serving as usher and standing along the outside wall.[27] Deacons usually wear white barongs or suits, and deaconesses, long-sleeved white dresses.[28] They may encourage people to move closer together in the pews to allow room for more occupants.[29] When the seats in an usher's rows are filled, his or her responsibility is fulfilled.[30] If the church does not have hymnals in

---

[23] Manalo, *Mga Leksiyong Ministeryal*, Lesson 15: 57f; Iglesia ni Cristo, "Worshipping God in an Acceptable Manner," video internet file http://www.iglesianicristo.ws (accessed April 6, 2009) ; Michelle Sarol-Valdez, "I Found the Way to God's Kingdom," *Pasugo*, 51, 10 (October 1999): 26 and 27; and Reototar, "Light Has Shone on Me at Last," 11.

[24] Author's observation on July 5, 2009; Sing Khaw Thawn, "Ethnographic Research Paper," graduate paper for New Religious Movements course taught by Anne Harper and Michael McDowell at Asian Theological Seminary, Quezon City, 2004, 2; Uk, "A Research," 2; and Zuñiga, "Ethnographic," 7.

[25] Author's observation on July 5, 2009; Ang, "Iglesia," 1; Thawn, "Ethnographic," 2; Kim, "Ethnographic," 1; Zuñiga, "Ethnographic," 2; Reototar, "Light Has Shone on Me at Last," 11; Uk, "A Research," ; and observation of convert James Johnson in *Pasugo*, "Converts: The Path to Peace and Salvation," 52, 5 (May 2000): 11.

[26] Author's observation on July 9, 2009; Thawn, "Ethnographic," 2; Zuñiga, "Ethnographic," 2; and Michelle Sarol-Valdez, "I Found the Way to God's Kingdom," 26.

[27] Author's observation on July 5, 2009.

[28] Uk, "A Research," 2; Ang, "Iglesia," 1; Khual, "My Observation," 2; and Kim, "Ethnographic," 1, 5, notes the barongs have green, white and red flat badges. Zuñiga, "Ethnographic," 2, notes that the male ushers at the service he attended wore blue suits with jackets and ties.

[29] Author's observation on July 5, 2009.

[30] Uk, "A Research," 1.

the pews, worshippers will be handed a hymnal or a sheet with the hymns for the service.[31]

Punctuality is not only valued but also required. People arrive within a half hour before the service officially starts. The choir of men and women will already be in place wearing robes, usually white ones.[32] The organist is playing solemn music quietly. During this half-hour pre-service time, every ten minutes or so the choir will stand together and sing a hymn.[33] The hymn number is noted on signs or poles in the front of the church on both sides.[34] Some worshippers may sing along quietly, but most remain in a meditative posture silently praying.[35] All worshippers must arrive prior to the announced worship time because the chapel doors are shut early, and the parking lot gates are closed approximately ten minutes prior to the service.[36] There is no talking or greeting

---

[31] Thawn, "Ethnographic," 2; Kim, "Ethnographic," 1; and Zuñiga, "Ethnographic," 2. In the service the author attended in the United States, the pew backs each had several racks with hymnals. In each rack were two bound Tagalog hymnals and two binders with English translations. Each of these hymnals and binders was labeled on the outside: female or male side, pew number and location. Inside was a label stating that the hymnal was the property of the Iglesia ni Cristo San Jose local with a number assigned.

[32] Uk, "A Research," 2; Zuñiga, "Ethnographic," 2, 7; and Kim, "Ethnographic," 4, notes the men wore black neckties over their choir robes.

[33] Author's observation on July 5, 2009; Ang, "Iglesia," 1; Kim, "Ethnographic," 1; and Zuniga, "Ethnographic," 2.

[34] Thawn, "Ethnographic," 2; Zuñiga, "Ethnographic," 2; and Khual, "My Observation," 2.

[35] Thawn, "Ethnographic," 2.

[36] Gino Rinaldo A. Garcia, "Ethnographic Research Paper," Graduate paper for New Religious Movements course taught by Anne Harper and Michael McDowell at Asian Theological Seminary, Quezon City, 2002, 1-2. When he arrived inside the church as the service was starting he was told if the pastor heard about it he would be *itiwalag* (expelled or punished). Author's observation on July 5, 2009.

others, and guests are warned to be quiet.[37] No one enters or leaves once the service proper has begun.[38]

Promptly at the assigned worship time, the ministers, workers and elders who will lead enter and sit on chairs on a raised platform behind the pulpit or podiums.[39] They wear western suits.[40] At this point, the deacons and deaconesses sit down in their assigned pews.[41] The choir stands again and leads the congregation in singing four or five hymns.[42] These are about the church, commitment to God, service, sinfulness, and God the Father's mercifulness.[43] The tunes sound Western, rather than Filipino or Asian.[44] They are sung in Tagalog in the Philippines, though in English in the United States.[45] The choir stands in unison with the hymnals under their arms on the left side; after singing, they place the hymnals back under their arms and sit down at the same time.[46]

Following the singing of hymns, there is a prayer led by a minister or evangelical worker lasting five to seven minutes.[47] Instructions to new members indicate they are to stand for prayer because "we stand in the presence of God;" they are to keep their

---

[37] Author's observation on July 5, 2009; Kim, "Ethnographic," 2; Thawn, "Ethnographic," 2; Zuñiga, "Ethnographic," 7; Khual, "My Observation," 1, 4; and Uk, "A Resesarch," 4.

[38] Author's observation on July 5, 2009; Thawn, "Ethnographic," 5, and Khual, "My Observation," 4, notes that no one goes in or out during the service.

[39] A description of typical chapels is included in the section below on Houses of Worship. Uk, "A Research," 2; and Ang, "Iglesia," 2.

[40] Thawn, "Ethnographic," 2; Uk, "A Research," 2; Ang, "Iglesia," 2; Zuñiga, "Ethnographic," 2; Khual, "My Observation," 2; and Kim, "Ethnographic," 1.

[41] Thawn, "Ethnographic," 2; and Uk, "A Research," 1.

[42] Author's observation on July 5, 2009; Uk, "A Research," 2; and Ang, "Iglesia," 1.

[43] Thawn, "Ethnographic," 2; Zuñiga, "Ethnographic," 2; and Thawn, "Ethnographic," 3.

[44] Author's observation on July 5, 2009; Uk, "A Research," 2; and Thawn, "Ethnographic," 3.

[45] Author's observation on July 5, 2009; and Zuñiga, "Ethnographic," 3.

[46] Author's observation on July 5, 2009; and Thawn, "Ethnographic," 3.

[47] Author's observation on July 5, 2009; and Uk, "A Research," 3.

eyes closed and "open their hearts."[48] Every time there is a pause the congregation responds in unison, loudly, with "Yes, Lord," or "Amen."[49] They are affirming agreement with the prayer.[50] Members are taught that there is a biblical basis for this affirming, and that they are expressing a conviction that the Lord "has accepted [their] prayers."[51] This general prayer may cover such topics as being faithful, being persecuted, or facing troubles; there will also be thanksgiving for the church and for Felix Y. Manalo.[52] This prayer is often emotional.[53] It is addressed to God the Father in Jesus' name or to Jesus as mediator.[54]

The lesson is presented by the minister. It is not called a sermon, and the minister explains that it was written and comes from the Chief Executive Minister.[55] Extremely well prepared and organized, it may be in a question and answer format using Bible verses as proof texts, or it may be a reading of several Bible verses with teaching on their central theme or church doctrine.[56] The minister will have several translations of the Bible on the pulpit and open them at appropriate points to read verses directly.[57] Iglesia ni Cristo members highly value this form of teaching and believe it is inspired. They look askance at sermons in other churches, which seem to involve nothing more than stories or the expressing of the

---

[48]INCWorld, "Manual for New Members," http://incworld.faithweb.com/info.htm (accessed June 29, 2007).
[49]Author's observation on July 5, 2009; Ang, "Iglesia," 2; Kim, "Ethnographic," 4; Uk, "A Research," 3; Zuñiga, "Ethnographic," 3; Thawn, "Ethnographic," 4; and Letters to the Editor, "Saying Our Amens," *Pasugo* 52 (June 2000): 2.
[50]Ang, "Iglesia," 2. Manalo, *Mga Leksiyong Ministeryal*, Lesson 24: 110.
[51]Editor, "Letters: Saying Our Amens," 2.
[52]Author's observation on July 5, 2009.
[53]Kim, "Ethnographic," 4; and author's observation on July 5, 2009.
[54]Author's observation on July 5, 2009; Thawn, "Ethnographic," 4; Zuñiga, "Ethnographic," 3; Khual, Manalo, *Mga Leksiyong Ministeryal*, Lesson 20:87;and Khual, "My Observation," 1. VJ, interview, May 20, 2004, called this "*Sa ngalan ni Jesus,*" or "in the name of Jesus prayer."
[55]Author's observation on July 5, 2009.
[56]Author's observation on July 5, 2009; Ang,"Iglesia," 2; Thawn, "Ethnographic," 4-5; and Uk, "A Research," 3.
[57]Author's observation on July 5, 2009; Zuñiga, 3.

speaker's opinion.[58] They believe they are receiving divine guidance through these messages. The length of the lesson varies from thirty to as long as fifty minutes.[59] In one observed service, two ministers spoke, one for thirty minutes and the other for twenty minutes.[60]

Those in the congregation do not bring Bibles with them.[61] They are taught that listening is the proper way to learn, not reading the Bible for themselves. "Even in Jesus' time He commanded his disciples to listen to Him rather than reading. Hearing is crucial so that people can understand what the Bible says."[62] They rely on the Chief Executive Minister and others in authority for the correct interpretation of Scripture because they are taught that not just anyone can understand the Bible.[63] If they are asked a question about biblical interpretation or confronted by someone saying their church teaches falsehoods, they will refer the person to one of their ministers or evangelical workers. They do not believe it is their place to respond.

Following the lesson, there is another lengthy prayer, which includes a request for guidance for the Church Administration.[64] This is followed by the collection of the offering with the choir singing.[65]

Offerings are an important part of Iglesia ni Cristo culture because of the high value placed on building new houses of worship and evangelistic outreach. There are several kinds of offerings. These are taken to cover chapel maintenance, operating expenses,

---

[58] *Pasugo*, "Converts: The Path to Peace and Salvation," 11.

[59] Author's observation on July 5, 2009; Thawn, "Ethnographic," 3; Kim, "Ethnographic," 2; and Uk, "A Research," 3.

[60] Garcia, "Ethnographic," 4.

[61] Author's observation on July 5, 2009; Kim, "Ethnographic," 3; Garcia, "Ethnographic," 5; and Uk, "A Research," 4.

[62] Khual, "My Observation," 3.

[63] Manalo, *Mga Leksiyong Ministeryal*, Lesson 13: 47-48; and Castro, "Those Given to Know the Mystery of God," 6.

[64] Author's observation on July 5, 2009, and Thawn, "Ethnographic," 4.

[65] Manalo, *Mga Leksiyong Ministeryal*, Lesson 24:109; author's observation on July 5, 2009, and Thawn, "Ethnographic," 4.

payment of ministers and evangelical Workers, care of retired workers, and the annual Thanksgiving offering (*handog*, discussed later) for new church buildings. The regular offering given during weekly worship services after the sermon is called *abuloy* (contribution). There are special offerings called *tanging handugan*. These are optional offerings used for special purposes such as missions, chapel repairs, one-time purchases, and other special needs of the locale congregation. Members make this special offering upon arrival before they enter the main worship hall. They enclose the funds in a small envelope with their name on it and drop it in a wooden chests located at the male and female entrances to the worship hall.[66]

For the offering during worship services, the deacons and deaconesses who served as ushers go through the two or three pews for which they are responsible. They hold an offering bag, usually white in color, in front of each person, one at a time. When they have completed their assigned rows, they move to the back of the church. The choir sings an offering hymn and the offerings bags are brought by the deacons and deaconesses, along with the boxes containing the special offerings to the front and placed in a large wooden box in front of the main pulpit.[67] One of the ministers prays over the offering.[68] Another hymn may be sung, and then the benediction is given.[69]

---

[66] Ang, "Iglesia," 3; and VJ, interview by author, Cainta, Rizal, April 1, 2003.

[67] Author's observation on July 5, 2009; QL, letter to the author, July 18, 2014; Ang, "Iglesia," 1; Kim, "Ethnographic," 4; Uk, "A Research," 3; and Garcia, "Ethnographic," 5. Zuñiga, Ethnographic," 4, notes that two men in suits brought smaller wooden boxes after the offerings bags were placed in the large box. He was told these boxes contained offerings for Ministers and church buildings.

[68] QL, letter to the author on July 18, 2014; author's observation on July 5, 2009; Ang, "Iglesia," 1; Uk, "A Research," 3; Zuñiga, "Ethnographic," 5; and Ang, "Iglesia," 3. Thawn, "Ethnographic," 5, notes that the prayer is for wise use of the funds by the Church Administration.

[69] Author's observation July 5, 2009; Garcia, "Ethnographic," 5; and Uk, "A Research," 3. Zuñiga, "Ethnographic," 5, notes the announcements came before the benediction in the service he attended..

Following the offering announcements about church activities are given. Depending on the size of the chapel, these may take as long as ten minutes.[70] Then the worshippers file out in an orderly fashion, pew by pew. They hand the song sheets and hymnals back to the ushers.[71] No one speaks while inside the chapel, and outside there is little talking and certainly nothing loud or boisterous or any laughing.[72]

Children, who have been meeting in another building, will join their parents in the parking lot following the service. A discussion of children's activity is found in the section on the Children's Worship Service later.

In summary, the worship services of the Iglesia ni Cristo are quite different from those in which the general Filipino population participates. Outsiders visiting these services for the first time are always amazed at this. The seriousness, silence, orderliness and lack of smiling are countercultural in a land in which people smile and laugh often and enjoy socializing with each other before, sometimes during and certainly after worship services. Joy would certainly be a characteristic of evangelical worship services, but no outward manifestations of joy are obvious during this group's experience of worship. The worship services of the Iglesia ni Cristo highlight the distinctiveness and separateness of this church's culture.

Beyond attending worship services, two overarching concerns characterize and motivate the daily, weekly, monthly and yearly activities of the Iglesia ni Cristo: building new houses of worship and evangelism.

---

[70]Author's observation on July 5, 200;, and Uk, "A Research," 4.
[71]Thawn, "Ethnographic," 3; Kim, "Ethnographic," 5; Ang, "Iglesia," 3; Uk, "A Research," 4; and Zuñiga, "Ethnographic," 5.
[72]Author's observation on July 5, 2009.

Houses of Worship

Every issue of *Pasugo* highlights the building and dedication of new houses of worship.[73] Pictures of different chapels appear each month. Called "the house of God," "the house of prayer," "the house of worship," "temple," or simply "chapel," these buildings are extremely important to Iglesia ni Cristo members. The church allocates millions of pesos each year for their construction and maintenance.[74] A minister commented to one of the author's students:

> The chapel is the dwelling place of God. So we have to build chapels better than our house, taller than an ordinary house... Psalm 11:4 says that 'the Lord is in His Holy Temple.' So we should build as big a chapel as we can.[75]

The Iglesia ni Cristo teaches that God's name and glory dwell in these special temples.[76] God himself cannot be contained in a building, but he has chosen and consecrated these buildings especially so that "His name, eyes and heart will dwell forever" in them.[77] Because of this, they should not be desecrated.[78] There is no buying and selling inside the house of worship or outside on its

---

[73]For example see Rogelio C. Dumangas, "Church Keeps Up Construction Boom," *Pasugo* 57, 1 (January 2005): 8; Rogelio C. Dumangas, "Renovation of Houses of Worship, Infrastructure Projects Continued," *Pasugo* 59, 2 (February 2007): 5; Rogelio C. Dumangas, "Highlights of the Church's Achievements: A Year After," *Pasugo* 56, 4 (April 2004): 8; Mariou Dabu, "Mississauga Dedicates House of Worship," *Pasugo* 53, 7 (July 2001): 34; and Rosemarie O. Carlos, "Cavite Greets 1999 with Renewed Inspiration and Devotion," *Pasugo* 51, 3 (March 2001): 26.

[74]Franklin T. Bunag, "The House of Worship: Its Importance to God and His People." *Pasugo* 57, 1 (January 2005): 10; and *God's Message* News Bureau, "Chronicles: Four New Chapels and Still Counting," *Pasugo* 56 (August 2004): 7.

[75]Khual, "My Observation," 5.

[76]Bunag, "The House of Worship," 13. See Jeffrey V. Rosquites, summary of the homily by the Deputy Executive Minister at the dedication of a new house of worship, in "EVM Officiates Brixtonville Thanksgiving, Dedicates New House of Worship," *Pasugo* 56, 2 (February 2004): 7.

[77]Feljun B. Fuentes, "Where His Glory Dwells," *Pasugo* 55, 7 (July 2003): 5.

[78]*Ibid.*

surrounding property.[79] This is different from Roman Catholic parishes in the Philippines, which sell religious paraphernalia and other merchandise on their properties, or Protestant churches, which often sell books, tapes and DVDs or tickets to special events.

The church teaches and members believe that God is especially attentive to the prayers of his people inside these buildings.[80] In times of trouble, members will flock to the chapels because they feel safer and because they believe God will hear them there.[81] They may go to the chapels to offer "devotional prayers" for special needs at times other than regular services.[82]

Keeping these buildings and their surrounding properties clean is a top priority, and there are regularly scheduled cleanings by officers and members.[83]

God's "mandate" is to continue to build more houses of worship "because of the responsibility of members to offer the sacrifice of praise to God."[84] These buildings are the only places exclusively designed for God's people to offer Him praises and worship.[85]

> For us the house of worship is a very important place; it is the religious center for the enhancement of our spiritual life. As a holy place, it is where we commune with God and say our prayers to Him. It is also the focal point of our

---

[79] *Ibid.*

[80] Bunag, "The House of Worship," 13; Rizza G. Mendoza, "Inside God's Holy Temple," *Pasugo* 56, 1 (January 2004): 1; and Rosquites, "EVM Officiates," 7.

[81] Marlex C. Cantor, "Survival of the Eldest: Pampanga District Revisited," *Pasugo* 56, 1 (January 2004): 37.

[82] For more on prayer see section on "Prayer" later in the chapter.

[83] Fuentes, "Where His Glory Dwells," 5; Joel V. San Pedro, "10 Tips for Helping Your Child Grow Spiritually," *Pasugo* 52, 9 (September 2000): 10; and R. M. Forro, Jr., J. B. Silva; and N. C. Caritativo, "Iloilo North Conducts Choir Day," *Pasugo* 56, 1 (January 2004): 8.

[84] Bunag, "The House of Worship," 14.

[85] Bienvenido C. Santiago, "Editorial: Building Houses of Worship for God's Glory," *Pasugo* 55, 7 (July 2003): 7; Bunag, "The House of Worship," 1; and Cantor, "Worshipping God in the Proper and Orderly Way," 9.

religious life because it is where we gather to worship the Lord. It is the place for our sanctification and edification.[86]

Special worship services are scheduled to dedicate new chapels and to rededicate renovated and expanded ones. There has been much fanfare and festivity associated with dedications, and whenever possible prior to his death in 2009, the Chief Executive Minister, Eraño Manalo, or his son, then Deputy Executive Minister Eduardo V. Manalo (Ka Eddie), attended and gave the homily. For new locals there is an official signing of a scroll by the CEM or DEM and their entourage of officials from the Central Office and the District.[87] The scrolls from the congregations in Jerusalem, Rome and Athens are displayed prominently in the church's museum at its central complex in Diliman, Quezon City, because their openings are viewed as fulfillment of biblical prophecies.[88]

These houses of worship are also regarded as landmarks to the Iglesia ni Cristo's faith.[89] Their tall spires rise above surrounding buildings, and the cleanliness and beautiful landscaping often stand in stark contrast with their barrios and neighborhoods. Members are justifiably proud of their accomplishment in building these structures.

In Metro Manila and throughout the Philippines diesel soot is endemic. Most buildings turn shades of grey within a few months after being painted. In a land where poverty is evident everywhere, frugality is necessary. So the paint applied to buildings is often watered down and thin. This is not the case with Iglesia ni Cristo chapels. They are painted in light pastel colors and regularly

---

[86]Fuentes, "Where His Glory Dwells," 4.
[87]Marie F. Ruiz, "Highway Hills," 25; Rebecca J. Flores, "Tinian Dedicates House of Worship," *Pasugo* 52, 5 (May 2000): 32; Antonio E. Bocobo, Jr. and Melissa C. Frani, "EVM Officiates Imus, Cavite Dedication," *Pasugo* 54, 3 (March 2002): 27; and *Pasugo* News Bureau, "Miscellany in the Districts: Students in Benguet Receive Words of Wisdom," *Pasugo* 54, 1 (January 2002): 38.
[88]Harper, "A Filipino Church at 80 Years," 429-450.
[89]Fuentes, "Where His Glory Dwells," 4.

cleaned and repainted. They appear as newly painted no matter how old the chapel. They are simply beautiful.

In a culture in which throwing litter on the ground is the norm, the cleanliness of the property surrounding the chapels is unique. In a tropical climate, leaves and plant debris also accumulate quickly; plants rapidly become overgrown. The landscaping around Iglesia ni Cristo temples shows little evidence of this; their regular maintenance is clearly evident.

Chapel properties are usually surrounded by a fence with large gates and a guard house. This is true even in the United States.[90] Parking is usually available in a lot with clearly marked spaces. Once, when the author was taking pictures of the chapel in Brookside, Antipolo, Rizal, the guard came out to check what she was doing. The group is protective of these buildings because of their significance.

One enters the chapel through a church foyer. In the foyer, there usually are some tables set up where deacons sit and provide attendance slips for those needing them. Cupboards holding registered members' nametags line the wall. The cabinet doors are opened prior to the services and closed once the services start. In some chapels, there will be a section of bank teller-like stalls.[91] These are for those who want to make deposits towards their annual Thanksgiving offering.[92]

There are entrances to the chapel proper on the left for the men and on the right for the women. Pews are comfortable and spaced far enough apart so that the ushers have enough room to pass between them for the offering. In the Philippines, most chapels are not air-conditioned, so fans may line the walls.[93] These are painted in light pastels. The ceilings are high, as in a cathedral.

---

[90] Author's observation of chapels in San Antonio, TX, and San Jose, CA, and pictures in issues of the *Pasugo*.
[91] Ang, "Iglesia," 3-4, and VJ, interview, April 1, 2003.
[92] For more on this see the section on "Thanksgiving" below.
[93] Ang, "Iglesia," 1; and Khual, "My Observation," 6.

Usually there are large, ornate chandeliers hanging from the ceiling. In the San Jose, CA, chapel, the floor was carpeted and the wooden pew seats and backs were upholstered in a pleasing geometric pattern of light green and blue.[94]

Inside the chapels, there are usually three levels:[95] that of the congregation's pews, a higher level with pulpits for the ministers and worship leaders,[96] and a third, still higher level for the choir with the organ placed at the center.[97] A large wooden box for the offering sits in the center front of the ministers' level.[98]

On the sanctuary's ministerial level, there are a number of chairs made of ornate wood.[99] One student who attended the Cubao, Quezon City, chapel was informed that the central chair was reserved for the Chief Executive Minister.[100] Another noted that this chair had the Iglesia ni Cristo seal on it.[101]

In the chapels, there are no crosses and no other religious symbols.[102] There may be some designs carved into the ornate wooden portions of the sanctuary, but these are decorative, having no symbolic meanings.[103] There are no statues, no candles are used

---

[94] Author's observation on July 5, 2009; Ang, "Iglesia," 1.
[95] Garcia, "Ethnographic," 31. Thawn, "Ethnographic," 6, notes a fourth level: in the chapel he visited the offering box was on a different level than the congregation.
[96] Kim, "Ethnographic," 4; and Ang, "Iglesia," 2. Thawn, "Ethnographic," 6, notes three pulpits.
[97] Author's observation on July 5, 2009; and Kim, Ethnographic," 4.
[98] Author's observation on July 5, 2009; Ang, "Iglesia," 2; and Zuñiga, "Ethnographic," 4.
[99] Author's observation on July 5, 2009; and Zuñiga, "Ethnographic," 5.
[100] Ang, "Iglesia," 1.
[101] Khual, "My Observation," 2.
[102] Author's observation on July 5, 2009; Kim, "Ethnographic," 4; and Uk, "A Research," 4. Khaul, "My Observation," 5, notes that when he asked a minister why there was no cross, the minister told him, "The cross is not a symbol of Christians; it is rather a sign of punishment."
[103] Zuñiga, "Observation," 5; and Kim, "Ethnographic," 5.

and only one student commented on artificial flower arrangements.[104]

In summary, the beauty, grandeur and cleanliness of Iglesia ni Cristo chapels are a distinctive cultural phenomenon for the group. The care of these places of worship is a high value for them and is at odds with the values and practices in typical Filipino culture, in which maintenance of buildings is only done when absolutely necessary, and worship may take place in multi-use buildings.

Church Expansion and Evangelism

> With modern communication technology, it becomes easier now than ever to go into the entire world and deliver the message of salvation. . . . Through its evangelical programs and with the help of its religious media—print, television and radio—its Ministers and workers deliver the gospel to the world to share the grace of salvation to all mankind.[105]

A Mission

The Iglesia ni Cristo is a church with a mission. That mission is to declare a message of salvation only through itself to the whole world because the Day of Judgment is fast approaching.[106] The multitude of activities and efforts at evangelizing family, friends, neighbors and neighborhoods is astounding.

By 2008, the Iglesia ni Cristo had extended its reach to ninety countries and territories with 5,000 congregations in the

---

[104]VJ, Interview by author, Antipolo, Rizal, April 1, 2003; and Zuñiga, "Ethnographic," 6.
[105]Feljun B. Fuentes, "Editorial: Spreading the Good News to the World," *Pasugo* 52, 2 (February 2000): 3.
[106]Bienvenido C. Santiago, "Getting the Good News Across," *Pasugo* 55, 10 (October 2003): 3.

Philippines and 600 abroad.[107] This expansion did not come out of a vacuum. It was intentional.[108]

Planning for evangelism takes place at all levels of the church. There is regular strategizing, and specific goals are set.[109] These objectives are clearly communicated from the top down to every member. All groups and individuals within the church are enlisted in the work of evangelism. There is a healthy competitiveness in it all. Those who are the most productive receive recognition[110] and, in the case of ministers and evangelical workers, the highest achievers receive opportunities to move to larger chapels or advance up the administrative ladder to the district level.[111] Efforts at outreach are highlighted in *Pasugo* to motivate and give ideas to the rest of the church. What do these efforts look like?

Media and Print

The Central Office spearheads evangelistic efforts by broadcasting programs on sixty-three radio stations, 218 cable TV and sixty-four relay television stations in the Philippines alone. Programs are broadcast in all the major Filipino languages.[112] The

---

[107]"Iglesia ni Cristo," http://www.absoluteastronomyu.com/topics/Iglesia_ni_Cristo (accessed April 15, 2009), and Gaynor Dumat-ol Daleno, "Celebrating 40 Years," *Pacific Sunday News*, March 15, 2009, http://www/guamdn.com/article/20090315/LIFESTYLE/903150319/1024 (accessed April 15, 2009).

[108]See Anne C. Harper, "New Religious Movements, Part Two: An Analysis of One Movement: The Iglesia ni Cristo of the Philippines," *Journal of Asian Mission* 10, 1-2: 100.

[109]Siegfred T. Gollayan, "More Districts Reap Bountiful Harvest," *Pasugo* 56, 9 (September 2004): 5, notes Northern California exceeded by 150% its assigned standard for baptisms.

[110]Gene N. Abella, "Northern California Celebrates Church's 87th Anniversary," *Pasugo* 53, 10 (October 2001): 34.

[111]*Pasugo* News Bureau, "Miscellany in the Districts: Oldest District Commemorates 77th Year," *Pasugo* 53, 4 (April 2001): 39; VJ, interview by author, Taytay, Rizal, February 4, 2004; and Benjie de los Reyes, "Church Commends Ministers," *Pasugo* 52, 5 (May 2000): 31.

[112]Santiago, "Getting the Good News Across," 3; and Fuentes, "Spreading the Good News," 3.

church prints a beautiful monthly magazine, *Pasugo*, ("God's Message"), in English and Tagalog.[113] They also print a wide variety of pamphlets and tracts, which members distribute worldwide.[114]

These materials are widely distributed by members regularly. Sometimes they are given to a family member or friend; other times there are large distribution drives such as one in Tarlac in which 32,000 pamphlets and 20,000 *Pasugo*s were given out.[115] A minister or evangelical worker may form a motorcade of members and go to a remote area to distribute these materials.[116] Door-to-door visitation is not unusual.[117] These efforts are mandated by the Central Administration and are carefully coordinated since they often happen during the same period and even on the same day in different locations.[118] Each year the Church Administration chooses a theme for the year. This theme may focus on families, on church leadership, or as in 2002, on evangelism: "Shine Brightly as Lights of Salvation to the World, Share the Message of Salvation to All."[119]

---

[113] Santiago, "Letter from the Editor," 2. Feljun B. Fuentes, in "Editorial: 60 Years of Heralding the Truth," 5, notes the meaning of "Pasug*o*:" "It means word or message coming from Almighty God that is being relayed to a person through His messenger." The magazine's purpose is to "propagate the faith; to expose false doctrines. . . to inform the brethren of the activities of the Church; to discuss religious issues; and to edify the brethren that they may be able to withstand persecutions and other forms of prejudice and discouragement."

[114] Santiago, "Getting the Good News Across," 3.

[115] *Pasugo* News Bureau, "Miscellany in the Districts: SCAN Launches 'Bantay Lansangan 2003,'" *Pasugo* 55, 6 (June 2003): 31.

[116] Tranquilino Sahagun and Lorenzo Mauel, "*Bagong Buhay* Brethren Brave Odds to Spread Gospel Truth," *Pasugo* 53, 10 (October 2001): 32-33.

[117] Edwin Guingab, Rebecca Flores and Rolando Zepeda, "Hawaii-Pacific Inducts 300 New Officers," *Pasugo* 53, 4 (April 2001): 34.

[118] Sahagun, "*Bagong Buhay*," 32-3. Dennis P. Eudela, "Virginia Beach Joins Worldwide Activity," *Pasugo* 53, 10 (October 2001): 36; and *Pasugo* News Bureau, "Miscellany in the Districts: Districts Join Worldwide Missionary Campaign," *Pasugo* 53, 10 (October 2001): 37.

[119] Norma Royeca and Janette Matugas, "Pacific Northwest Beats the Cold Weather," *Pasugo* 54, 4 (April 2002): 32.

Grand Evangelical Missions

Large evangelistic rallies take place several times a year—often in January, at the start of the year, and in July, the month during which the church celebrates its reemergence in the Philippines.[120] Members are "exhorted" and encouraged to invite their families,[121] friends and acquaintances to these events, called Grand Evangelical Missions (GEMs). These usually take place at the district level, and publicity for them will include banners hung across major roads and highways.[122] Smaller events, called Evangelical Missions (EMs), take place at the locale level.

The GEMs involve a great deal of preparation[123] and may have special features to attract attendees such as a large choir, a musical competition, video presentations, and historical, photo and art displays.[124] The event itself will always include an exposition from

---

[120] For example, Marlex C. Cantor, "Districts Worldwide Open 2004 with Fruitful Missions," *Pasugo* 56,3 (March 2004): 5, notes over 3000 Grand Evangelical Missions and missionary events held throughout the world in January. Benjie de los Reyes, "Metro Manila Districts Baptize More than 2,000," *Pasugo* 51,10 (October 1999): 33, notes that seven million tracts were distributed prior to "simultaneous grand missions held in all the ecclesiastic districts of the archipelago" during July. S. Gollayan, "Districts Intensify Missionary Activities," *Pasugo* 56, 8 (August 2004): 6-7, describes the distribution of invitation cards prior to districts holding simultaneous Evangelical Missions in their locals.

[121] One family is held up as an example for distributing religious pamphlets to relatives at a large family reunion and for inviting Iglesia ni Cristo Ministers to attend! Marie F. Ruiz, "A Family Bequeaths a Priceless Heirloom," *Pasugo* 53,1 (January 2001): 12.

[122] VJ, interview, February 4, 2004.

[123] Jeffrey V. Rosquites, "*Iglesia ni Cristo* Children's Choir featured in Grand Evangelical Mission," *Pasugo* 55, 6 (June 2003): 11, describes some of the preparations for a January GEM. These preparations promote unity and reinforce church values.

[124] For example, *Pasugo* News Bureau, "Miscellany in the District: Samar South Pushes Forward," *Pasugo* 55, 2 (February 2003): 35, shows a picture of female members from Cebu South wearing elaborate dresses in a dance competition similar to *sinulong* competitions. *God's Message* News Bureau, "Chronicles: INC Music Video Festival—Year 3," *Pasugo* 56 (September 2004): 5, highlights the annual music video festival. Astrophel P. Caraig, Rosemarie O. Carlos and Villamore S. Quebral, "330,000 Receive Gospel,"

the Bible about Iglesia ni Cristo teachings and an invitation to pursue Bible studies focusing on the church's doctrines.[125] These Bible studies are discussed below.

Smaller evangelistic gatherings show a lot of creativity. These are called *Pamamahayag,* from the Tagalog verb *pahayag,* "to declare."[126] They are often held during a weekday, and members are asked to bring non-members with them. Some gatherings are called Bible Missionary Parties.[127] There may be videos about church teachings or testimonies of Iglesia ni Cristo members;[128] there may also be themes such as a Hawaiian luau[129] or a café night.[130]

Social Assistance

As part of its outreach efforts the Iglesia ni Cristo holds *Lingap sa Mamamayan* ("Care for People") programs.[131] On a set day members of the church will offer services to designated communities—a barrio, a prison,[132] a home for the aged,[133] a major

---

Pasugo 52, 6 (June 2000): 26, notes a 2,200-member choir. Dahlia Baldonade, Bella Agustin and Danilo Ramos, "Kowloon Launches 'Operation FYM 50,'" *Pasugo* 51, 1 (January 1999): 26, describes a photo exhibit of the history of the church, its locations, and world leaders' greetings to the church.

[125] VJ, interview, April 1, 2003.

[126] VJ, interview, February 4, 2004.

[127] Siegfred T. Gollayan, "Southern Europe Steps Up Activities," *Pasugo* 55, 5 (May 2003): 31.

[128] Rebecca Flores, Norma Royeca, Marites Miranda and Edna Domingo," Locales Propel Propagational [*sic*] Activities," *Pasugo* 53, 1 (January 2001): 35; and Eva B. Velasco and Rosette C. Dawson, "Southern California Shares Faith," *Pasugo* 54, 11 (November 2002): 32.

[129] Velasco and Dawson, "Southern California Shares," 32.

[130] Eva Velasco, Gabriel Cabasada, and Anne Marie Sandoval, "Southern California Youths Take the Lead," *Pasugo* 55, 5 (May 2003): 32.

[131] "Iglesia ni Cristo," http://absoluteastronomyu.com/topics/Iglesia_ni_Cristo; Marie F. Ruiz, "The Methuselah of Anaheim," *Pasugo* 52, 2 (February 2000): 23; and Gary P. Barrientos, "Helping People in Times of Need," *Pasugo* 53 (July 2001): 10.

[132] Frani and Villafuerte, "Metro Manila South Assists Rehabilitation Institutions," 33.

[133] El P. Buelva, "NEU Conducts Outreach Program for the Aged," *Pasugo* 51, 4 (April 1999): 31.

street,[134] or a Muslim community.[135] These services may include any or all of the following: free medical care,[136] distribution of medicines,[137] free dental services,[138] free legal services,[139] optical services,[140] circumcisions,[141] blood collection drives,[142] food distribution,[143] donation of clothing,[144] dengue prevention and education,[145] anti-drug campaigns,[146] and blood pressure monitoring.[147]

---

[134]*Pasugo* News Bureau, "Muslim Community Benefits from *Lingap*," *Pasugo* 52, 5 (May 2000): 34.

[135]*Ibid.*; and E.P. Buelva, "Church Extends *Lingap* to Muslims in QC," *Pasugo* 51, 5 (May 1999): 25.

[136]*Pasugo* News Bureau, "Muslim Community Benefits," 34; *Pasugo* News Bureau, "Miscellany in the Districts: Zamboanga Central Pulsates Youth, Community Projects," *Pasugo* 51, 1 (January 1999): 29; Buelva, "Church Extends *Lingap* to Muslims," 25; and Feljun B. Fuentes, "Editorial: More than an Expression of Compassion," *Pasugo* 51, 8 (August 1999): 3.

[137]Ruiz, "The Methuselah, 23, and Buelva, "Church Extends *Lingap* to Muslims," 25.

[138]*Pasugo* News Bureau, "Muslim Community Benefits," 34; *Pasugo* News Bureau, "Zamboanga Central Pulsates," 29; Buelva, "Church Extends *Lingap* to Muslims," 25; and *Pasugo* News Bureau, "Miscellany in the Districts: Summer Kindergarten Program Graduates 9, 224," *Pasugo* 51, 8 (August 1999): 37. Tooth extractions are done fairly frequently due to poor dental hygiene.

[139]Fuentes, "More than an Expression," 3.

[140]Buelva, "Church Extends *Lingap* to Muslims," 25.

[141]In the Philippines circumcisions are routinely performed on boys about age twelve during summer holidays in April or May. *Pasugo* News Bureau, "Summer Kindergarten Program," 37.

[142]*Pasugo* issues will often have stories or highlighted boxes showing how much blood was collected during drives. See, for example, *Pasugo* News Bureau, "Recently Conducted Blood Drives," *Pasugo* 53, 2 (February 2001): 39; and Siegfred T. Gollayan, "HK Brethren on the Go," *Pasugo* 53, 5 (May 2001): 36.

[143]Ruiz, "The Methuselah," 23; *Pasugo* News Bureau, "Zamboanga Central Pulsates," 29; and Buelva, "Church Extends *Lingap* to Muslims," 25.

[144]Ruiz, "The Methuselah," 23.

[145]*Iwas* Dengue is a government program in which the church supports and actively participates. Jennifer Bringas-Tuazon, "Church Youth Leader and Organizations Recognized," *Pasugo* 52, 6 (June 2000): 23.

[146]Anti-drug campaigns are also government-instituted but heavily supported by the church. Jennifer Bringas-Tuazon, "Church Youth Leader," 23.

[147]*Pasugo* News Bureau, "Miscellany in the Districts: Districts Promote Literacy for Less Fortunate," *Pasugo* 51, 3 (March 1999): 29.

Other community projects include *Linis Bayan* ("Clean Town") clean up drives,[148] tree planting projects,[149] English classes to prepare children for school,[150] distribution of goods such as toilet bowls,[151] aid to victims of typhoons and other disasters,[152] summer schools,[153] and free summer kindergarten programs.[154]

In summary, Iglesia ni Cristo members are passionate about bringing their message of salvation by any means available to others nearby and abroad. Thinking, planning, praying and spreading their church's gospel consumes much of their lives. This occurs at the individual, local (chapel), district, national and international levels. The church and its members are serious and intentional in proclaiming the truth of the church through words and deeds.

---

[148]These "promote cleanliness and environmental consciousness." *Pasugo* News Bureau, "Miscellany in the Districts: *KADIWA*'s 26th Year Remembered," *Pasugo* 52, 2 (February 2000): 35; *Pasugo* News Bureau, "Muslim Community Benefits," 34; Bringas-Tuazon, "Church Youth Leader," 23; *Pasugo* News Bureau, "Miscellany in the Districts: Districts Promote Literacy," 29; Rogelio C. Dumangas, "Monerey Joins Marina Cleanup Drive," *Pasugo* 51, 7 (July 1999): 25; and Rizza G. Mendoza, "Scan Int'l Conducts Environmental Activities," *Pasugo* 56 (January 2004): 6.

[149]Bringas-Tuazon, "Church Youth Leader," *Pasugo* 52, 6 (June 2000): 23; and Perlino Pineda and Filomena Alcon, "Melbourne Joins Conservation Project," *Pasugo* 51, 2 (February 1999): 33.

[150]Erlinda L. Kimura, "Tokyo Launches English Class for Children." *Pasugo* 52, 9 (September 2000): 24.

[151]*Pasugo* News Bureau, "Zamboanga Central Pulsates," 29.

[152]*Ibid.*; Ronnie C. Gonzales and Sesina G. Besa, "Church Sends Relief to Calamity Victims," *Pasugo* 51, 5 (May 1999): 24; and Fuentes; "Editorial: More than an Expression," 3.

[153]Glenn David, Bienvenido Magtuto, Jr. and Filomena Alcon, "Australia Holds First Summer Class, Senior Citizens Day," *Pasugo* 51, 5 (May 1999): 23.

[154]"SKP is part of the church's effort in extending a helping hand in developing young children and helping to curb the costly preschool education; ". . . teaches academics and aims to instill good value sin children and enhance their artistic skills; it is a yearly project of the church open to member and nonmembers alike." *Pasugo* News Bureau, "Summer Kindergarten Program Graduates," 34; G. C. Gaddi, "So. California Launches Kindergarten Program, Livens Up Missionary Efforts," *Pasugo* 56, 1 (January 2004): 4.

Joining the Iglesia ni Cristo

Those interested in joining the Iglesia ni Cristo undergo a lengthy and multi-step process of indoctrination and observation.

Bible Studies

When someone becomes interested in investigating or joining the church, they are invited to attend doctrinal Bible studies.[155] Inquirers are carefully shepherded to these studies, which are usually held weekly, often in a church member's home. A deacon or deaconess will accompany them and make sure they have transportation.[156] In areas where there are long distances between chapels and few Iglesia ni Cristo members, a minister may come to the individual's home and give the studies there.[157]

These Bible studies are actually doctrinal lessons taken from the book, *Mga Leksiyong Ministeryal* ("Doctrinal Lessons for Ministers") written by Eraño Manalo himself. These are not available to the general public but only given to ministers and evangelical workers. There are twenty-four lessons used in the Philippines, with an additional three added in overseas locations to cover the history of the church.[158]

The lessons follow the typical teaching style of the church: a question is asked, such as, "How do you join the church according

---

[155]Daniel Dautrey, "The Dawn of Eternal Life," *Pasugo* 51, 2 (February 1999): 25; and Rudolf Konrad Reiter, "A Life of Spiritual Purpose," *Pasugo* 53, 2 (February 2001): 31.

[156]Alma L. Catayay, "In Love, They Will Always Be," *Pasugo* 54, 1 (January 2002): 28; Robert Tapales, "He Led Me to Truth," *Pasugo* 54, 10 (October 2002): 32; Clarence F. Bridges, Jr., "I Found the True Church," *Pasugo* 52, 2 (February 2000): 24; Sarol-Valdez, "I Found the Way to God's Kingdom," 27; and Robert F. Pellien, "The Lord Gave Me Another Chance," *Pasugo* 54, 6 (June 2002): 26.

[157]Larry Small, "God's Message Piqued My Curiosity," *Pasugo* 55, 12 (December 2003): 9; and Sledge, "My Guide to Eternal Life," 12.

[158]Manalo, *Mga Leksiyong Ministeryal*, and "Iglesia ni Cristo," http://www.absoluteastronomyu.com/topics/Iglesia_ni_Cristo.

to the Bible?" Bible verses are then quoted and expounded in answer to the question.[159] Lessons take from thirty minutes to an hour.[160]

Probation

Following satisfactory completion of the lessons, those who desire to join the church must pass through a probationary period of six months. During this time, they must faithfully attend the twice-weekly services. Absence for any reason means they must take the lessons again and start a new six-month probation.[161] They are also required to attend fifteen prayer meetings during that period.[162] Their lives are carefully watched and must be above board: they should live as Iglesia ni Cristo members do. That means no gambling, no public drinking, keeping unity, and so on. At the end of the probation period they are screened; they are asked questions about the doctrines they were taught during the Bible studies. Those passing the screening will proceed to baptism.[163]

Baptism

Having satisfactorily passed their probation, they will be baptized by immersion as part of a mass baptism in a pool or lake. The number of baptisms in different regions was usually reported monthly in *Pasugo* until the magazine's revamping in January 2004. There is a special push for baptisms performed in January and July. Those baptized in January include Iglesia ni Cristo youths aged about twelve who have taken the lessons during the summer (April-

---

[159] Manalo, *Mga Leksiyong Ministeryal*, Lesson 10: 39, and Reototar, "Light Has Shone on Me at Last," 10.
[160] "Iglesia ni Cristo," http://www.absoluteastronomyu.com//topics/Iglesia_ni_Cristo.
[161] Steven Michael Deen, "My Dream to Find Fulfillment Came True," *Pasugo* 54, 2 (February 2002): 27; and Sarol-Valdez, "I Found the Way," 27.
[162] "Iglesia ni Cristo," http://www.absoluteastronomyu.com//topics/Iglesia_ni_Cristo.
[163] *Ibid.*; and Sarol-Valdez, "I Found the Way," 27.

May) and passed the six-month probationary period. The youths' lessons are given every day, and, as with the adults attending Bible studies, they are not allowed to miss any of them.[164] The July baptisms are held in conjunction with the anniversary celebrations of the church's founding (its re-emergence, according to their teaching).[165]

There are no *ninongs* and *ninangs* ("sponsors" or "godparents") for the ones being baptized.[166] Pictures in *Pasugo* show everyone dressed in white, men and women, both those being baptized and those performing the rite.[167] A person is not saved until they have passed through the waters of the Iglesia ni Cristo's own baptism,[168] so those wishing to join look forward to their baptism with anticipation.

The last of the doctrinal lessons covers the expected behavior and responsibilities of church members. This includes worship attendance, prayer, involvement in assigned weekly prayer groups and Christian Family Organizations, and the giving of offerings.[169]

Prayer

Regular prayer takes place during worship services and weekly prayer groups. The church also teaches members to pray throughout the day and to set regular schedules for prayer.[170]

---

[164]VJ, interview, February 4, 2004. See *Pasugo* 52, 5 (May 2000): 13, for a photo of the youth baptism held on January 1, 2000, in San Jose, CA. Cromwell W. Correa, "Pampanga Baptizes 1,001 Converts, Adds 1,015 Officers," *Pasugo* 53 (January 2001): 33.

[165]De los Reyes, "Metro Manila Districts Baptize," 33.

[166]VJ, interview, April 1, 2003.

[167]For example, see photo in Dumangas, "Special Report: Highlights of the Church's Achievement," 8; and photos in *Pasugo* 55, 10 (October 2003): 37; and *Pasugo* 55, 3 (March 2003): 29.

[168]Manalo, *Mga Leksiyong Ministeryal*, Lesson 19: 77-82.

[169]*Ibid.*, Lesson 24: 103-127. See section later in this chapter on "Thanksgiving" for additional information.

[170]Manalo, *Mga Leksiyong*, Lesson 20: 85; Michael Alexander Peter Adams, "How My Life Turned Out for the Better," *Pasugo* 56, 4 (April 2004): 28; Melissa C. Frani, "Church Member Ranks 8th in Bar Exams," *Pasugo* 54,

Parents are to train their children to have regular times of prayer and the proper way to pray.[171] The doctrinal lessons explain this regularity as "morning, noon or evening,. . .[and]. . . every time you eat, before going to work or school, . . .after you arrive at work or school, before sleeping, when waking up, when asking for forgiveness, for protection from temptation."[172]

Repetitive and nonsense prayers are forbidden, and prayer is to be in Christ's name.[173] Members are encouraged to pray for healing and to tell God all their needs.[174]

Special devotional prayers may be scheduled to seek God's guidance or help during times of hardship and danger.[175] These devotional prayers are also offered prior to evangelistic activities that family and friends may join the church and that God may bring church growth.[176]

The Iglesia ni Cristo believes that God will hear and answer the prayers of its members because it is the true church. However, God will not answer the prayers of those who are remiss in their duties.[177] As noted earlier, there seems to be an understanding that God especially hears prayer offered in the church's houses of worship.[178]

---

12 (December 2002): 23; Imelda Llana-dela Cruz, "A Woman's Faith in Spirit and Practice" *Pasugo* 51, 11 (November 1999): 1; and Fuentes, "Learning How to Pray," 5.

[171]Imelda Llana-dela Cruz, "Portrait of a Fruitful Church Member," *Pasugo* 52, 8 (August 2000): 23; San Pedro, "10 Tips," 10.

[172]Manalo, *Mga Leksiyong Ministeryal*, Lesson 20: 85-86.

[173]*Ibid.*, 87.

[174]*Ibid.*, 85.

[175]Marie F. Ruiz, "A Promise Fulfilled," *Pasugo* 55, 11 (November 2003): 9; *Pasugo* News Bureau, "Zamboanga Central Pulsates," 29; and Noel I. Ilan, "Are You Patient Enough?," *Pasugo* 55, 1 (January 2003): 11.

[176]Myrna V. Santiago, "Haifa, Israel Becomes New Locale," *Pasugo* 53, 3 (March 2001): 27; and Eudela, "Virginia Beach Joins Worldwide Activity," 36.

[177]Antonio E. Bocobo, Jr., "The People Whom God Recognizes," *Pasugo* 55, 8 (August 2003): 9.

[178]Melville-Laborde, "I Found," 31; Amelie L. Danganan, "A Picture of Unwavering Faith," *Pasugo* 58, 11 (November 2006): 29; and Marlex C. Cantor, "How Their Lives Have Changed." *Pasugo* 56, 11 (November 2004): 11.

CHAPTER 7

THE IGLESIA NI CRISTO—A DISTINCT CULTURE
PART II

Church Meetings and Organizations

An important part of Iglesia ni Cristo culture are groups that promote faithfulness, connection to other group members and service.

Weekly Prayer Groups

Every Iglesia ni Cristo member is involved in a weekly group comprising several families. He or she is assigned to this group by the locale secretary.[1] These groups meet in members' homes,[2] and they are overseen by a deacon or deaconess or an overseer being trained to be a deacon.[3] The meetings may include listening to sermon tapes, prayer, and anointing the sick with oil. If a member has a problem, it will be shared in this context.[4]

---

[1] Manalo, *Mga Leksiyong Ministeryal*, Lesson 24: 104.

[2] *Ibid.*, 105. This lesson seems to imply that members may be required to use their homes: "There might come a time it will be held in your own home. You must recognize it as a blessing. . ."

[3] INCWorld, "Manual," 4, and Manalo, *Mga Leksiyong Ministeryal*, Lesson 24: 105.

[4] INCWorld, "Manual," 4; Ronnie Cadiz Gonzales, "Port of Call: The Ecclesiastical District of the Pacific Northwest in Retrospect," *Pasugo* 57, 1 (January 2005): 35; and Dawes, "Iglesia Ni Cristo," quoting a district secretary's statement on http://www.canadianchristianity.com/cgi-bin/bc.cgi?bc/bccn/0897/iglesia.

Christian Family Organizations

Members are required to be involved in the Christian Family Organization corresponding to their age and marital status.[5] These are:

Buklod – meaning "united in marriage," for all married members.[6]

KADIWA – meaning "youth with pure intent," for those single, aged eighteen and older.[7]

Binhi—meaning "seed," for youth from thirteen to seventeen years of age who have been baptized.[8]

These organizations meet about once a month.[9] At their meetings, they may receive messages and assignments from the Church Administration, such as service projects and evangelistic activities; they may also undertake social activities such as sports events and competitions of different kinds. These organizations exist to build families, strengthen relationships and maintain harmony within the locals and districts.[10] At the district or local level, *Buklod* may hold seminars on marital relationships, raising

---

[5] INCWorld, "Manual," 3.

[6] Feljun B. Fuentes, "Milestones in the History of the Church," *Pasugo* 55, 4 (April 2003): 7; and Bien Santiago, http://aboutiglesianicristo.blogspot.com, blog of a church member (accessed April 15, 2009).

[7] This group was originally called *Kapisanan ng Maligayang Pagtatagumpay* (Association of Happy Triumph or Victory) and renamed *Kabataang may Diwang Wagas* or *KADIWA* in 1973. *Pasugo* News Bureau, "*KADIWA's* 26th Year Remembered," 33; Marie F. Ruiz, "Happily Facing the Sunset," *Pasugo* 56, 8 (August 2004): 24; Fuentes, "Milestones," 7; and Santiago, http://aboutiglesianicristo.blogspot.com.

[8] Santiago, http://aboutiglesianicristo.blogspot.com, and Fuentes, "Milestones," 7; VJ, May 20, 2004.

[9] Santiago, http://aboutiglesianicristoo.blogspot.com.

[10] Bienvenido Santiago, "Editorial: Preserving and Strengthening the Family," *Pasugo* 56, 2 (February 2004): 2; Feljun B. Fuentes, "Editorial: Strengthening the Christian Family Organizations," *Pasugo* 53, 1 (January 2001): 3; Aileen B. Quilang, "Metro Manila North Holds '*Musikapisanan*,'" *Pasugo* 55 (March 2003): 28; Alma L. Catayay, "DNM Launches Annual Website Contest," *Pasugo* 51 (March 1999): 26-27; and *Pasugo* News Bureau, "Miscellany in the Districts: *KADIWA* Promotes Fellowship through Healthy Competition," *Pasugo* 52 (July 2000): 34-39.

children and finances, or schedule romantic banquets and field trips.¹¹ Similarly, at the district or local level *KADIWA* will schedule events for young people such as courtship seminars.¹² *Binhi* will have activities attractive to teens that address issues facing this age group such as personality development, drug addiction, study habits and teenage relationships.¹³

*Pagsamba ng Kabataan*¹⁴ ("Children's Worship Service") nicknamed *PNK,* is a Sunday school class designed to teach children aged four to twelve the doctrines of the church and the proper way to behave and to prepare them for baptism.¹⁵ These classes often take place while parents are in regular worship services, but may also be held during the summer in preparation for baptism.¹⁶

Other Groups

Ilaw ng Kaligtasan ("Light of Salvation") is a church association in which members learn how to share their faith.¹⁷ Christian Brotherhood International is an organization of campus chapters for college students. Members of the Iglesia ni Cristo attending various colleges and universities meet to participate in activities

---

¹¹For example, see John Bolinas and Marc Quiambao, "Mississauga Goes Sailing," *Pasugo* 53, 2 (February 2001): 34; *Pasugo* News Bureau, "Miscellany in the Districts: Church Serves Payatas Tragedy Victims," *Pasugo* 52, 9 (September 2000): 29; and Gene N. Abella, "San Jose Couples End 1999 with Great Zeal," *Pasugo* 52, 3 (March 2000): 25.

¹²For example, see *Pasugo* News Bureau, "Zamboanga Central Pulsates," 29.

¹³For example, see *Pasugo* News Bureau, "Miscellany in the Districts: Education program Produces Graduates in Three Districts," *Pasugo* 52, 3 (March 2000): 27; Abella, "Northern California Baptizes 81 Converts," 31; and Fuentes, "Strengthening," 3.

¹⁴Today in popular Tagalog usage *kabataan* refers strictly to young people, not to children.

¹⁵Editor, "Letters," 2; and Feljun B. Fuentes, "Let Us Give Them a Better Future," *Pasugo* 54, 2 (February 2002): 3.

¹⁶Iglesia ni Cristo, "Worship Service Schedule," http://www.insacramento.org/service_schedules.html (accessed April 15, 2009); and David, Magtuto, and Alcon, "Australia Holds First Summer Class," 23.

¹⁷Manalo, *Mga Leksiyong Ministeryal*, Lesson 24: 125.

dealing with moral values, managing stress, or spiritual development, and to hold evangelistic activities.[18]

SCAN, the Society of Communicators and Networkers International, was founded by Eduardo V. Manalo, who is the honorary chairman.[19] This group has an interest in CB radios as a way of assisting motorists and the general public during times of emergency. In addition, the group offers seminars and holds special worship services on the anniversary of its founding.[20]

Other groups include a wide variety of special interest and professional groups, including the Association of Christians in Information and Communication Technology, the Emergency and Rescue Assistance Group (ERA), the Social Services Livelihood Group, the Nurses and Midwives Group, the Christian Lawyers' Association (CLASS), the Christian Dental Society (CDS) and the Association of Christian Physicians, Inc. (ACPI).[21]

Officers

Each of the above groups is led by a variety of officers: president, chairperson, secretary, finance secretary, teacher (in the

---

[18] Christian Brotherhood International, "Constitution," http://www.freewebs.com/cbi_bacolod/ (accessed June 30, 2007). For example, see *Pasugo* News Bureau, "Miscellany in the Districts: Tarlac CBI Receives Award," *Pasugo* 52,6 (June 2000): 27; and *Pasugo* News Bureau, "Education Program," 27.

[19] *Pasugo*, "SCAN Int'l Conducts Environmental Activities," *Pasugo* 56, 1 (January 2004): 6.

[20] *Pasugo* News Bureau, "Samar South Pushes Forward," 36; *Pasugo* News Bureau, "SCAN Launches '*Bantay Lansangan* 2003,'" 28-29; *Pasugo* News Bureau, "Miscellany in the Districts: Districts Commemorate FYM's 117th Anniversary," *Pasugo* 53, 7 (July 2003): 35; *Pasugo* News Bureau, "Miscellany in the Districts: Minister Receives Plaque of Appreciation," *Pasugo* 51, 5 (May 1999): 29; and *Pasugo* News Bureau, "Miscellany in the Districts: Youth Captures National Title," *Pasugo* 53, 2 (February 2001): 37.

[21] *Pasugo* News Bureau, "Muslim Community Benefits," 34; Marie F. Ruiz, "Celebrating 25 Years of CLASS: Honoring the Newly Appointed Secretary of Justice," *Pasugo* 52, 8 (August 2000): 32; and *Pasugo* News Bureau, "*Lingap* Missions Held in Mindanao," *Pasugo* 53, 1 (January 2001): 37.

case of CWS) and more.[22] Each district and local will have a similar range of officers. This is described in more detail below under Church Administration. Members are recommended for these positions by friends who write notes on their behalf to the *pamamahala*, the local governing body of the chapel, in response to which a person may be asked to serve.[23]

Deacons and deaconesses are also called "officers." There are usually several head deacons and deaconesses, the number dependent on the size of the local.[24] Those desiring to become deacons and deaconesses attend special seminars to prepare them for their roles.[25] Additional training programs to ensure officers' "quality service" may be held from time to time over the course of the year.[26]

Organization officers will usually have monthly meetings.[27] Deacons and deaconesses meet weekly, usually on Saturdays.[28] Opportunities for involvement in the church and its organizations are manifold. It is easy to see why members have little time for activities and relationships outside the group.

---

[22]For example, see Marie F. Ruiz, "Never Remiss in Serving the Lord," *Pasugo* 52, 5 (April 2000): 25; Stephen Kent Smith, "A New Beginning for All of Us," *Pasugo* 53, 1 (January 2001): 29; Marie F. Ruiz, "Paragons of Benevolence," *Pasugo* 53, 3 (March 2001): 26; Ronald Cayabyab, "Western Sydney Gives Officers a Treat," *Pasugo* 51, 1 (January 1999): 27; and Abella, "San Jose Couples," 25.

[23]VJ, February 4, 2004.

[24]For example, see Bridges "I Found the True Church," 24.

[25]Clayton M. Knight, Jr., "The Iglesia ni Cristo Enriched My Life," *Pasugo* 51, 12 (December 1999): 25.

[26]*Pasugo* News Bureau, "Miscellany in the Districts: Rizal GEM Draws Over 25,000; Pangasinan West Dedicates New House of Worship," *Pasugo* 55, 11 (November 2003): 37.

[27]Ronald Cayabyab, "Western Sydney Gives Offices a Treat," *Pasugo* 51, 1 (January 1999): 27.

[28]VJ, interview, April 1, 2003, and Rogelio C. Dumangas, "A Deaconess Makes Her Mark," *Pasugo* 55, 11 (November 2003): 33.

Oaths of Office

All of these officers—group and association leaders, deacons, and deaconesses as well as teachers, organists and choir members—take oaths of office annually at special worship services.[29] The fulfillment of their duties is pledged as a solemn commitment before God and recognized as such by the entire church. For those taking these positions there is a strong desire to be heavily involved in the church and in caring for others. These roles are perceived as bringing special blessings.[30]

Male and Female Roles/Marriage

The church teaches that males and females are called to different roles. In the church, only males may be ministers and evangelical workers; females are limited to non-pastoral roles such as singing in the choir, being organists and serving as deaconesses. However, females can be leaders and officers in the Christian Family Organizations.[31]

It is God who joins a man and a woman in marriage, and a special blessing occurs during the marriage ceremony.[32] "God hates

---

[29]For example, see *Pasugo* News Bureau, "Miscellany in the Districts: Metro Manila North PNK Inducts New Officers," *Pasugo* 54, 3 (March 2002): 28; Dennis P. Eudela and Evangeline G. Galvez, "Southeastern Seaboard Sets Pace for 2000," *Pasugo* 52, 4 (April 2000): 32; *Pasugo* News Bureau, "Miscellany in the Districts: Districts Intensify Edification Programs," *Pasugo* 52, 4 (April 2000): 37; Guingab, Flores and Zepeda, "Hawaii-Pacific Inducts 300 New Officers," 34; *Pasugo* News Bureau, "Muslim Community Benefits," 37; El P. Buelva, "Metro Manila Enlists 1,000 PNK Officers," *Pasugo* 51, 2 (February 1999): 30, 31; and Benjie de los Reyes, "Ministers, Church Workers Take Oath of Office," *Pasugo* 51 (April 1999): 30.

[30]*Pasugo*, "Converts: The Path to Peace and Salvation," *Pasugo* 52,5 (May 2000):12; and *Pasugo* News Bureau, "Metro Manila North PNK Inducts," 28.

[31]See, for example, Bringas-Tuazon, "Church Youth Leader," 3; Ang, "Research," 5; and Ang, "Iglesia," 3.

[32]Iglesia ni Cristo, "The Iglesia ni Cristo and the Bible: Divine Rules for Marriage," Internet video file, http://iglesianicristo.ws (accessed April 6, 2009), also teaches that premarital sex and homosexuality are against the will of God.

divorce so it is sin when a couple thinks of divorce; only death can separate them."[33] The church regularly offers seminars on strengthening marriage and on the separate roles for men and women.[34]

In marriage, expectations for men and women are separate.[35] Men are not to be harsh with their wives, and women are expected not to dominate, but be submissive.[36] The husband should provide for the physical needs of his family, and the wife is to oversee the home, including "comings and goings, house help, and the household budget." She is "custodian of her husband's honor and should do nothing to hurt his name."[37] Members are forbidden to marry outside the church.[38] Family planning is encouraged so that couples are not overextended financially.[39]

Parenting/The Family/Whole Family Involvement

The family is highly valued and supported by the church. This is seen in the number of family activities the church offers and in the teaching it provides on parenting.[40] Harmony and peace within

---

[33] Iglesia ni Cristo, "Divine Rules;" and Cantor, "How Their Lives Have Changed," 13.
[34] *Pasugo* News Bureau, "Metro Manila North Strengthens," 37.
[35] Joanne Dianne S. Banawa," A Story of a Locksmith Unlocked," *Pasugo* 55, 1 (January 2003): 29; and *Pasugo* News Bureau, "Metro Manila North Strengthens Family," *Pasugo* 52, 10 (October 2000): 37.
[36] Iglesia ni Cristo, "Divine Rules."
[37] *Ibid.*
[38] VJ, interview, April 1, 2003, and Letters to the Editor, "On Marrying Unbelievers and Youngest Victims of Murder," *Pasugo* 51 (June 1999): 2.
[39] Iglesia ni Cristo, "Divine Rules."
[40] See, for example Richard R. Rafols, "King William's Town Focuses on the Family," *Pasugo* 54, 1 (January 2002): 35; Feljun B. Fuentes, "Editorial: Preserving Christian Values," *Pasugo* 53, 10 (October 2001): 3; Ronnie C. Gonzales, "Church Supports National Family Week," *Pasugo* 53, 10 (October 2001): 30; Samuel Estopito, "*Bago Bantay* Holds Parent-Child Communication Seminar," *Pasugo* 52, 11 (November 2000): 33; and Rebecca Jinco-Flores, "Saipan Fosters Family Solidarity," *Pasugo* 53 (July 2001): 33.

the home are greatly esteemed, sought after and made a focus of teaching.[41]

Parents are entrusted with providing for both the physical and the spiritual needs of their children.[42] They are expected to teach them God's words and train them to be respectful, obedient, trustworthy, and honorable.[43] Most importantly, parents are responsible to see that family members do not turn away from God, but remain active in the church.[44] Many issues of *Pasugo* are filled with stories highlighting specific families and their involvement in the church.[45] In one interview, a former member noted that someone cannot remain a minister, an employee of the church or an officer if their family members are not also active.[46] This presents a huge obstacle to anyone considering leaving the Iglesia ni Cristo because their departure or marriage to a non-church member would greatly affect their entire family.

Children are not baptized as infants, but dedicated to the Lord's service during a worship service in which the minister lays hands on the child. As noted above, there are no godparents (*ninongs* and *ninangs*), contrary to Philippine custom.[47]

---

[41] Arthur P. Agag, "Building a Happy Home," *Pasugo* 51, 12 (December 1999): 6; and Lloyd I. Castro, "What Makes Up a Blessed Home?" *Pasugo* 53, 8 (August 2001): 10.

[42] Iglesia ni Cristo, "What God Expects of All Parents and Children," http://www.iglesianicristo.ws; Agag, "Building," 6; and Marlex C. Cantor, "The Spiritual Upbringing of Children," *Pasugo* 52, 6 (June 2000): 9.

[43] Fuentes, "Let Us Give Them a Better Future," 2; Marlex C. Cantor, "Making Our Parents Proud," *Pasugo* 57, 1 (January 2005): 30; and Iglesia ni Cristo, "What God Expects."

[44] Santiago, "Preserving and Strengthening the Family," 2; Tomas C. Catañgay, "A Reminder to Parents," *Pasugo* 53, 7 (July 2001): 13; and Joel San Pedro, "10 Tips," 10.

[45] See, for example, Ruiz, "A Promise Fulfilled," 8; Dumangas, "A Deaconess Makes Her Mark," 33; Smith, "A New Beginning,"29; *Pasugo*, "Converts: I Could Ask for Nothing More," *Pasugo* 52, (July 2000): 25; and Elsa P. Cariaso, "Hurdling God's Crucial Test," *Pasugo* 51, 9 (September 1999): 20-21.

[46] VJ, interview by the author, Taytay, Rizal, January 21, 2003.

[47] VJ, interview, April 1, 2003; "Iglesia ni Cristo," http://www.absolute astronomyu.com/topics/Iglesia_ni_Cristo; Bienvenido C. Santiago, "Worshipping

Church Administration

The Iglesia ni Cristo has a distinct administrative structure, which tightly controls the church's agenda and activities.

The Central Administration

The clearly-defined, hierarchical organizational structure of the Iglesia ni Cristo begins at the top with the Chief Executive Minister and the Central Administration. This structure stretches down through the districts to the locals. As in Philippine culture, members know their place and role and feel most comfortable when responding out of that context. For instance, as noted earlier, an ordinary church member would not feel comfortable answering questions about Bible interpretation; they would refer an inquirer to a minister or evangelical worker. Local officers or district group leaders might brainstorm and plan, but the authority for approval of those plans and any necessary resources would come from the local or district minister who is responsible for their organization.

Iglesia ni Cristo members are taught and believe that their leaders are chosen by God to look after their spiritual welfare. They are to submit to this authority.[48] The Presiding Elder or Chief Executive Minister (CEM) is the overseer of the church. Eraño Manalo, son of Felix Manalo, was the CEM from 1963 until his death on August 31, 2009. Eraño's son, Eduardo Manalo, served as the Deputy Executive Minister and was groomed to take the Chief Executive Minister position following his father's death.

---

the Lord from the Days of Youth," Pasugo 54, 12 (December 2002): 3; Feljun B. Fuentes, "Dedicating Our Children in the Service of the Lord," *Pasugo* 54, 12 (December 2002): 5; and Feljun B. Fuentes, "Editorial: A Heritage from the Lord," *Pasugo* 53, 6 (June 2001): 3.

[48]Manalo, *Mga Leksiyong Ministeryal*, Lesson 21: 88-92. Feljun B. Fuentes, "Editorial: The Church under a Centralized Administration," *Pasugo* 54 (July 2002): 3; and Feljun B. Fuentes, "Editorial: Our Fellowship with the Central Administration," *Pasugo* 55 (February 2003): 4-5.

The Deputy Executive Minister, known as *Kanang Kamay*, "Right Hand of the Executive Minister," oversees all church activities abroad and represents the Executive Minister. The General Evangelist, known as *Kaliwang Kamay* or "Left Hand of the Executive Minister," is the spokesman for the CEM on all public matters and oversees the church's evangelistic programs.

Under Eraño Manalo there were nine senior offices under and reporting directly to him:

1. The General Secretary, who handles all paperwork, correspondence and communication. In public ceremonies he is the *Taga Basa* "Reader of the Bible") for the CEM.
2. The General Treasurer, who is responsible for all church funds and their disbursement.
3. The General Auditor, who audits financial activities at all levels of the church to ensure that funds are handled properly.
4. The District Ministers. There are currently eighty-eight of these.
5. The Administrative Secretary, who is in charge of security, properties and engineering.
6. The Propagation of the Faith Minister, who is responsible for evangelistic activities.
7. The Minister for members eighteen years and older, who oversees policies and activities for this age group. This officer supervises the *KADIWA* organization.
8. The Minister for members thirteen to seventeen years old, who oversees policies and activities for this age group. This officer supervises the *Binhi* organization.
9. The Minister for children four to twelve years old, who oversees policies and activities for this age group. This officer supervises the *Pagsamba ng Kabataan* (PNK).

Immediately below these offices is that of the President of New Era, who oversees New Era University, the College of Evangelical Ministry, which trains ministers, as well as New Era Hospital.[49]

Districts

An Ecclesiastical District is comparable to a Roman Catholic Diocese, and a Supervising or District Minister oversees it."[50] Each Supervising Minister reports directly to the CEM;[51] he will have offices under his authority similar to the nine under the CEM. There will be a District Secretary, a District Treasurer, a District Auditor, and a *Katiwala sa Pagtitibay* "Defender of the Faith.")"[52] The District Minister is responsible for various locales headed by resident ministers.[53]

Locals[54]

A local is similar to a Roman Catholic parish, a single congregation to which those living in a particular area are assigned, and is overseen by a resident minister.[55] The resident or presiding minister will have additional ministers and evangelical workers on his staff depending on the size of the local.[56] Below and responsible to the resident minister are lay offices and a variety of deacons and

---

[49] Ang, "Research," 3-4, 7. He notes that this structure is a recent reorganization.

[50] *Pasugo*, "Facts & Figures: A Brief Profile of the Church," *Pasugo* 55, 4 (April 2003): 13.

[51] INCWorld, "Manual," 3; and Ang, "Research," 7.

[52] Ang, "Research," 4.

[53] *Pasugo*, "Facts & Figures," 13; *Pasugo*, "A Brief Profile of the Church," http://geocities.com/truthfinder_inc/profile.htm (accessed April 15, 2009).

[54] "or locale." I recognize that many Iglesia ni Cristo members prefer the term "locale," however, I have chosen to use "local" in most places in this book to avoid confusion with the normal English usage of these terms.

[55] *Pasugo*, "Facts & Figures," 13.

[56] Ang, "Research," 4, 7. The Resident Minister is also called the "the Presiding Elder or Administrator" in Feljun B. Fuentes, "Editorial: Esteeming Them Highly in Love," *Pasugo* 52, 1 (January 2000): 3.

deaconesses with assigned duties such as overseeing weekly prayer groups, Light of Salvation associations, the choir, and Sunday school.[57] Each local is further subdivided into areas such as barrios and subdivisions, each administered by an area leader; these are subdivided again into groups supervised by a leader who may be a deacon, a deaconess or an overseer being groomed for the diaconate.[58]

Ministers

Becoming an ordained minister in the Iglesia ni Cristo is a long and arduous process. It begins with six years of training at the College of Evangelical Ministry (CEM).[59] During the last years, students have practical or field work assignments in different locals and live in designated church housing. They continue to attend classes while carrying a full-time ministry load of teaching daily Bible studies, visitation, counseling and overseeing church ministries. They don't receive a BEM degree (Bachelor of Evangelical Ministry) after completing their years of formal classes. This degree is only given after five years of probation as a regular evangelical worker.[60] During this time, they are under the close observation of the entire local to which they have been assigned. If someone is unhappy with their behavior and writes a critical note to the Administration, they may not be ordained.[61] Ministers are

---

[57]For example, see Gary Haack, "My True Wealth," *Pasugo* 54, 1 (January 2002): 30; VJ, interview, April 1, 2003; Smith, "A New Beginning," 29; and Manalo, *Mga Leksiyong Ministeryal*, Lesson 24: 113.

[58]INCWorld, "Manual," 4.

[59]Founded in 1974 as a school for Ministers, the CEM was originally known as the Ministerial Institute of Development. In 1995 it became the CEM. Joel V. San Pedro, "The CEM: Continuing the Work of the Messenger," *Pasugo* 51, 10 (October 1999): 4; and Feljun B. Fuentes, "Editorial: CEM: 25 Sterling Years," *Pasugo* 51, 10 (October 1999): 3.

[60]San Pedro, "The CEM," 7.

[61]VJ, interview, May 20, 2004.

ordained by the Chief Executive Minister by the laying on of hands at a special worship service at the Central Temple.[62]

Ministerial training is a lifelong process. Resident ministers, ministers and evangelical workers within a district meet for weekly planning and attend monthly training seminars.[63] A yearly conference for ministers is held at the Central Temple in the New Era complex on Commonwealth Avenue, Diliman, in Quezon City. This is a national conference for those working throughout the Philippines;[64] there is also a yearly video conference for those working overseas.[65] These conferences include a yearly oath-taking,[66] and ministers who have performed in an outstanding way in "propagation" and "edification" are recognized.[67]

Ministers' wives are considered partners in the ministry. They also attend regular seminars on topics such as their duties, overcoming stress, strengthening the marital relationship, cooking,

---

[62]Benjie R. de los Reyes, "Church Ordains 52 Ministers," *Pasugo* 55, 5 (May 2003): 33; and Benjie de los Reyes, "118 New Ministers Ordained," *Pasugo* 52, 6 (June 2000): 25.

[63]Henry Capuno and Alex Tolentino, "EVM Visits Enlivens Laguna," *Pasugo* 55, 10, (October 2003): 33; and Rudy Pumar and Amy Simon, "Northeastern Seaboard Renews Vigor for 2001," *Pasugo* 53, 2 (February 2001): 36; and *Pasugo* News Bureau, "Metro Manila North PNK," 28. See for example, photos and captions in *Pasugo* 56, 4 (April 2004): 39, *Pasugo* 56, 7 (July 2004): 40, *Pasugo* 56, 8 (August 2004): 40, and *Pasugo* 56, 9 (September 2004): 40.

[64]De los Reyes, "Church Commends Ministers," 31; and Benjie de los Reyes, "19 Ministers Sworn into Office," *Pasugo* 52, 10 (October 2000): 33.

[65]Benjie R. de los Reyes, "42 Ministers Take Oath During 8th Ministerial Conference," *Pasugo* 53, 4 (April 2001): 32.

[66]De los Reyes, "42 Ministers," 32; October 2000: 22; and de los Reyes, "Church Commends," 31.

[67]De los Reyes, "Church Commends," 31.

and family planning.[68] Special gatherings are held only for ministers, evangelical workers and their families.[69]

Housing projects and settlements are built to provide accommodations for active ministers and evangelical workers and for those who have retired.[70]

District and Local Activities

Every *Pasugo* reports an astounding number of church activities at the district and local levels. Most of these are spearheaded by the various Christian Family Organizations and their officers. Here is a small sampling: Christian music festivals and vocal competitions,[71] sports tournaments,[72] Bible and *God's Message* quizzes,[73] video boot camps,[74] livelihood seminars,[75] game and skit

---

[68]*Pasugo* News Bureau, "Muslim Community Benefits," 35; Pamela B. Pascual, "A Vow of Love Remembered," *Pasugo* 52, 10 (October 2000): 32; *Pasugo* News Bureau, "Metro Manila North PNK," 31; and *Pasugo* News Bureau, "Miscellany in the Districts: Districts Focus on Family Activities," *Pasugo* 54, 11 (November 2002): 34.

[69]*Pasugo* News Bureau, "Miscellany in the Districts: Religious Program Gives Birth to New Locale," *Pasugo* 53, 3 (March 2001): 30, 31.

[70]Rogelio C. Dumangas, "Construction, Renovation of Houses of Worship, Infrastructure Projects Continued," *Pasugo* 59, 2 (February 2007): 7; and Ronnie Cainglet and Abegail dela Cruz, "NEU Perks Up Elderly in Dasmariñas," *Pasugo* 52, 6 (June 2001): 25.

[71]Gonzales, "Port of Call," 38; Marie Ruiz, Ronald Acob, and Glenn David, "Metro Manila South Sings Praises in One Voice," *Pasugo* 56, 2 (February 2004): 9; and Aileen Bouilang, "Metro Manila North holds '*Musikapisanan*,'" *Pasugo* 55, 3 (March 2003): 28.

[72]Lizerne Guiting and Jennifer Pineda-Doyrit, "Southern California Sets Annual Volleyball Tourney," *Pasugo* 59, 2 (February 2007): 11; M. Tam, "Washington, D.C., Turns a Decade Old," *Pasugo* 56, 1 (January 2004): 5; Siegfred T. Gollayan, "Locales in Asia Press Forward," *Pasugo* 55, 6 (June 2003): 27; and Norma O. Royeca and Rhodora D. Rigor, "Pacific Northwest Builds on Family Quality Time," *Pasugo* 55, 8 (August 2003): 31.

[73]G. N. Abella, "Northern California Showcases *Tagisanng Talino*," *Pasugo* 56, 2 (February 2004): 5.

[74]Y. Fomocod and S. Gollayan, "Anaheim Hosts first US 'Digital Video Bootcamp,'" *Pasugo* 56, 5 (May 2004): 5.

[75]Livelihood seminars offer training in how to earn additional income. Some of the topics covered are mushroom growing, cosmetology, dressmaking, fish processing and swine raising. *Pasugo* News Bureau, "SCAN Launches '*Bantay Lansangan* 2003,'" 31.

nights,[76] music writing training and competitions,[77] seminars on how to stop smoking,[78] leadership training,[79] family finance management,[80] raising children,[81] strengthening spirituality and anniversaries of the locale's founding.[82]

These activities are designed to build relationships, foster unity and assist members in daily living and raising their families.[83]

Holidays and Celebrations

The distinctiveness of Iglesia ni Cristo culture is evident in the holidays it does not recognize as well as its own celebrations.

Non Participation

The church does not observe many of the events and holidays of the general Philippine population. Members are forbidden to participate in barrio fiestas because the food is said to have been offered to idols.[84] Since fiestas are expensive community endeavors, the Iglesia ni Cristo's lack of support sets them at odds with their neighbors and locale leaders.

---

[76] *Pasugo* News Bureau, "Districts Commemorate FYM's 117th Anniversary," 35.

[77] Melissa C. Frani, "KADIWA Celebrates 28th Year through Music Writing Tilt," *Pasugo* 54, 2 (February 2002): 35.

[78] *Pasugo* News Bureau, "Metro Manila North PNK," 29.

[79] *Pasugo* News Bureau, "Miscellany in the Districts: Districts Boost Officer Leadership: Swear in 10,600 Officers," *Pasugo* 53, 5 (May 2001): 37-38.

[80] Norma O. Royeca, "Pacific Northwest Symposium Focuses on the Family," *Pasugo* 52, 12 (December 2000): 26.

[81] *Pasugo* News Bureau, "Miscellany in the Districts: Arayat, Gumaca Locales Celebrate Diamond Year," *Pasugo* 51, 9 (September 1999): 30.

[82] Royeca, "Pacific Northwest," 26. Cromwell S. Correa, "Pasay Celebrates 43rd Year," *Pasugo* 51 (February 1999): 36, Guampdn.com, "Celebrating 40 Years, http://gumadn.com/article/20030315//LIFESTYLE/903150319/1024 (accessed April 15, 2009); and Joji S. Crisostomo, "Hong Kong West Turns 18: Brethren Foster Harmonious Relations," *Pasugo* 53 (July 2001): 36.

[83] Gollayan, "Locales in Asia," 27.

[84] VJ, interview, April 1, 2003.

Another striking distinctive is that they do not observe the Christmas season or Christmas Day. They teach that this is because Jesus' birthday is not recorded in the Bible, and he was not born in December. They argue that because December 25 was the birthday of the Roman sun god, Sol Invictus, the celebration of Christmas on that date is of pagan origin. They also believe that Christmas celebrations have incorporated many pagan practices.[85]

Neither do they celebrate or participate in Lent or the Holy Week activities, which are an important part of Filipino life. In the Philippines, flagellations and crucifixions are given more press coverage than Easter itself. The Iglesia ni Cristo believes that it is "not correct that Jesus rose on Sunday morning because three days after Friday is not Sunday morning." They recognize that Jesus rose again, but they do not celebrate Easter day.[86] Since Holy Week activities and the Christmas season are important observances in Philippine culture, this lack of participation sets the Iglesia ni Cristo as a culture apart.

Finally, the group does not participate in Halloween celebrations,[87] and they "do not celebrate Valentine's Day because its practices and customs bear close association with paganism."[88]

A Calendar of Celebrations

What does the Iglesia ni Cristo offer in place of these typical Filipino holidays and celebrations? It has a year full of occasions to which members look forward. These are described in the order in which they occur during the calendar year.

---

[85] *Pasugo*, "Frequently Asked Questions," 10, and VJ, interview, April 1, 2003.

[86] VJ, interview, April 1, 2003.

[87] Editor, "Mailbox," *Pasugo* 56, 2 (February 2004): 3. The author has not found any documentation regarding the group's stance on All Saints' Day, which is an important holiday in the Philippines when families visit the graves of loved ones.

[88] *Pasugo*, "Frequently Asked Questions," 11; and Editor, "Letters: On Valentine's Day," *Pasugo* 55, 2 (February 2003): 2.

Eraño Manalo's Birthday

The year begins in January with recognition of the birthday of the former Chief Executive Minister, Eraño Manalo. During this time, attention is focused on the Church administration with special services and prayers for its members.[89] *Pasugo* will feature editorials and articles about the importance of the Church administration.[90] As mentioned previously, there will be mass baptisms and Grand Evangelical Missions during the month. Even after his death, Eraño Manalo's birthday continues to be celebrated.

Santa Cena

Once a year, in February or March, the *Santa Cena* or Lord's Supper is celebrated. Partaking is a requirement for salvation and the forgiveness of sins. Only those who have been baptized may participate, and only ordained ministers in good standing may serve the elements. The service will begin with a procession of the choir and ministers, and following the sermon the minister will break a large loaf of unleavened bread and place the fragments on several platters. This breaking of bread is intentional since the church teaches that Jesus broke the bread and then distributed it; this is different from the procedure in the Roman Catholic Church in which the priest serves people individually. Juice or diluted wine from a large container is poured into glasses with handles.[91]

---

[89]Eraño Manalo's birthdate was January 2, 1925. As noted earlier Eraño Manalo passed away on August 31, 2009. Bienvenido C. Santiago, "Editorial: 'Onward to Spiritual Maturity and Perfect Unity,'" *Pasugo* 55, 1 (January 2003): 3.

[90]For example, see Bienvenido C. Santiago, "Editorial: The Church Administration: Ministering to a Global Flock," *Pasugo* 56, 1 (January 2001): 2-3; Ruben D. Aromin, "Being United with the Church Administration," *Pasugo* 56, 1 (January 2004): 13-16; Feljun B. Fuentes, "Editorial: Keeping Us Strong in the Faith," *Pasugo* 54, 1 (January 2002): 3; and Fuentes, "Esteeming Them Highly," 3.

[91]VJ, interview, April 1, 2003; DR, conversation with author, Cainta, Rizal, October 6, 1998; Cora interview by Kevin Alamag, Quezon City, October 1998; Syliva E. Nepomunceno, "Holy Supper in Southeast Asia," *Pasugo* 45, 5 (September-October 1993): 34, and Adorado A. Apostal, "A Brief History of the Congregations in Israel," *Pasugo* 49, 7 (Special Issue, July 1997): 55; also see photo on the same page.

Felix Y. Manalo's Birth Anniversary

May 10 brings the celebration of Felix Y. Manalo's birth anniversary. Since Felix is the Last Messenger of God who was instrumental in the re-emergence of the true church, the group teaches that commemorating his birthday is "in line with apostolic instruction."[92] *Pasugo* will usually feature articles and editorials commending his life and service.[93] In addition to special worship services,[94] GEMs and baptisms are conducted,[95] and community services are offered.[96] The two biggest celebrations are the church's anniversary in July and the Thanksgiving celebration in December.

Iglesia ni Cristo Day

July 14, 1914 is the date the Iglesia ni Cristo was registered with the Philippine government, and this is the date they believe the true church re-emerged.[97] The author has observed the banners that are strung in front of every chapel and across major roads announcing the year—eighty-seventh, ninetieth, etc.—of the anniversary commemoration. Major newspapers in the Philippines are sure to publish articles about this occasion.[98] Greetings from

---

[92] Bienvenido C. Santiago, "Editorial: Reflections on the Man Who Spoke God's Words to Us," *Pasugo* 56, 5 (May 2004): 2.

[93] For example, see Feljun B. Fuentes, "Editorial: Lest We Forget Him," *Pasugo* 54, 5 (May 2002): 3; Santiago, "Reflections on the Man," 2; and Dennis C. Lovendino, "Remembering the Messenger of God in These Last Days," *Pasugo* 53, 5 (May 2001): 10-11.

[94] Dabu, "Mississauga Dedicates New House of Worship," 34.

[95] For example, see Ronnie C. Gonzales, "Northern, Southern Europe Commemorate," *Pasugo* 55, 7 (July 2003): 32; and Baldonade, "Kowloon Launches 'Operation FYM 50,'" 26.

[96] Margie Castigo, "Kula Lumpur Promotes Health, Reaches Out to Children," *Pasugo* 55, 8 (August 2003): 30.

[97] Feljun B. Fuentes, "From the Managing Editor: Anniversary Greetings, et al." *Pasugo* 53, 7 (July 2001): 2.

[98] For example, see Sandy Araneta, "Mammoth Crowds Gather for Iglesia ni Cristo Day," *Philippine Star*, July 28, 2009), 1-3, http://philstar.com /Article.aspx?articleID=490894&publicationsSubCategoryID=63 (accessed July 28, 2009); *Inquirer* News Service, "Iglesia to Mark 87th Year Sans Fanfare," *Newbreak Magazine*, July 24, 2001, http://archive.inq7.net /archive/2001-p/nat/2001/jul/25/nat_15-1-p.htm (accessed February 5, 2003); Isabelo T. Crisostomo, "Felix Manalo and His Mission," *The Philippine Star*,

major politicians will be read during services and special commendations noted in *Pasugo* and newspapers.[99] There are church- and district-wide celebratory activities,[100] and often GEMs will be conducted.[101] The annual census of membership is taken at worship on the Sunday closest to that day.[102] In recognition of this important occasion for the church, in 2009 Philippine President Gloria Macapal Arroyo made July 27 a special national working holiday.[103]

Thanksgiving Day/Pasalamat

The church's biggest and most important celebration is its year-end Thanksgiving celebration *Pasalamat*.[104] The faithful save for the whole year and that is called *pagsisimpan* or *pagbubukod* (setting aside). They do this by making regular weekly deposits to the treasurer of the local before or after the worship services. Every deposit is logged into a libretta, a type of savings deposit passbook. The total amount of this offering is tallied on Thanksgiving Day, and a piece of paper which resembles a check with that amount is

---

July 27, 2001: 13; E. T. Suarez, "Officials Greet INC on 88th Year Today," *Manila Bulletin*, July 26, 2002, http://www.mb.com.ph/news.php?search=yes&sect=1&fname=MAIN/2002-07/MN0207261726159890.txt (accessed February 5, 2003); and Philstar.com, "Mammoth Crowds Gather for Iglesia ni Cristo Day," *Philippine Star*, July 28, 2009, http://philstar.com/Article.aspx?articled=490894&publicationSubCategoryID=63 (accessed July 28, 2009).

[99] For example, see the greetings from U.S. President George W. Bush, Philippine President Gloria Macapagal Arroyo, U.S. Vice President Dick Cheney, Philippine Vice President Noli de Castro, in that order in *Pasugo*, "Messages," *Pasugo* 56, 7 (July 2004): 2-7.

[100] For example, see *Pasugo* News Bureau, "Chronicles: INC Music Video Festival—Year 3," *Pasugo* 56, 9 (September 2004): 5; Pamela Agular and Aliw Pablo, "Northern California Fosters Brotherhood," *Pasugo* 51, 9 (September 1999): 25; and VJ, interview, April 1, 2003.

[101] Marlex C. Cantor, "Worldwide GEM Caps Church's 90th Anniversary Commemoration," *Pasugo* 56, 9 (September 2004): 8.

[102] Announcement following worship service the author attended on July 5, 2009. Members were told to worship only at the local in which they were registered. Instead of turning over their attendance tags, they were to place them in a box provided.

[103] Araneta, "Mammoth Crowds," 1.

[104] Rosquites, "EVM Officiates Brixtonville Thanksgiving," 7, and VJ, interview, April 1, 2003.

given to the member. That is then ceremonially given during the Thanksgiving Day service.[105] Locals and districts compete among themselves to see if they can increase the amounts given in previous years and give more than each other gives. During the special worship service when the offerings are presented, the congregation praises and thanks God for the previous year, and prays for healing, protection and blessings in the coming year.[106] There is a family day with games and programs. Other activities such as beauty contests may take place the day before or after.[107] Since the Christmas season is so important in Philippine culture, it is not surprising that the Iglesia ni Cristo would hold a major celebration during the same time of the year.[108]

Anniversaries

Throughout the year the Christian Family Organizations, other organizations and locals and districts will celebrate anniversaries of their foundings. Every issue of *Pasugo* is filled with notices of these celebrations and the activities that accompany them.[109] Every barrio

---

[105]QE, email to the author July 18, 2014; VJ, interview, April 1, 2003; Ang, "Iglesia," 3-4; and Marlex C. Cantor, "With Thanksgiving to God comes the Offering of Sacrifices," Pasugo 55, 12 (December 2013): 7 indicates there are rules on how one should give and that this offering is a sacred duty. Members are to plan their giving and not just give on the spur of the moment.

[106]Bienvenido C. Santiago, "Editorial: Thanksgiving to God: Our Solemn Vow," *Pasugo* 53, 12 (December 2003): 3. See photo in *Pasugo* 46, 3 (March 2004): 31.

[107]VJ, interview, April 1, 2003.

[108]Another possible reason for the year-end celebration is that regularly employed workers in the Philippines receive "13th month." This is an extra month's salary given at Christmas-time to assist workers with Christmas-expenses. It is somewhat like receiving a Christmas bonus, but is required by law.

[109]For example, see Frani, "KADIWA Celebrates 28th Year," 35; Alyssa V. See, "Europe Celebrates 25th Year," *Pasugo* 51, 1 (January 1999): 28; Pasugo News Bureau, "Miscellany in the Districts: Officers Recognized for Long Years of Service," *Pasugo* 51, 2 (February 1999): 35, 36; Cristino V. Chico, "Nueva Ecija Marks 9th Year," *Pasugo* 51, 3 (March 1999): 27; Gene N. Abella, "San Jose Plays Host to Significant Events," *Pasugo* 51, 4 (April 1999): 32; and Ronnie C. Gonzales, Bella Q. Agustin, and Maylene D. Zapatero, "Singapore Celebrates 20th Year; Kowloon Moves Forward," *Pasugo* 51 (December 1999): 31.

in the Philippines has an annual barrio fiesta celebrating its patron saint; these anniversaries would seem to take the place of those activities.

Other Facets of Iglesia ni Cristo Culture

There are a number of other distinctive features in Iglesia ni Cristo culture.

Health

Members who are sick will ask a church minister, elder or officer to anoint them with oil and pray for them. In addition, members are also encouraged to seek medical help.[110] The church has its own hospital, New Era Hospital, located in the New Era complex in Quezon City, Philippines.

Persecution

The Iglesia ni Cristo teaches and members expect to face persecution for their faith. This is so that they may be "worthy of God's grace and blessings." It is a privilege to suffer for the sake of one's faith.[111] Worship service hymns, prayers and lessons as well as *Pasugo* editorials and articles regularly describe that suffering and persecution are to be expected. Members of the group believe they experience these for the glory of God and as a sign that they are members of the true church. They are to endure suffering as did Christians during the first century, and persecution is a part of God's plan and purpose for them.[112]

---

[110]Editor, "Mailbox," *Pasugo* 56, 5 (May 2004): 4; Imelda Llana-Dela Cruz, "Unwavering Devotion to the Lord's Service," *Pasugo* 53, 11 (November 2001): 11; and San Pedro, "10 Tips," 10.

[111]Benvenido C. Santiago, "Editorial: Blessed Are Those Who Persevere," *Pasugo* 54, 11 (November 2002): 3, 5; and Fuentes, "In the Face of Suffering," 5.

[112]Aromin, "The Heirs of God," 16-18; Fuentes, "In the Face of Suffering," 5; Santiago, "Blessed Are Those Who Persevere," 3; and Letters to the Editor, "Overcoming Persecution," *Pasugo* 51 (November 1999): 2.

Iglesia ni Cristo Terminology

As a distinct culture, the Iglesia ni Cristo has its own vocabulary of terms with special meanings. It is known for its use of old, formal Tagalog particularly in its terminology of church activities.[113] Several examples include:[114]

TABLE ONE

English	Filipinos Commonly Use	Iglesia ni Cristo Members Use
Church	*Simbahan*	*Iglesia* (organization) *Kapilya* (edifice)
Leadership	*Pamahalaan*	*Pangangasiwa* (officials)
Hymn	*Kanta*	*Awit*
Offering	*Alay*	*Abuloy* (weekly) *Simpan* (year-long savings for the thanksgiving offering)
Attend a service	*Magsisimba*	*Sasamba*
Non-member	*Hindi Katoliko*	*Taga-sanlibutan* (belonging to earth)

The group also uses a number of familiar words and phrases, though with different meanings than these have in general Philippine culture or orthodox Christianity. A short dictionary of commonly-used words and phrases can be found in Appendix A.

Understanding a Different Culture

Many observers, especially detractors writing from outside the Iglesia ni Cristo, have reacted against its beliefs and behaviors, which are at odds with general Philippine culture or orthodox

---

[113] QL, personal interview with author, digital recording. San Juan, Metro Manila, Philippines, January 23, 2010.
[114] QL, e-mail to the author, March 7, 2010.

Christianity. Instead of merely reacting and criticizing, those desiring to engage with members of this group need to attempt to understand its culture.

Missiologists' study of anthropology over the last half century has illustrated the importance of recognizing and understanding cultural differences.[115] When missionaries see that different cultures perceive, understand and interact with their physical and spiritual environments in distinct ways, new avenues for communication of the gospel become evident. Gaining knowledge about the Iglesia ni Cristo as a distinct culture offers the opportunity for greater understanding and therefore more effective communication of the Christian message.

Learning the group's vocabulary will lessen misunderstandings and provide new ideas for communication. Studying its activities, beliefs, and values will help identify similarities, which can serve as bridges and new avenues for sharing the good news in ways that may be embraced, not rejected. Moreover, knowledge takes away fear. It is much easier to approach and dialogue with people we see as like ourselves, with the same desires to honor God, the same needs, the same life experiences and families, rather than as enemies to criticize, shun or fear.

---

[115]For example, see David J. Hesselgrave, *Communicating Christ Cross-Culturally: An Introduction to Missionary Communication* (Grand Rapids, MI: Zondervan Publishing House, 1991); Paul Hiebert, *Anthropological Reflections on Missiological Issues* (Grand Rapids, MI Baker Books, 1994); Charles H. Kraft, *Christianity in Culture: A Study in Dynamic Biblical Theologizing in Cross-Cultural Perspective* (Maryknoll, NY: Orbis Books, 1979); and Eugene Nida, *Customs and Cultures: Anthropology for Christian Missions* (Pasadena, CA: William Carey Library, 1954).

CHAPTER 8

MISSIOLOGICAL RESEARCH ON CULTURALLY APPROPRIATE STRATEGIES AND METHODOLOGIES[1]

This chapter reviews relevant missiological literature discussing ideas, research and methodologies, including current thinking regarding various evangelistic approaches to members of NRMs, people and insider movements, hospitality and incarnational ministry, and bridges to communication. A brief discussion of the nature of conversion is presented to provide a basis for an understanding of religious conversion as a process involving much more than mere replacement of one set of religious ideas with another.

Current Thinking on Reaching NRM Members

The 1980 Lausanne Committee for World Evangelization Thailand Report on *Christian Witness to New Religious Movements* was one of the first evangelical documents to define "mystics and cultists" as "unreached groups" needing intentional strategies for conversion.[2] This was partly the result of the increasing number of

---

[1] Phrases used in this paper such as "the gospel," "good news," "the evangelical community," and "evangelical Christianity" refer to the presentation of and participants in an orthodox form of Christianity consistent with the Lausanne Covenant. In the Philippines, this may be called "biblical Christianity," and adherents are often called "born-again Christians." See Lausanne Committee for World Evangelization, "Lausanne Covenant," http://www.lausanne.org/covenant (accessed May 2, 2010).

[2] Lausanne Committee for World Evangelization, "Christian Witness to New Religious Movements," Lausanne Occasional Paper 11, Mini-Consultation on Reaching Mystics and Cultists, Pattaya, Thailand, 1980, http://www.lausanne.org/all-documents/lop-11.html (accessed April 18, 2010).

NRMs that began springing up in the west starting in the late 1960s. That report stated:

> Many have seen in the growth of various new religious movements a hopeful sign of deep spiritual hunger. The Christian church, if it were guided by the Holy Spirit and the Word, could do much to lead those involved, their families and friends, to full repentance and new life in Christ. There is an element of opportunity here which it dare not miss.[3]

This proliferation of New Religious Movements led to a great deal of sociological, anthropological, psychological and theological research. The evangelical community in particular responded to the invasion of what it termed "cults" with a number of approaches which noted apologist Philip Johnson summarizes in six categories: heresy-rationalist apologetics; end-times prophecy and conspiracies; spiritual warfare; apostate testimonies; cultural apologetics; and behavioralist apologetics.[4] These approaches have been characterized as ineffective tools for evangelism because those using them are often negative and confrontational in their interactions with members of NRMs.[5] Their focus has been on refutation, not on presentation of the gospel.[6] Rather than reaching out in love to members of these groups, they have built walls between the

---

[3] *Ibid.*

[4] Johnson, "Apologetics, Mission and New Religions: A Holistic Approach," 10-101.

[5] Harold W. Turner, "New Mission Task: Worldwide and Waiting," *Missiology* 13, 1 (January 1985): 14; John W. Morehead,"A Fresh Agenda for Apologetics in the 21st Century," http://www.neighboringfaiths.org/Articles.html (accessed November 3, 2009).

[6] Gordon Lewis, "Our Mission Responsibility to New Religious Movements," *International Journal of Frontier Missions* 15, 3 (July-September 1988): 116-117; and J. Gordon Melton, "Emerging Religious Movements in North America: Some Missiological Reflections," *Missiology* 28, 1 (January 2000): 94.

evangelical community and those it should be trying to reach. Fear has often been the result, not compassion and love.

In the late 1990s, some apologists in the evangelical community attempting to reach people involved in the new spiritualities and also in the Church of Jesus Christ of Latter-Day Saints began to consider new ways of approaching members of these groups. Their first step was to end use of the word "cult" when describing and discussing these and other such groups and begin referring to them more neutrally as "New Religious Movements," "New Religions" and "New Spiritualities." "New Religious Movement" or NRM is the term which is now used most often.[7]

The years between 2003 and 2005 were a focal point for the transition in perception of these groups from "the enemy" to unreached neighbors in need of missiological study and new approaches using missiological tools. First, in 2003, a DVD and group study book, *Bridges: Helping Mormons Discover God's Grace; Training Program: How to Reach Mormons Effectively with the Good News of Jesus Christ*, was produced by Salt Lake Theological Seminary.[8] Then in 2004, *Encountering New Religious Movements: A Holistic Approach*,[9] edited by Irving Hexham, Stephen Rost and John Morehead, was published, a year later being named as the best Missions/Global Affairs book by *Christianity Today*. Also in 2004, the invitation-only Lausanne Forum, held in Pattaya, Thailand, included a study group charged specifically with the task of studying outreach to "New Spiritualities (the New Age)." This

---

[7]Melton, "Emerging Religious Movements," 93-94; Stephen Rost, "Paul's Areopagus Speech in Acts 17," in *Encountering New Religious Movements: A Holistic Evangelical Approach*, eds. Irving Hexham, Stephen Rost and John W. Morehead, II (Grand Rapids, MI: Kregel Academic and Professional, 2004), 128-129, and Hesselgrave, "Traditional Religions, New Religions, and the Communication of the Faith," 140.

[8]Salt Lake Theological Seminary, *Bridges: Helping Mormons Discover God's Grace*.

[9]Hexham, Rost and Morehead, eds., *Encountering New Religious Movements*.

group discussed outreach methods not just to the New Age but also to NRMs in general.[10]

The cumulative message of these three pivotal works as well as a myriad of articles, discussions and blogs that followed was a challenge to the evangelical community to view and approach NRMs and their devotees in new ways. Their strong conclusions were:

1. That NRMs are unreached people groups needing evangelization;[11]
2. That old apologetic methods have not worked well as evangelistic tools;[12]
3. That NRMs are unique cultures, not merely people with different sets of beliefs or understandings of truth;[13]

---

[10] The author was a member of this study group. Johnson, Harper and Morehead, *Religious and Non-Religious Spirituality in the Western World.*

[11] Philip Johnson, "Reaching the Christadelphians," in *Encountering New Religious Movements: A Holistic Evangelistic Approach,* eds. Irving Hexham, Stephen Rost and John W. Morehead, II (Grand Rapids, MI: Kregel Academic and Professional, 2004), 188; Johnson, Harper, Morehead, *Religious and Non-Religious,* 33-4; and John W. Morehead, "Reflections on the Divide in LDS Evangelism in Utah: Why I Practice an Incarnational Missions Strategy," 2, http://www.neighboringfaiths.org/html (accessed May 21, 2008).

[12] John Morehead, "Where Do We Go From Here?" in Irving Hexham, Stephen Rost and John W. Morehead II, eds., *Encountering New Religious Movements: A Holistic Evangelistic Approach* (Grand Rapids, MI: Kregel Academic and Professional, 2004), 287; Johnson, Harper, Morehead, *Religious and Non-Religious* 7, 10, 12; Morehead, "A Fresh Agenda," 3, and John W. Morehead, "From 'Cults' to Cultures: Bridges as a Case Study in a New Evangelical Paradigm on Religions," 4, paper presented at The Center for Studies on New Religions Conference, Salt Lake City, UT, June 13, 2009.

[13] Kenneth Mullholland, "Bridging the Divide: Cross-Cultural Missions to Latter-day Saints," in *Encountering New Religious Movements: A Holistic Evangelistic Approach,* eds. Irving Hexham, Stephen Rost and John W. Morehead, II (Grand Rapids, MI: Kregel Academic and Professional, 2004), 162; Johnson, Harper, Morehead, *Religious and Non-Religious,* 10; Morehead, "From 'Cults,'" 6-8; John W. Morehead, "Transforming Evangelical Responses to New Religions: Missions and Counter-Cult in Partnership," 2, 20, http://www.emnr.org/papers/Transforming_Evangelical.pdf (accessed December 3, 2002); Morehead, "Where Do We Go," 298-299; and John W. Morehead, "Ministry to Alternative Spiritualities in Religiously Plural America: Moving

4. That these groups need to be studied missiologically—that is, viewed through the variety of lenses that any missionary uses when encountering and attempting to reach a new culture: anthropological, sociological, linguistic, theological, etc.;[14]
5. That the gospel needs to be presented not necessarily in a Western truth-versus-falsehood way but in a receptor-oriented way that considers how the message will be received;[15]
6. That this cross-cultural engagement means looking for bridges and contextual methodologies in presenting the gospel to each particular culture,[16] which includes contextualized world-view contrast and apologetics;[17]
7. That the gospel needs to be presented relationally,[18] holistically[19] and incarnationally.[20]

Beyond Confronting Cults," *Occasional Bulletin,* Fall 2003. http://www.neighboringfaiths.org/Articles.html (accessed May 2, 2009).

[14]Lewis, "Our Mission Responsibility," 116; Stephen Rost, "Paul's Areopagus Speech," 133; Morehead, "Where Do We Go?" 297; John W. Morehead, "Can You Hear Me Now? Insights from Communications and Missions for New Religions," 2, http://www.neighboringfaiths.org/Articles.html (accessed September 10, 2009); Morehead, "From Cults," 6, and Morehead, "Transforming Evangelical Responses," 16, 21.

[15]Johnson, Harper, Morehead, *Religious and Non-Religious,* 12-13, 33-34; Morehead, "Where Do We Go?" 279.

[16]Philip Johnson and John Smulo, "Reaching Wiccan and Mother Goddess Devotees," in *Encountering New Religious Movements: A Holistic Evangelistic Approach,* eds. Irving Hexham, Stephen Rost and John W. Morehead, II (Grand Rapids, MI: Kregel Academic and Professional, 2004), 210; Morehead, "Where Do We Go?" 291.

[17]Morehead, "A Fresh Agenda,"1-2; Harold Netland, "Toward Contextualized Apologetics," *Missiology* 16, 3 (July 1988): 289-303; John Smulo, "Missional Apologetics"; Morehead, "Reflections on the Divide," 10, and Morehead, "From 'Cults,'" 5.

[18]Johnson, Harper, Morehead, *Religious and Non-Religious,*12-13, 22-23, and Morehead, "Can You Hear," 3.

[19]Morehead, "Can You Hear," 3, and Morehead, "From 'Cults,'" 5

[20]Gailyn Van Rheenen, "Foreward," in *Encountering New Religious Movements: A Holistic Evangelistic Approach,* eds. Irving Hexham, Stephen Rost and John W. Morehead, II (Grand Rapids, MI: Kregel Academic and Professional, 2004), 14; Mikel Neumann, "The Incarnational Ministry of Jesus: An Alternative to Traditional Apologetic Approaches," in *Encountering New*

While this new thinking has not been uniformly embraced, particularly by those in the apologetics community, it has influenced this author's understanding of the Iglesia ni Cristo and encouraged a broader examination of possible evangelistic methods and tools for reaching out to the group's members. A discussion of important issues, possible strategies and modalities follows.

The Missional Spiral

Noted missiologist Gailyn Van Rheenen has proposed a theoretical model for evangelism and church planting in the shape of a spiral.[21] He urges the evangelical church to be "theologically-informed, Christ-centered, [and] Spirit-led" as it seeks to manifest Christ to the world and call others to him.[22] He views the church's mission as an interactive process which involves theological, cultural, historical and strategic reflection not as a straight line, one-way process but as a helix which involves the repeated interactions of these four activities.[23] By study, planning, experimentation, and examination of results the church should continually re-evaluate the effectiveness of its methods.[24] Ministry models must be refined to reflect each particular cultural context.

Religious Movements: A Holistic Evangelistic Approach, eds. Irving Hexham, Stephen Rost and John W. Morehead, II (Grand Rapids, MI: Kregel Academic and Professional, 2004), 25-41.

[21]Gailyn Van Rheenen, "Monthly Missiological Reflection #26: The Missional Helix: Example of Church Planting," http://www.missology.org/mmr/mmr26.html (accessed May 2, 2009).

[22]Van Rheenan, "Reflection #26;" Gailyn Van Rheenen, "Monthly Missiological Reflection #34: Contrasting Missional and Church Growth Perspectives," http://www.missiology.org/mmr/mmr34.htm (accessed May 2, 2009).

[23]Gailyn Van Rheenen, "Monthly Missiological Reflection #25: From Theology to Practice: The Helix Metaphor," http://www.missiology.org/mmr/mmr25.htm (accessed May 2, 2009).

[24]By the word, "effective" the author means several important things. Real communication must take place; the timeless gospel message is presented to a people through contextualized means. Those receiving the message hear it in ways and terms they truly understand and in ways that make the message truly good news to them so that they want to accept it.

The challenge is to utilize this method in developing incarnational ministries to New Religious Movements (NRMs) such as the Iglesia ni Cristo. So far, the focus has been on theological reflection in determining how the group's teachings deviate from orthodox Christian belief. Little or no consideration has been given to building bridges using beliefs that are not contrary to sound understanding of the Holy Scriptures. Similarly, there has been little or no examination of cultural concerns in communication methods,[25] and there has been no documented evaluation of what has been effective in reaching members of the group. The next chapter provides some broad observations on the latter point in an analysis of case studies of those who have left the Iglesia ni Cristo and embraced evangelical Christianity. The last chapter offers some strategic reflections on bridges and communication methods.

Group Conversion

The question most frequently raised about the Iglesia ni Cristo is whether there is any possibility that it might change its Christology and become more theologically orthodox, as the Worldwide Church of God (WCG) did in the late 1990s. To evaluate this possibility several missiological themes and areas of research and practice must be reviewed, and the particular case of the WCG must be examined more closely.

---

[25]The author has previously published an article looking at the Iglesia ni Cristo as the receptor in communication attempts by Evangelicals and considering how the forms of Evangelicals' communication have influenced the Iglesia ni Cristo's viewpoint in Anne C. Harper, "The Iglesia ni Cristo and Evangelical Christianity," *Journal of Asian Mission* 3 (March 2001):101-119. The author has also noted the different understanding members of the Iglesia ni Cristo hold for certain words commonly used in evangelistic efforts in Harper, "Iglesia ni Cristo," 2-3. Similarly, Filipino Apologist and Pastor Jun Divierte has stressed the necessity of understanding the meaning of terms and vocabulary when dialoguing with Iglesia ni Cristo members in Benito D. Divierte, III, "Understanding the Christology of the Iglesia ni Cristo for Better Dialogue," in *Naming the Unknown God,* ed. Abelard O. Gorospe (Manila: OMF Literature, Inc., 2006), 227-238.

People Movements

"To Christianize a whole people, the first thing not to do is to snatch individuals out of it into a different society."[26] So writes Donald McGavran in the mid-1950s. McGavran, a third generation missionary to India with three decades of service there, wrote *The Bridges of God* in order to challenge the existing model of church planting, which extracted converts from their existing social networks by seeking individual decisions for Christ and then placing those converts in churches of similarly extracted individuals. He proposes promulgating a different strategy aimed at encouraging what he calls "people movements."[27] His thesis is that throughout church history and even today in non-Western cultures most people come to Christ not as individuals but through a group choice, which involves multi-individual decisions to follow a culture's natural leaders.[28] This is because in non-Western cultures individuals do not make such decisions on their own.[29]

The result of a people movement is that those coming into a relationship with Christ and becoming members of a church maintain existing social networks and leadership structures and therefore do not face the problem of ostracism as do those won by the individual-convert method.[30] Further, McGavran notes that people movement churches are more stable and more likely to survive even when facing extreme persecution. This is because the group provides relational support and social cohesion.[31]

---

[26]Donald Anderson McGavran, *The Bridges of God: A Study in the Strategy of Missions* (Eugene, OR: Wipf & Stock Publishers, 2005), 10.
[27]*Ibid.*, 13.
[28]*Ibid.*, 12. See, Alan R. Tippett, "Conversion as a Dynamic Process in Christian Mission," *Missiology* 5 (April 1977): 203-221, for an overview of his analysis of people movements to Christianity in oceanic societies.
[29]McGavran, *Bridges*, 8-9.
[30]*Ibid.*, 8-13.
[31]*Ibid.*, 77. As I was completing my dissertation I became aware of a new book dealing with the issue of social networks and conversion in Asia. It contains a number of essays on family networks in Buddhist cultures and may offer additional insight for this discussion. Paul De Neui, ed., *Family and Faith*

Missiologist Alan Tippett, in his analysis of people movements to Christianity in Pacific Oceanic societies, notes several stages in the group conversion process: 1) a period of awareness; 2) a period of decision; 3) a point of encounter; and 4) a period of incorporation.[32] The period of awareness is the interval during which a society first begins to realize there are other "contexts" or possible belief systems and lifestyles than their own. Next, there is a period of decision as people discuss and come to general agreement on whether to keep existing allegiances or change them through conversion. When the decision is to convert there comes the point of encounter, when subcultures within the group decide to accept or reject the group's decision. For those accepting the change, separation from the old context occurs. Then follows a period of incorporation as a new group identity is developed with new behavioral norms, activities and rituals.[33]

Insider Movements

In the past few years, the idea of sparking people movements has generated serious discussion in the arena of Muslim evangelism under the rubric of "insider movements."[34] Initially, this term was applied to contextualization in Muslim contexts, but it has become a more widely-used term for groups of people who become

---

in Asia: The Missional Impact of Social Networks (Pasadena, CA: William Carey Library, 2010).

[32] Tippett, "Conversion as a Dynamic Process," 207.

[33] Ibid., 208-213.

[34] See, for example: Rebecca Lewis, "Insider Movements: Honoring God-Given Identity and Community," International Journal of Frontier Missiology 26, 1 (Spring 2009): 16-19. She further describes insider movements as "any movement to faith in Christ where 1) the gospel flows through pre-existing communities and social networks, and where 2) believing families, as valid expressions of the Body of Christ, remain inside their socioreligious communities, retaining their identity as members of that community while living under the Lordship of Jesus Christ and the authority of the Bible;" and Rebecca Lewis, "Promoting Movements to Christ within Natural Communities," International Journal of Frontier Missiology 24, 2 (Summer 2007); 75, www.ijfm.org/PDFs_IJFM_2_PDFs/24_2Lewis.pdf (accessed May 17, 2010).

believers and followers of Jesus Christ without leaving their own social contexts. Rebecca Lewis defines insider movements "as movements to obedient faith in Christ that remain integrated with or inside their natural community."[35] In investigating appropriate ideas and strategies for reaching members of the Iglesia ni Cristo, the discussion of "fruitful practices"[36] in Muslim outreach is important for two reasons. First is the fact that both are extremely close-knit cultures in which individuals do not make decisions without considering family, social and leadership networks and obligations. Second is the ostracism and persecution that an individual experiences when he or she decides to leave either group.

Recent articles in the *International Journal of Frontier Missiology* have offered some observations about practices which appear to be "fruitful" in encouraging movements to Christianity within Muslim cultures. Those that seem relevant for outreach to members of the Iglesia ni Cristo and even for encouraging whole families and social networks to decide to follow Christ include:

- The gospel should be shared contextually so that it is seen as strengthening social networks, not tearing them down.[37]
- The stronger the contextualization, the likelier it is to cause development of a people movement as converts keep more of their cultural identity.[38]

---

[35]Lewis, "Insider Movements," 16.

[36]Don Allen, Rebecca Harrison, Eric and Laura Adams, Bob Fish and E. J. Martin, eds., "Fruitful Practices: A Descriptive List," *International Journal of Frontier Missiology* 26, 3 (Fall 2009): 111-122.

[37]Andrea Gray and Leith Gray, "Paradigm and Praxis, Part I: Social Networks and Fruitfulness in Church Planting," *International Journal of Frontier Missiology* 26, 1 (Spring 2009): 26-27; Leith Gray and Andrea Gray, "Paradigm and Praxis Part II: Why Are Some Workers Changing Paradigms?" *International Journal of Frontier Missiology* 26, 2 (Summer 2009): 66.

[38]Rick Brown, Bob Fish, John Travis, et al., "Movements and Contextualization: Is There Really a Correlation?" *International Bulletin of Frontier Missiology* 26, 1 (Spring 2009): 21-23. Leith Gray and Andrea Gray note contextualization in such externals as growing a beard, use of language, application of the Bible to the felt needs of the community in Leith Gray and Andrea Gray, "Part II," 65.

- Evangelization efforts should target existing social networks.[39]
- Workers should intentionally reflect on and choose practices which will encourage the extension of the gospel through social connections.[40]
- Whole families should be discipled, not just individuals.[41]
- Consideration should be given whether to or not to plant a separate culture-specific church rather than moving converts into existing churches outside their culture or social networks.[42]
- Messengers should behave in culturally appropriate ways.[43]
- Messengers should hold a transformational[44] rather than an attractional model of church,[45] because this promotes growth of church structures within the culture rather than parallel to it.[46]
- Workers should go where people normally gather rather than meeting them on the worker's own turf.[47]
- Faith communities should share meals and practice hospitality both to express love within their communities and to reach outside them.[48]

---

[39] Allen et al, "Fruitful Practices," 114.
[40] Andrea Gray and Leith Gray, "Part I," 20, 28.
[41] *Ibid.*, 27.
[42] Leith Gray and Andrea Gray, "Part II," 70.
[43] Allen, "Fruitful Practices," 113.
[44] A transformational model views church as "an existing social network that has been transformed by Christ." Workers using this model may encourage evangelism and discipleship through social relationships that are already in place or intentionally share with a group of people. Andrea Gray and Leith Gray, "Part I," 20.
[45] An attractional model of church is one in which people come together because they are Christians not because they have a previous social connection. They may have little in common. Andrea Gray and Leith Gray, "Part I," 20.
[46] Andrea Gray and Leith Gray, "Part I," 20.
[47] Leith Gray and Andrea Gray, "Part II," 70.
[48] Allen, "Fruitful Practices," 121.

Some thoughts on the practical implications of these "fruitful practices" in an Iglesia ni Cristo context appear in the last chapter.

The Worldwide Church of God

The Worldwide Church of God (WCG) is often raised as an example of a New Religious Movement that has changed dramatically and even come to accept Christian orthodoxy. A brief summary of its history and the series of events that led to such change is necessary before considering whether the Iglesia ni Cristo might follow its model. It is important to recognize that the WCG's metamorphosis took place gradually over almost a decade. Also, according to the church only 40% of membership remained in the group throughout its change.[49]

The WCG was established in the 1930s by the ardent ministry of Herbert W. Armstrong. Mainstream Christians considered the church to hold heretical teachings and to be a "cult" because of its reliance on Armstrong as the sole authoritative interpreter of Scripture, its faulty understanding of God and salvation, its legalistic lifestyle requirements and its control over members' lives.[50] The group circulated Armstrong's teachings through many publications and aired them over television and radio broadcasts worldwide. Following his death in 1986, there was an earnest seeking for the Lord and a quest for biblical truth among the WCG's leadership.[51] The first crack in the church's cocoon was the questioning and discarding of the belief in Armstrong's "absolute

---

[49] Grace Communion International, email to the author, February 9, 2011.

[50] See, for example, Walter Martin, *Kingdom of the Cults* (Minneapolis, MN: Bethany House Publishers, 1985), 303-305.

[51] Insiders have published two books describing what happened. Joseph Tkach, Jr., *Transformed by Truth* (Colorado Springs, CO: Multnomah Books, 1997), was written by the son of Armstrong's named successor, Joseph Tkach, Sr., who himself became the denomination's leader when his father died. The second book was written by Tkach's right-hand man, the editor of *The Plain Truth*, the WCG's primary publication. J. Michael Feazell, *The Liberation of the Worldwide Church of God* (Grand Rapids, MI: Zondervan, 2001).

insight on the Scriptures."[52] His hand-picked successor, Joseph W. Tkach, Sr., who held the office of "God's apostle, the only person on earth through whom God brings doctrine into his church," began to alter the church's previously unquestioned authoritarian leadership structure.[53] In their search for the Lord and for truth, J. Michael Feazell, Tkach's executive assistant, and other WCG leaders began to attend the C.P. Haggard Graduate School of Theology at Azuza Pacific University. Tkach notes that the school's dean was the first evangelical leader who would have anything to do with WCG leadership, and that other professors and administrators at the school never interfered. "They never pushed. They never tried to change or 'convert us.' They simply taught the Bible in all the joy and enthusiasm the Lord provides those who love him, and they did it at a time when no other Christian graduate school would ever consider admitting us."[54]

As the leaders explored biblical truth they began to make significant changes in the church's official teachings. Most notable were:

- in 1991, redefining what it means to be born again by rejecting the idea that people can become gods; acknowledging the divinity of the Holy Spirit;
- in 1993, announcing an orthodox understanding of the Trinity;
- in 1994, removing the requirements to keep covenant laws, observe the Sabbaths, and contribute multiple tithings.[55]

These shifts in the church's doctrines and self-understanding naturally resulted in a huge upheaval. Not all could accept such radical changes, and in 1995 a large group of ministers and members left to form a new denomination.[56] Well-known cult

---

[52] Feazell, *The Liberation,* 21.
[53] *Ibid.,* 23.
[54] *Ibid.,* 28.
[55] Grace Communion International, "Transformed by Christ," http://www.wcg.org/lit/aboutus/history.htm (accessed April 21, 2010).
[56] *Ibid.*

researcher Hank Hanegraaff of the Christian Research Institute notes over one hundred splinter groups forming during the years of the group's doctrinal transformation.[57] Those remaining in the Worldwide Church of God came to understand and embrace evangelical Christianity. By 1997, most evangelicals had reciprocated by acknowledging the WCG's orthodoxy, and it was accepted into membership in the National Association of Evangelicals.[58] In 2009, the Worldwide Church of God changed its name to Grace Communion International.[59]

Standing out in this story are several important factors: 1) the death of the group's founder; 2) the questioning and earnest seeking after God and biblical truth by the church's leadership; 3) the pivotal role of welcoming acceptance and non-confrontational teaching by evangelicals at Azuza Pacific University before the WCG's leaders were "converted;" 4) the long duration of the process; and 5) the inability of all to accept the results.

The Iglesia ni Cristo has long passed the death of its founder, Felix Y. Manalo. However, it is now entering a new transition begun by the death of Felix's son and ecclesiastical heir, Eraño G. Manalo, late in August 2009 and the ascension to leadership of

---

[57] Walter Martin; Hank Hanegraaff, ed, The *Kingdom of the Cults*, 30th Anniversary Edition. (Minneapolis, MN: Bethany House Publishers, 1997), 471-472.

[58] Grace Communion International, "Transformed by Christ," and Grace Communion International, "Global Lessons from the Worldwide Church of God," http://ww.wcg.org/lit/aboutus.media/global.htm (accessed October 22, 2009). For a fuller description of the changes and emerging understanding and spiritual growth of this group, see Feazell, "The Liberation," 49-147; for a first-person account of one member's spiritual and emotional crisis amidst these changes see, "Case Studies—God Is Still at Work, Revealing Himself and His Truth to Those Who Sincerely Seek Him," *Kenya Church Growth Bulletin*, January 1, 1997, http://www.strategicnetwork.org/index.php ?loc=kb&view =v&id= 9900&fto=9& (accessed November 3, 2009).

[59] Grace Communion International, "Worldwide Church of God Announces Name Change," news release April 16, 2009, http://www.wcg.org/ (accessed October 26, 2009).

Eraño's son, Eduardo V. Manalo.[60] As Eduardo brings his leadership team on line, will they seek and accept biblical Christianity, or will they rely on the undisputed teachings of the group's founder? Will evangelical Christian leaders welcome them, seeing the Iglesia ni Cristo as a field ripe for dialogue and harvest? Recently an Iglesia ni Cristo minister sought to register for some courses at an evangelical seminary in metro Manila. However, he wished to remain anonymous, with his name kept out of the institution's records. Because the school felt it could not admit a student under those conditions, the minister decided not to enroll.[61] Was this a missed opening?

Hospitality

In recent years, there have been a number of significant studies of the biblical understanding of hospitality as an essential component of the church's mandate, mission and methodology. Those with the spiritual gift of hospitality tend to think of this as exclusively their domain and often see it as limited to feeding and housing others. However, recent works by writers such as Christine Pohl, John Koenig, Michele Hershberger, and Abraham Malherbe[62] have examined the biblical, cultural, and historical dimensions of the church's collective call to hospitality. A number of the ideas and themes in these publications are relevant to the discussion of outreach to those in the closely-knit culture of the Iglesia ni Cristo.

---

[60]*Manila Bulletin*, "Happy Birthday to Iglesia ni Cristo Executive Minister Eduardo V. Manalo," *Manila Bulletin*, October 30, 2009, http://www.google.com/#hl=en&q=Eduardo+manalo+news&aq=f&aqi=&aql=&oq=&gs_rfai=&fp=a2bb30ecf4f91972 (accessed December 1, 2009).

[61]Author's conversation with seminary administrator on January 25, 2010.

[62]Christine D. Pohl, *Making Room: Recovering Hospitality as a Christian Tradition* (Grand Rapids, MI: William B. Eerdmans Publishing Company, 1999); John Koenig, *New Testament Hospitality: Partnership with Strangers as Promise and Mission* (Eugene, OR: Wipf and Stock Publishers, 1985); Michele Hershberger, *A Christian View of Hospitality: Expecting Surprises* (Scottsdale, PA: Herald Press, 1999), and Abraham J. Malherbe, *Social Aspects of Early Christianity* (Philadelphia: Fortress Press, 1983).

These authors have concluded that hospitality is God's call to the church, both as redeemed individuals and as a community, to invite strangers and outsiders into its life. Outsiders should not be approached as mere objects for conversion but as people deserving our friendship. With vulnerability, evangelical Christians are to encounter outsiders as friends who bring gifts to our lives and to expect that through mutual, trusting relationships God will reveal himself both to the outsider and to themselves.

In Michael Green's analysis of evangelism in the early church, he describes the household, composed of "blood relatives, slaves and freedmen," as the essential unit of society. Evangelism took place largely through the hospitality extended within the home.[63] John Koenig explores this idea more thoroughly, noting the "sacred bond between guests and hosts" while espousing the view that the "strangers" to whom we offer hospitality often bring us blessings.[64] He describes Jesus' association with those at the margins of society: the tax collectors, the sinful woman who washed his feet, and others.[65] Further, Koenig sees the book of Acts as a series of "guest and host stories."[66] He calls "local churches. . . [to] function as 1) banquet communities which attract nonbelieving neighbors and 2) home bases for missionaries. . . [to] promote mutual concern among. . . churches," offering financial and physical assistance to those in need.[67] Hospitality begins with communities who understand themselves to be "guests of God,"[68] and then pushes beyond the communities' boundaries.[69]

---

[63] Michael Green, *Evangelism in the Early Church* (Grand Rapids, MI: Wm B. Eerdmans Publishing Co., revised edition, 2004), 318-319. Malherbe also notes the household as the "basic political unit," including "servants, laborers and business associates" in Malherbe, *Social Aspects*, 67.
[64] Koenig, *New Testament Hospitality*, 2-3.
[65] *Ibid.*, 20-29.
[66] *Ibid.*, 87.
[67] *Ibid.*, 119.
[68] *Ibid.*, 132.
[69] *Ibid.*, 126.

The noted Roman Catholic writer Henri Nouwen sees hospitality in the context of movements in our own spiritual lives. In the first of these, he proposes that Christians move from loneliness to solitude. He describes solitude as a place in which we no longer see our interaction with the world as interruption, but as a vocation. We allow God to create an inner space in which "compassionate solidarity with our fellow human beings becomes possible."[70] When we reach to our inner selves, we are led to reach out to the stranger.[71] Nouwen sees hostility and hospitality as opposite ends of a spectrum.[72] We need to be receptive to others, allowing them to become friends.[73] Like other authors, Nouwen notes Old and New Testament stories that illustrate our obligation to welcome others into our homes and lives; he observes that through those encounters God brings gifts and blessings to the hosts as well as the guests.[74] He challenges us to see hospitality as an attitude toward others, which creates a space in which a stranger "can enter and become a friend instead of an enemy. *Hospitality is not to change people, but to offer them space where change can take place.*"[75]

Methodist missiologist Joon-Sik Park sees hospitality as the core of evangelism. While evangelism must include proclamation by word, more importantly, it must include incarnation—as demonstrated by Jesus, the Word become flesh. As such, it is a "boundary-crossing event," and to be effective it must be the fruit of our spiritual lives. Hospitality then gives the gospel credibility, because Christ is the real host, and it is his table which we offer to others.[76]

---

[70]Henri J. Nouwen, *Reaching Out* (London: Fount, 1975), 38-39.
[71]*Ibid.*, 43.
[72]*Ibid.*, xx.
[73]*Ibid.*, 54.
[74]*Ibid.*, 44.
[75]*Ibid.*, 46-53; italics added.
[76]Joon-Sik Park, "Hospitality as Context for Evangelism," *Missiology* 30, 3 (July 2002): 386-7.

In Christine Pohl's study of hospitality, she challenges the church to respond to the physical needs of outsiders for "food, shelter and protection." She stresses the importance of table fellowship, shared meals, throughout the church's history. The act of eating together recognizes the "equal value and dignity of persons."[77] It is interesting that she then points to the challenge of Jesus in Luke 14 and Matthew 25 to invite to our tables, not our friends and relatives, but the poor, maimed, and disabled—those we consider to be lower than ourselves. By inviting them to share our meals, we extend to others the same hospitality and welcome God has extended to us as undeserving sinners.[78] Pohl challenges the church to recover table fellowship in the context both of the home and of the congregation, not as occasional events but as an intentional practice, which is "fundamental to our identity as Christians."[79]

Pentecostal theologian Amos Yong reflects on the story of the Good Samaritan as an example of a welcoming attitude and actions toward those of other faiths. He rightly urges that while proclamation of the gospel message is essential to the church's calling, the evangelical community can still learn from members of other faiths. The Samaritan showed a more godly attitude and lifestyle than did those who were perceived as being the most religious and therefore the most righteous in the Jewish community of that time.[80] Further, Yong notes that "it was the multiculturally formed deacon Philip" who was the first to preach the gospel effectively beyond the borders of Judea; the apostles, all of them Jews, began with a much more parochial vision, though God later

---

[77]Pohl, *Making Room*, 5-6.
[78]*Ibid.*, 19-21.
[79]*Ibid.*, 171-177.
[80]Amos Yong, "The Spirit of Hospitality: Pentecostal Perspectives toward a Performative Theology of Interreligious Encounter," *Missiology* 35, 1 (January 2007): 60. For additional discussion of interaction with members of other religions see John W. Morehead, "Amos Yong Interview: Pneumatology, Hospitality and Religious Pluralism," Morehead's Musings, February 2, 2007, http://johnmorehead.blogspot.com/2007/02/amos-yong-interviewpneumatolory.html (accessed April 23, 2010).

expanded their horizons. Yong challenges the evangelical community to give its members permission to dialogue with and learn from those of other religions.[81]

What are the implications of these insights into hospitality for the evangelical community's interaction with members of the Iglesia ni Cristo? First, an attitude change is essential. Evangelicals must become more welcoming and accepting of those in this group. This acceptance does not mean incorporating or acquiescing to false beliefs, but merely viewing those who hold such beliefs as potential friends rather than necessary enemies. When others are invited to be friends, there is the possibility of learning from each other and of receiving as well as giving. Second, we must actively engage in dialogue with those in the Iglesia ni Cristo. What is needed is not debate but discussion, so that we may learn of their faith as they see it, coming to understand their felt needs and what is truly important to them. Third, we must make a conscious, deliberate effort to offer table fellowship to these outsiders. Churches should plan specific events to which Iglesia ni Cristo members can be invited not to hear preaching aimed at them but to experience the fellowship of God's family. These events should demonstrate that evangelicals accept and value Iglesia ni Cristo members as fellow human beings who have something to offer to evangelicals in return. Fourth, we must base these efforts on a renewed spirituality—on the work of the Holy Spirit in the evangelical community and in the lives of its individual members. We must seek the Holy Spirit as both the impelling and the enabling force who alone can bring about these transformed attitudes and transforming activities.

---

[81]Yong, "The Spirit of Hospitality," 61-66.

The Holy Spirit, Strategy and the Spirituality of the Messenger

Park believes that:

> Evangelism is not about methods or techniques. It is not simply a task of memorizing and reciting salvation prescriptions. The Christian witness is to be born out of the depth of our being: it is to be an encounter at the deepest level. It thus involves our spirituality more than any other ministries of the church.[82]

God the Holy Spirit opens hearts and makes them receptive to the good news. The Spirit convicts people of sin (John 16:8-11), restores their spiritual sight, and frees them from the power of Satan (John 3:5; 1 Corinthians 1:14-16; 2 Corinthians 4:3-4; Titus 3:5).[83] Further, the Spirit calls and equips the church to pray for both the harvest and the harvesters (Matthew 9:37-38).

The Spirit calls and prepares some to be his special messengers. Jesus called the disciples who would become his apostles. In Acts 13 members of the church in Antioch, led by the Spirit, laid hands on Paul and Barnabas, sending them out. Those called must rely on the Spirit for empowering, insight, opportunities, and protection. Reaching out to strangers, becoming their friends and meeting their needs in evangelistic contexts is hard work. The equipping prior to ministry and the empowerment for ongoing service can only come from a mature, sustained spiritual life.[84]

Missiologist Don Allen notes that those having the most fruitful ministries among Muslims are people who "mobilize

---

[82]Park, "Hospitality as Context for Evangelism," *390-391*.
[83]Netland, "Toward Conceptualized Apologetics," 289-303.
[84]Pohl, *Making Room*, 13; Gailyn Van Rheenen, "Monthly Missiological Reflection #39: Spiritual Formation in Church Planting," http://www.missiology.org/MMR/mmr39.pdf (accessed November 1, 2009).

extensive, intentional, and focused prayer."[85] Similarly, those seeking to reach members of the Iglesia ni Cristo must be people with deeply nourished prayer lives who have the prayer support of others behind them.

The evangelical community must not shy away from developing strategies while recognizing the need for balance between detailed planning and trust in the sovereignty of God. Throughout Acts it is the Holy Spirit who orchestrates the church's expansion.[86] While God often brings surprises, he has also gifted some with the ability to strategize in church planting. For example, Paul recognized his gift for laying foundations and building young churches. He encouraged others to be similarly wise in their ministries (1 Corinthians 3:10-11).[87] He was also intentional in his travel strategy, though he listened as the Holy Spirit sometimes redirected him (Romans 1:13; Acts 16:6-10).

People with a spiritual life of constant encounter with God will manifest the fruit of the Spirit: love, joy, peace, patience, kindness, faithfulness, gentleness, goodness and self-control. They will thus attract people to themselves and therefore to God. An attitude of humility will pervade their encounters with others. Noted NRM scholar John Morehead describes two dimensions of humility: "rhetorical humility," avoiding needless cultural offense; and empathy, showing compassion for those in NRMS. This does not mean agreeing with them theologically but really loving those we engage in ministry.[88] Park notes Jesus' willingness to be a guest of Zaccheus, a despised tax collector, and challenges missionaries to have the same attitude.[89] The *Bridges* video suggests speaking from vulnerability rather than strength.[90]

---

[85] Allen, "Fruitful Practices," 113.
[86] Park, "Hospitality as a Context ," 391.
[87] Van Rheenen, "Contrasting Missional," 3.
[88] Morehead, "Reflections," 8-9.
[89] Park, "Hospitality as Context," 393.
[90] Salt Lake Theological Seminary, *Bridges*.

First impressions are important. A recent article in the *Philippine Star* describes three characteristics Filipinos look for in a salesperson:

> The salesperson must be neat and clean. . .
> [He or she] must speak gently and politely.
> [He or she] must be well-mannered.[91]

The article notes that Filipinos are more sensitive to the person than to what that person may be selling. They base their decision to purchase on whether they like and have a rapport with him or her.[92] In light of this, how much more important are the character and attitude of the one bringing the good news?

Incarnational Ministry

The New Testament describes the incarnational ministry of Jesus Christ, who though God, emptied himself and became like us in order to communicate God's love in ways and a language that humans could understand. Jesus is our primary model for doing incarnational ministry, but there also have been others throughout church history.

Discovering and Meeting Needs

Throughout Jesus' life and ministry, he met the tangible needs of those around him. Both Mikel Neumann and Harold Taylor stress the necessity of incarnational ministry to members of NRMs.[93] Neumann approaches the topic via an examination of

---

[91] *Philippine Star*, "Why Pinoys Behave the Way They Do," *Philippine Star*, May 11, 2003, 16.

[92] "Why Pinoys," 16.

[93] Neumann, "The Incarnational Ministry of Jesus," 25-42; and Harold Taylor, "Contextualized Mission in Church History," in *Encountering New Religious Movements: A Holistic Evangelical Approach*, eds. Irving Hexham, Stephen Rost, and John Morehead, II (Grand Rapids, MI: Kregel, 2004), 43-62.

narratives in the Gospels and Acts, while Taylor examines contextualization in church history, describing St. Francis of Assisi's ministry to Muslims as one in which his actions revealed the love of Jesus.[94] Christine Pohl notes in the writings of John Chrysostom his charge to meet basic human needs, to give food even to robbers and murderers. She reflects on the church's insulation from those in real need, stressing that it is important not to wait for people to ask for help "but to run to them, and be given to finding them."[95]

Parallel to people's physical needs are their spiritual, emotional and social needs. Evangelicals ministering to NRM members must understand these and show how biblical Christianity can answer their questions and fulfill their needs so that they really hear the gospel as good news. This means the starting point for reaching those involved in NRMs—including the Iglesia ni Cristo—must be identifying their questions and felt needs.[96]

Relationships and Communication

While some needs may be obvious, others are not. Discovering needs requires building relationships. Jesus mixed with ordinary people; he shared their life experiences and understood their beliefs. Relationship-building was at the core of his ministry. An incarnational approach to adherents of NRMs must involve interaction in daily life and a long-term commitment to friendship.[97] This means coming to know their culture, customs and language as well as their beliefs. It means liking them and wanting to associate with them. Ken Mulholland describes how one evangelical pastor communicates that he likes his Mormon neighbors and their children: he coaches the community youth

---

[94]Taylor, "Contextualized Mission," 53-55.
[95]Pohl, *Making Room*, 70.
[96]Turner, "New Mission Task: Worldwide and Waiting," 5.
[97]Neumann, "The Incarnational Ministry," 27.

football team.⁹⁸ Are there similar opportunities to show Iglesia ni Cristo members that they are liked?

Harold Netland notes that while in the West it is not uncommon for a person to become convinced about Christianity through reading a book or an article, in Japan truth is always communicated through personal relationships.⁹⁹ The deepening of those relationships and thus of cultural understanding will uncover appropriate ways of communicating. In Philippine culture, direct confrontation is an offense that diminishes the stature of those being confrontational in the eyes of others. Such individuals are viewed with disdain, having incurred *hiya* (shame) for their aggressive behavior. Instead, a friend may gently offer indirect correction or suggest a different viewpoint. It is better to present and praise right beliefs rather than to attack wrong beliefs.¹⁰⁰

The Use of Testimonies

To evangelize is to make Christ known in such a way as to prompt conversion. Arguing does not foster interest in the gospel; in fact, it often leads non-Christians to dig in their heels rather than opening their minds. In incarnational ministry, it is important to listen in order to learn about the lives of others, but it is just as important to speak vulnerably, sharing our own lives. In ministry to Jehovah's Witnesses, missionary John Fisher urges evangelicals to discover some common attitudes and desires and then eagerly communicate what Christ has done in their own lives.¹⁰¹ Michael Green points out the recurrent use of personal testimony by the New Testament writers as they describe the difference Christ has made in their lives.¹⁰² Ken Mulholland suggests the use of such

---

⁹⁸Mulholland, "Bridging the Divide," 166.
⁹⁹Netland, "Toward Contextualized Apologetics," 300-301.
¹⁰⁰Salt Lake Theological Seminary, *Bridges*.
¹⁰¹John Fisher, "The Why and How of Reaching Jehovah's Witnesses," *Evangelical Missions Quarterly* 12 (October 1974): 123.
¹⁰²Green, *Evangelism in the Early Church*, 316.

personal testimony in a "gospel sandwich," a portion of Scripture being shared along with personal experiences such as descriptions of promises claimed and prayers answered, of struggles with sin and growth in godliness, and stories about how the Holy Spirit has encouraged them through the reading of a portion of Scripture.[103]

Bridges

The idea of building on what people already know is old in Asia. Sometime between 600 and 531 B.C. Chinese poet Lao Tzu wrote,

> Go to the people
> Live among them
> Learn from them
> Love them
> Start with what they know
> Build on what they have[104]

The strategy of searching for bridges by which to communicate the gospel is not new. Don Richardson describes discovering "redemptive analogies" in the cultures of aboriginal peoples in his books, *Peace Child* and *Eternity in Their Hearts*.[105] Missiologist J. Dudley Woodberry discusses adapting the five pillars of the Islamic faith in ministry to Muslims.[106] Samuel Zwemer dialogued with Muslims, seeking keys in their literature and ways of reasoning to open their eyes to Christ.[107]

---

[103]Mulholland, "Bridging the Divide," 171.

[104]A Chinese poem by Lao Tzu quoted in Taylor, "Contextualized Mission," 59. See also, Lao Tzu, "Go to the People," http://thinkexist.com/quotation/go-to-the-people-live-with-them-learn-from-them/348565.html (accessed April 26, 2010).

[105]Don Richardson, *Peace Child*, ((Ventura, CA: Regal Books, 1975), and Don Richardson, *Eternity in Their Hearts* (Ventura, CA: Regal Books, 1984).

[106]Dudley J. Woodberry, "Contextualization among Muslims: Reusing Common Pillars," in *The Word Among Us: Contextualizing Theology for Mission Today*, ed. Dean S. Gilliland (Dallas: Word, 1989), 282-312.

[107]Taylor, "Contextualized Mission," 58.

Finding common ground is a necessary step in communicating with members of NRMs. The *Bridges* approach to Latter-day Saints advocates discovering "points of contact within that culture."[108] Finding common ground does not mean accepting heresy or non-biblical ideas, but rather identifying and focusing initially on the right beliefs a person already has. In his ministry to the Christadelphians, Philip Johnson advocates an approach which sees them as "God-fearers" with faulty or incomplete knowledge of God rather than as "purveyors of false doctrine."[109] He points to the way in which the apostles and Philip interacted with God-fearers throughout the book of Acts and sees common ground with Christadelphians in their high view of Scripture.[110]

Filipino pastor and apologist Jun Divierte applies this principle with his argument that it is "important to establish common ground to foster better understanding—areas such as Christ's Lordship, being Messiah, his true humanity and virgin birth. Knowing the Iglesia ni Cristo is a vital key."[111] Some additional bridges will be discussed later in the last chapter.

Barriers

Similarly, it is important to discover barriers to communicating and comprehending the good news and to clarify areas of misunderstanding that give rise to these barriers. What prevents members of the Iglesia ni Cristo from hearing the gospel? The Iglesia ni Cristo's writings in its official magazine, *Pasugo* (*The Message*), show a deep distrust of evangelicals.[112] In an earlier publication, the author has noted some reasons for this: the paternalistic, racist attitudes of Protestant missionaries in their

---

[108] Mulholland, "Bridging the Divide," 159.
[109] Johnson, "Reaching the Christadelphians," 187.
[110] *Ibid.*, 189.
[111] Divierte, "Understanding the Christology," 190-191.
[112] See, for example, Ferdinand P. Alcid, "The Rightful Preachers of God's Word," *Pasugo* 50, 8 (August 1998): 8-12, and Donald Pinnoch, "The Charismatic Movement," *Pasugo* 51, 1 (January 1999): 5-8.

interactions with Felix Manalo; evangelicals' vitriolic and sometimes false portrayals of the group and its beliefs; and the inappropriate and sometimes disastrous methods evangelicals have used to evangelize members of the Iglesia ni Cristo.[113] Evangelicals who have built relationships of trust with the group's leadership have betrayed that trust by writing negatively about the group.

There has been little attempt to understand members of this group as receptors of gospel communication. Some aspects of Filipino culture and that of the Iglesia ni Cristo that have served as barriers to the gospel message include: the Filipino relational approach to life, amplified by the Iglesia ni Cristo's clannishness; the strong collectivism of this relational culture; values such authority and class structure; the normal cultural reaction to confrontation; and the huge cultural distance between Western missionaries and cult researchers and members the group.[114]

Harold Netland notes that most Christian apologists today are American or European. Their message is implicitly intended for those holding a Western understanding of the world, one that is "influenced by post-Enlightenment secularism and scientism." This means that what is being presented is probably not geared to the needs and questions of a non-Western Iglesia ni Cristo audience. Further, Iglesia ni Cristo members may not understand what is

---

[113]Harper, "The Iglesia ni Cristo and Evangelical Christianity," 103-112, and Harper, "Iglesia ni Cristo," 3-4. I would note here an excellent book recently published which contrasts Iglesia ni Cristo teachings with the whole of what Scripture has to say and examines the biblical context of passages that the group has used inappropriately. However, this book has a title which is off-putting even to those who are not members of the Iglesia ni Cristo! Tino C. Ruivivar, *The Absurd Claims and Biggest Mistakes of the Iglesia ni Cristo* (Quezon City: Evangelical Life Publications, 2005). No member of the group would pick up, much less read, a book with such a title; so the possibility of using the book evangelistically is unrealistic.

[114]In Harper, "The Iglesia ni Cristo and Evangelical Christianity," 114-119, I use two cultural distance scales to show the breadth of this distance. These are David Hesselgrave's "Seven Dimensions of Cross Cultural Communication" and David Hofstede's "Four Major Cultural Distance Dimensions."

being said or "respond favorably unless some of [their] basic presuppositions are first altered."[115]

The Process of Conversion

Before proceeding to specific case studies of those who have converted to evangelical Christianity from the Iglesia ni Cristo, it is important to understand the nature of conversion as a process, not simply an exchange of one set of religious ideas or theories about life for another. Andrew Buckser and Stephen Glazier observe that, "To change one's religion is to change one's world, to voluntarily shift the basic presuppositions upon which both self and others are understood."[116]

Too often Paul's Damascus Road experience is considered a universal norm for a conversion model. However, there are other biblical models such as the conversion of the disciples themselves, members of the households of Cornelius and Lydia, and Priscilla and Aquila. Further, anthropological and sociological research points to conversion usually as involving a change in viewpoint, a transformation, which takes place over a period of time. Earlier Tippett's work on group conversion process was discussed. A consideration of the process involved in individual conversion follows.

Christian anthropologist Lewis Rambo describes conversion as a multi-layered process in which a series of elements interact over time.[117] Cultural, social, personal and religious factors accumulate in varying degrees, possibly culminating in particular moments of commitment.[118] These commitment points may be ritualized

---

[115]Netland, "Toward Contextualized Apologetics," 296-297.

[116]Andrew Buckser and Stephen D. Glazier, eds., *The Anthropology of Religious Conversion* (London: Rowman and Littlefield Publishers, Inc., 2003), xi.

[117]Lewis R. Rambo, *Understanding Religious Conversion* (New Haven, CT: Yale University Press, 1993) 16-17.

[118]*Ibid.*, 124.

through such actions as baptism or in public demonstrations such as the giving of testimony. Further, conversion is affected by context; that is, the expectations of a given cultural and religious context shape the experience and description of such turning points.[119]

Noted professor and writer Gordon T. Smith urges the evangelical community to reconsider the way in which it frames conversion. He believes conversion does not take place at a single point in time but is a progressive process of faith formation.[120] Sociologists John Lofland and Rodney Stark propose a model of conversion, which includes what they call the "predisposing conditions" of persons prior to their contact with a new religion. These include 1) a tension created by the discrepancy between real life and idealized belief; 2) a problem-solving approach which "imposes religious meaning on events;" 3) the discovery that their institutional religion is inadequate; 4) a turning point at which they realize they face an opportunity to change; 5) initial interaction with those in the new religion; 6) friends' and relatives' frequent unawareness that a conversion is in process and therefore their inability to intercede; and 6) the development of relationships and friendships with those in the new group.[121]

Lofland and Normand Skonovd describe a variety of "motifs" which interact to bring about different types of conversion, including:

- Intellectual conversion: an individual investigates different viewpoints without the social involvement of others.
- Mystical conversion: an individual has an experience

---

[119]Rambo, *Understanding Religious Conversion*, 5.

[120]Gordon T. Smith, *Transforming Conversion: Rethinking the Language and Contours of Christian Initiation* (Grand Rapids, MI: Baker Academic, 2010).

[121]John Lofland and Rodney Stark, "Becoming a World-Saver: A Theory of Conversion to a Deviant Perspective," *American Sociological Review* 30 (December 1965): 864-873.

through which he or she suddenly gains a new understanding of life and sense of change in self; Paul's Damascus Road experience would be one example.
- Experimental conversion: a person "tries on" a new worldview, religious identity and associated behaviors while withholding final judgment.
- Affectional conversion: interpersonal relationships bring about changing allegiance and commitment.
- Revivalist conversion: a person experiences transformation in the midst of an emotionally-charged mass gathering.
- Coercive conversion: though rare, brainwashing and "mind control" can cause adherence to a new religion.[122]

Lofland and Stark propose two classes of converts: "verbal converts," those who verbally acquiesce to a group's teachings and beliefs, but take no active role; and "total converts," those whose lives exhibit commitment in word and deed.[123]

The life stories of former Iglesia ni Cristo members recounted in the next chapter illustrate both these classes of converts as well as many of the elements in the descriptions above. In none of these cases did conversion happen at a single point in time, when the truth of the Trinity or the claims of Christ were initially presented, when an unbiblical teaching of the Iglesia ni Cristo was aggressively confronted, or when a book debunking the group's teachings was read.

In conclusion, there is much we can apply from the experience of those engaged in ministry to other people groups with similar characteristics. But, we must begin with attitudes and perspectives molded by Scripture and the Holy Spirit.

---

[122] John Lofland and Normand Skonovd, "Conversion Motifs," *Journal for the Scientific Study of Religion* 20 (1981): 375-381.
[123] Lofland, "Becoming a World-Saver," 864.

CHAPTER 9

CASE STUDIES

The author has had many interactions with Iglesia ni Cristo members over the course of sixteen years. Her students have also interacted with the group's members and reported to her their findings. For this study, twelve former members of the Iglesia ni Cristo who subsequently joined evangelical churches were interviewed about their experiences and insights using a questionnaire. This sample is limited by the small number of people interviewed and by how few are part of the lowest socio-economic strata from which the Iglesia ni Cristo draws the bulk of its membership.[1] This sample includes representatives of all but the highest socio-economic level of Philippine culture.

Lawyer[2]

CA[3] is the legal manager of a pharmaceutical company and unmarried. She grew up in the Iglesia ni Cristo as a *handog*[4] and was baptized at the age of twelve. Her father was a Roman Catholic before he converted to marry her mother, whose entire family were Iglesia ni Cristo members. CA's mother and other family members were active in the Iglesia ni Cristo, holding officer positions in the

---

[1] I believe this small sample is a reflection of the low number of converts from the Iglesia ni Cristo to Evangelical Christianity, despite the fact the Evangelical Protestant population in the Philippines has passed the five percent mark.

[2] CA, interview by author 5 February 2010, Quezon City. Digital recording.

[3] In all cases, the real names have been withheld for security purposes.

[4] A *handog* ("gift" or "offering") is someone whose parents are Iglesia ni Cristo members, and who was dedicated to God during a worship service as an infant and raised in the group.

Christian Family Organizations and serving as deacons, deaconesses, organists, choir members, and a *pananalapi*.[5] When she was young her parents held *panatas*[6] for the family, but this stopped as she and her siblings grew up.

She first considered leaving the Iglesia ni Cristo when her parents were on the verge of separating.[7] An evangelical friend helped her family to pray, and through this CA realized that God was there to help her. "That was a different point of view. Before in the Iglesia ni Cristo we understood God as a discipliner who was formal and humbled us. Now I realize God loves you for who you are. He's there to pick you up." The same friend gave her a Bible, which CA read every night in the midst of the family crisis. Evangelical family members invited her to visit Greenhills Christian Fellowship (a large Conservative Baptist church with multiple congregations in the Philippines). She began to attend not only its worship services but also Bible studies in which she felt free to ask questions and heard about the experience of others. The Bible studies were in the home of an uncle and aunt. "*Ate* Cindy stuffed us with food and then fed us with the Word of God afterwards."

When CA stopped attending Iglesia ni Cristo worship services, the *kapatid*[8] visited her, worried about her salvation. She was told that this was just a phase she was going through, and that they would give her another chance to remain a member. She declined. Today she is a member of Greenhills Christian Fellowship, but because of distance often attends Victory Christian Fellowship Malate with her fiancé.

---

[5] A *pananalapi* counts contributions.

[6] *Panata* is a devotional time of prayer.

[7] Divorce is not allowed in the Philippines. However, couples often do separate and then live with new "spouses" without the benefit of legal recognition.

[8] Members of the Iglesia ni Cristo call one another *kapatid* (brother). When someone misses worship services a *kapatid* is assigned to visit the person to find out the cause and woo them back.

Evangelical Pastor[9]

PW is the pastor of a church with 150 to 200 members located in Cavite, the province just south of metro Manila. His oldest sister was the first in the family to convert from the Iglesia ni Cristo to evangelical Christianity after she left home and came to metro Manila to find work. PW went to stay with his sister because she was able to support him in high school. He went forward during an altar call in her church: "I raised up my hands and said, 'I surrender to you.' I was filled with the Spirit of God—it was an intervention of the Holy Spirit."

Following his conversion he returned home to evangelize his family. Initially his father persecuted him, so PW began by teaching his younger sister and brothers Christian songs. When his younger sister became blind, in faith PW prayed and laid hands on her. His sister believed and received back her sight. His parents and brothers became evangelical Christians soon afterward.

PW had never questioned the teaching that those in leadership in the Iglesia ni Cristo must be obeyed. However, the actions of a leader when he was preparing for baptism at age twelve bothered him. It is required that those joining the church by baptism, even youth raised in the group, attend the doctrinal lessons first. His minister told him to lie to the Division Office and say he had completed the lessons so that the minister could meet his quota for baptisms.

When asked what attracted him to evangelical Christianity PW noted several things: The way of salvation—that this is solely the work of Christ—as well as the power and availability of the Holy Spirit. Having a relationship with Christ that was not dependent on church membership, salvation by grace apart from fulfilling duties, and being able to read the Bible for himself also appealed to him.

---

[9]PW, interview by author, 6 February 2010, Imus, Cavite. Digital recording.

Sales Agent[10]

MI was also raised in the Iglesia ni Cristo. His family was involved in the group's activities, participating not only in weekly worship services but in weekly prayer groups and Christian Family Organization meetings. They distributed literature door-to-door every two weeks and were regularly involved in evangelistic meetings.

During his college years, MI rented a room near campus. Another boarder exposed him to the Bible in a new way, and they studied Scripture together for over a year. When his family learned he had started attending an evangelical church his sister spoke to their Iglesia ni Cristo minister, and MI was expelled from the group.

The teachings and beliefs in evangelical Christianity which appealed most to him were the promise of salvation, the gifts and fullness of the Holy Spirit and the opportunity to have a relationship with Christ that is not dependent on church membership.

Call Center Worker[11]

A *handog* baptized in the Iglesia ni Cristo at the age of thirteen, OA graduated from college with a degree in tourism and now has ten professional certifications. While she was growing up her mother was one of the top ten financial givers in her locale with her name posted on a banner in the entryway of the chapel; her father was a military man who guarded the offerings at chapel events. Following her parents' separation and the annulment of their marriage, OA began to have questions about the Iglesia ni Cristo such as why they didn't care for families, why her father was

---

[10]MI, interview by author, 5 February 2010, Imus, Cavite. Digital recording.

[11]OA, interview by author, 31 January 2010, Katipunan, Quezon City. Digital recording.

promiscuous yet still in the group, and why she didn't see "fruits" in her parents' lives if the Iglesia ni Cristo "really were the chosen ones." She "didn't feel the Holy Spirit at church anymore; something was missing. . . .[She] was praying, 'Tell me how to really know God.'"

While she was working as a sales associate for a resort on Boracay Island other colleagues who were evangelical Christians talked about their faith and invited her to church. Her company later transferred her to Hong Kong, where she was deeply moved by Connie Reyes' testimony on CBN Asia's "700 Club" program. After she was transferred back to another location in the Philippines an officemate told her about "being born again" and gave her a cassette of Christian songs. These had a powerful effect on her, and she "received the Lord."

When asked what about evangelicalism appealed the most to her, OA responded:

- "the peace and truth in Connie Reyes' face—the fruit in Connie's life was plain to see;"
- reading the Bible for herself—before she was afraid to read it because she "might sin by adding or deleting something;"
- the manner of pastors teaching from the pulpit using only one Bible and proving something else than what she was taught previously;
- a cell group where the group could discuss questions about salvation—not needing to wait for the pastor—a lot of people were equipped to teach the faith.

OA is married to an evangelical co-worker she met during her period of searching.

Auto Mechanic[12]

DP became involved in the Iglesia ni Cristo because of the influence of a girlfriend. Baptized into the group at the age of twenty-two, he remained a member for almost thirteen years. Working as a day laborer in the auto shops of an uncle, he was regularly transferred to locations throughout Luzon far from his home in Manila. Each time he moved, he would record his new work location with the locale from which he was transferring. Church administration would notify the chapel closest to his new location; members would visit him and bring him to services there. He transferred his membership to different locales seven times.

After his seventh move he "grew cold" and "didn't like the new place." He also broke up with his girlfriend. So when his uncle moved him back to work in Manila, he didn't re-register. His sister, an evangelical Christian, invited him to her church. Because he didn't want to offend her, he went. Eventually he became an evangelical Christian and is now a member of a small Pentecostal church in which he serves as custodian, although he has limited involvement.

He likes being able to read the Bible for himself and being able to eat blood again.[13] He is not married because he struggles to earn enough to feed just himself.

---

[12]DP, interview by author, 29 January 2010, Katipunan, Quezon City. Digital recording.

[13]The Iglesia ni Cristo teaches that blood cannot be eaten. *Dinuguan*, a cooked blood dish that is a favorite of Filipinos, is off limits to members of the group.

Operations Supervisor[14]

DE grew up in the Iglesia ni Cristo but lived a double life. He describes his life then as one of "wickedness—I was a drunkard. I was being good in front of my minister, but there was this other side of me [that] when the minister wasn't looking. . . let's go; let's do some bad things."

Two years ago DE became ill and was hospitalized for three months. He describes the time as a major crisis in his life: "I needed a serious operation. My parents and friends turned their backs on me. They texted me on my cell phone telling me, 'We will leave you behind in the hospital whether you survive this operation or not; we don't have the money to support you.' They abandoned me in the hospital."

His family did this because they were unhappy about his lifestyle. They were also aware that DE had been married for five years to a woman who was not a member of the Iglesia ni Cristo. Prior to their marriage he had persuaded her to agree to join the group, but afterward she had stuck to her own faith instead. She read the Bible and encouraged her husband to do the same. DE also notes that a superior at work gave him tracts and shared Bible verses with him. DE had been talking with other evangelical Christians at work about the Bible, beginning to "discover this hope," and suddenly came his hospitalization. He couldn't stand as he was bedridden, so he read the Bible much of the time and began to understand its message of salvation.

"I completely surrendered to the Lord in the hospital. I've seen help keep coming from the Lord. My daily maintenance medicine was 550 pesos [about $10.50] per day.[15] I had the operation, and the Lord made a way for me to get out of that hospital without any

---

[14]DE, interview by author, 28 January 2010, Alabang, Muntinlupa City. Digital recording.

[15]This far exceeded his weekly earnings.

single cent owed. I told the Lord, 'If you want me to have this second life, I offer it to you.'"

When DE's family discovered he was attending an evangelical church they announced this at their chapel. Officers charged with the task of checking on the membership came to him and said, "Come back to the faith. You're on the wrong path. The Lord will curse you. You're not in the true church right now. You need to come back." When he didn't return the group expelled him. What has been most heart-wrenchingly difficult for DE is that his immediate and extended family will not speak with him. He has been entirely cut off from them. In the midst of his devastation he is praying for them and studying the Bible so that he can convince them of its truth.

Former Security Guard Now a Pastor[16]

FM had come to Manila from the province looking for work and was hired by a security firm. Though not raised in the Iglesia ni Cristo, he had relatives on his mother's side of the family who were active in it. However, he states that they lived far away,

> "so they didn't have time to work on my mother." When a girlfriend brought him to Iglesia ni Cristo meetings, he attended the doctrinal lessons, was baptized and joined. However, he describes his time with the group as one of personal struggle; although "the minister was teaching me about perfect living, during that time it's impossible for me to accomplish."

He also could not fully accept that Jesus was only a man.

His aunt introduced him to a "born again pastor. He gave time for me: he met with me daily, every night for almost a year. We opened the Bible and looked at it together so that I saw the whole

---

[16]FM, interview by author, 28 January 2010, Quezon City. Digital recording.

Bible and not just a verse. He taught me about the Bible and showed me that Christ is a true human, and then about his divinity. Christ is also God. From that teaching I agree, and I had the power to leave the Iglesia ni Cristo."

The promises of God, particularly that He will never leave us (Matthew 28:20 and Hebrews 13:5) and the assurance of salvation (John 1:12), were attractive to him.

Retired Nurse[17]

FL is shy, soft-spoken and a gracious hostess. She was a *handog*, and as an active Iglesia ni Cristo member attended twice-weekly services, weekly prayer groups and Christian Family Organization meetings. She and members of her immediate family held important leadership positions such as deacon, deaconess and locale secretary. She left the group at age twenty-nine when she married an "unbeliever." Her husband was a non-practicing Roman Catholic. "I asked him to join the Iglesia ni Cristo, but he wouldn't. I left because I wanted to avoid arguments and being asked questions. I seldom attended services by that time because I had questions about salvation."

An American missionary couple came door-to-door and invited them to a Bible study. Her husband attended the study for two years and became a born-again Christian before her. FL says he never pushed her, but she would occasionally attend church with him. The missionary wife visited her regularly for two years and became her friend. FL began to read the Bible and "saw the difference." She was attracted by evangelicals' openness and vulnerability in talking about their problems. Like a number of other former Iglesia ni Cristo members, she found it hard to accept the divinity of Christ, but the divinity of the Holy Spirit was

---

[17]FL, interview by author, 27 February 2010, Fairview, Quezon City. Digital recording.

attractive. She "accepted right away the power and availability of the Spirit."

FL is active in her church. In addition to participating in worship services, she attends a weekly Bible study and an adult Sunday school class and serves on a fund-raising committee for the church's building fund.

Securities Representative[18]

QL describes himself as "super *handog*, hard core, not just born into it, solid, my whole family is Iglesia." He held, and members of his immediate and extended family continue to hold, leadership positions in all the Christian Family Organizations at the locale and national levels, including the ordained ministry. His family regularly gives twenty to twenty-five percent of their income to the church.

He describes the process of leaving the Iglesia ni Cristo as "a long conversion that took about three years. It was not a leap of faith." He began dating a "non-Iglesia" in secret and attended her church with her. His girlfriend asked him to accompany her to weekly cell group meetings and then a Bible study. At the same time, because of his musical gifts he was asked to coach the choir at her church. He started to make friends.

He began to notice that the Bible studies were conducted differently than those of the Iglesia ni Cristo. They involved "reading whole stories and chapters. That was not the way the Iglesia would read and interpret the Bible." The pastor "did a good job by being passive. We just talked about the Bible. He wasn't aggressive and didn't tell me to convert now. We just read the Bible. There was no confrontation. So I didn't have to debate him. I would come with my list of phrases, and ask 'what can you say about this?' Instead of just reading the verse, he would read the

---

[18]QL, interview by the author, 23 January 2010, San Juan, Metro Manila. Digital recording.

whole chapter and show the whole context. . . . That opened my eyes little by little."

He said,

> "It was so easy for me to convert in this particular church. If I went to [several churches mentioned] I wouldn't have been converted as easily because I didn't like the concept of people jumping, bands, speaking in tongues. . . . My concept of a worship service then was the Iglesia concept: solemn, prayerful, quiet, disciplined, reverent. It was like that. The only difference was that the men weren't separated from the women. The music was the same; even the pews were almost the same. The format is almost exactly the same."

QL's doubts about the Iglesia ni Cristo weren't doctrinal but were "more about the culture. . . . I hated some things; the system of reporting, *ulat* in Filipino. This is the culture where if you do something wrong, somebody will report straight to the church administration without any due diligence or investigation." He also disliked the attitude of looking down on others.

He describes the process of leaving the Iglesia ni Cristo as,

> "a battle and very slow. . . There were times I would come here fully convinced that this is the right interpretation. Then they [the Iglesia ni Cristo ministers] would talk to me again, and I'd say they have a point too. If I do this I break my family. At night I would cry by myself. It was a long, long struggle."

After his conversion he "lost them for a while." His family was upset and did not talk with him for a long time. "I know they're still praying for me. I'm the subject of their prayers."

Computer Business Owner[19]

NN's family migrated to the United States when he was seven. His first girlfriend in high school brought him to the Iglesia ni Cristo, and he "felt very much like I belonged." At that stage in his life he wanted to be involved with other Filipinos. He attended doctrinal lessons, was baptized and quickly became deeply involved in the group, becoming president of his local's *KADIWA*, the group for singles aged eighteen and older, and even serving as the driver for the minister. Following college, he migrated back to the Philippines and continued his involvement in the Iglesia ni Cristo. However, he describes himself as beginning to grow "cold." His focus was on starting up his business, so he was busy.

His cousin introduced him to the woman who would become his wife. She was an evangelical. "We jumped from one church to another until we found something solemn like the Iglesia ni Cristo. It took me two or three years down the road before I was baptized." The pastors talked and had Bible studies with him. "Through them I learned what faith really means. . . .I learned to talk to him directly and read and understand the Bible for myself."

In the beginning he was put off by the behavior of one of the pastors. NN describes that pastor as "*kumukulit*—too persistent, pushing too much. . . .Going into this Christian religion I told myself I would take it slowly. . . .His persistence repelled me a lot actually—wanting me in a cell group, campus group." NN wanted to take things at his own pace.

---

[19]NN, interview by author, 8 February 2010, Katipunan, Quezon City. Digital recording.

Husband: Farmer and Security Guard;[20]
Wife: Fish Processor[21]

SE joined the Iglesia ni Cristo at age twenty-eight due to the "persuasion of in-laws" who were members. He was active in the church and served as a deacon. However, his wife was unfaithful, divorcing him and remarrying. SE married CC, another Iglesia ni Cristo member with whom he now has five children. However, the group did not recognize SE's divorce or the new marriage and expelled (*tiwalag*) the couple from the church. Despite repeated requests for reinstatement (*balik loob*) over two years, the Iglesia ni Cristo refused to restore them to membership. "The church was making it hard for us. They tried to impose an unreasonable policy against us. They would not solemnize marriage for us because my husband's former wife is still alive—even if they are already divorced and the woman has another husband." A family that was close to the couple brought them to an evangelical church. What appealed to them the most were "salvation by faith in Jesus Christ and not salvation through the church" and being able to read the Bible for themselves.

Summary of Observations from Interviews

In looking at these case studies as a whole several things become readily apparent. First, most conversions from the Iglesia ni Cristo to evangelical Christianity took place during the individuals' late teens or twenties; none took place after the age of thirty-four. This would suggest that the optimal period of life for conversion is

---

[20]CR, interview by Edgardo Santos, 29 April 2010, Saipan, Northern Mariana Islands. Transcript.

[21]CC, interview by Roger Abe, 29 April 2010, Saipan, Northern Mariana Islands. Transcript. She has completed three years of college, but is underemployed as a fish processor.

in the late teens and early twenties. Currently more than half the population of the Philippines is under the age of twenty-two.[22]

Two-thirds of these converts fall within the middle-class socio-economic bracket, which is not the norm for Iglesia ni Cristo membership. Sample bias reflects the fact that Protestantism in the Philippines is largely a religion of the middle class while Iglesia ni Cristo's membership is drawn primarily from the lower classes. A similar bias is evident in the educational level of those interviewed. According to the Philippine National Statistics Office, only one-half of one percent of the population of the Philippines are college graduates. Seven of the twelve converts interviewed have completed college or have at least some higher education. Comparable figures for primary school attendance and high school graduation rates are not available. However, in the author's experience during her time in the Philippines many in the poorer classes may only have completed elementary school (grade 6) and many more have even less education. So conclusions regarding the openness to conversion of those with less schooling cannot be made with certainty.

Two-thirds of the converts interviewed had a high or extremely high level of involvement in the Iglesia ni Cristo, indicating that strong group involvement is not a barrier to attraction to evangelical Christianity. The personal giving levels of those in the group also indicate a high level of commitment to the Iglesia ni Cristo. The length of their involvement in the group varied greatly, so again this does not seem to be a barrier to conversion. While eight (two-thirds) were the first in their families to leave the group, only four (one-third) had other family members who had left. Nine (three-fourths) still have relatives involved in the Iglesia ni Cristo.

---

[22]Norimitsu Onishi, "Imelda Marcos Seeks," *New York Times*, May 8, 2010, http://www.nytimes.com/2010/05/08/world/asia/08marcos.html?emc=eta1 (accessed May 8, 2010). The statistics from the 2000 census indicate half the population is under the age of twenty-one. National Statistics Office. "Philippines: Population Expected to Reach 100 Million Filipinos in 14 Years," http://www.census.gov.ph/data/pressrelease/2002/pr02178tx.html (accessed May 12, 2010).

Below are some additional observations based on converts' responses.

Dissatisfaction with the Iglesia ni Cristo

Interviewees noted the following particular beliefs and practices of the Iglesia ni Cristo to which they objected:

- Seven people said the refusal to allow romantic relationships with non-Iglesia ni Cristo members;
- Six people said the demand for unquestioning obedience to leadership, its conduct requirements and decisions;
- Two people said judgmental attitudes;
- Two people said monitoring of church attendance.

From the few comments about this, it is clear that discontent with group practices and beliefs was not a major consideration or catalyst for leaving the group; frustration at not being allowed to date or marry non-Iglesia ni Cristo members is the one exception. In the section below on the process involved in their conversion to evangelicalism, note that the seven who raised this objection were in fact involved in romantic relationships with non-members.

Process of Conversion

In descriptions of their conversion experiences, the following common elements were noted:

- Ten people said an evangelical friend or officemate;
- Nine people said participating in evangelical Bible studies;
- Eight people said reading the Bible themselves;
- Seven people said a family member sharing/inviting them;
- Seven people said romantic relationships with non-Iglesia ni Cristo members;

- Five people said a missionary or pastor meeting regularly with them;
- Five people said a welcoming evangelical church community;
- Five people said hearing testimonies/hearing experiences of others;
- Five people said a personal or family crisis;
- Four people said personal seeking.

Eleven of the twelve described the process of conversion to evangelicalism as taking two or more years.

Attractiveness/Difficulty

Participants were asked what they found most attractive in evangelical Christianity and with which teachings or practices they initially had difficulty. They were asked about specific teachings and practices, but were also given the option to add others.[22] Their responses appear in the table on the next page.

---

[22]Where numbers do not add up to the total of those interviewed, it is because the respondent was ambivalent about whether the teaching or practice was either attractive or difficult to accept.

TABLE TWO
Converts' Responses[23]

Teaching / Practice	Found Attractive	Had Initial Difficulty Accepting
Relationship with Christ not dependent on church membership	10	1
Salvation	9	
Freedom from sin	9	
Being able to read and understand the Bible themselves	8	4
Power and availability of the Holy Spirit	8	
Salvation by grace (not having required duties)	7	4
Divinity of the Holy Spirit	6	3
Joy	6	
Freedom in worship (being able to smile and show joy)	6	3
Worship songs	4	
Divinity of Christ	3	7
Style of preaching	3	
Promise of God to never leave or forsake	2	
God's unconditional love (not through deeds)	2	
The Trinity	1	3
Faith	1	
Noisiness in services (musical instruments)		9
Lack of orderliness and discipline in services		5
Speaking in tongues		2
Being asked to pay in public		2

---

[23]Republic of the Philippines National Statistics Office. *Philippines in Figures 2010.* http://www.census.ph/data/publications/2010PIF.pdf (accessed May 5, 2010).

The possibility of having a personal relationship with Christ without the church as a necessary intermediary was most often appealing. The importance of salvation as relief from sin is also readily apparent. Iglesia ni Cristo members are taught a high standard of conduct and personal morality, which is difficult to attain or maintain. They are aware of "falling short" of God's requirements. Also attractive was being able to read the Bible themselves. The Iglesia ni Cristo teaches that the Bible is a mystery, and that only those qualified (that is, the group's leadership) can accurately interpret and teach from it. When those interviewed began to read the Bible for themselves they made a number of unexpected discoveries: that it was possible to have personal contact with God, that they could understand the Bible themselves and that when reading longer stories and passages it was clear that many of the proof texts the Iglesia ni Cristo uses to support its doctrines have a different meaning in their original context.

It is interesting to note that the divinity and accessibility of the Holy Spirit were more attractive and more easily accepted than the divinity of Christ. It took many of these converts a long time to accept the Christ's divinity and the doctrine of the Trinity. The noisiness of musical instruments, particularly guitars and drums, was a major difficulty because of the solemnity and quiet atmosphere of Iglesia ni Cristo worship services. These give much more opportunity for personal reflection and private prayer.

Current Church Membership/Involvement of Converts[24]

The current church membership and involvement of those interviewed include four Baptist, four Charismatic,[25] three

---

[24]Total number is higher than number interviewed because one had membership in a Baptist church, but was also regularly attending a Charismatic church.

[25]Charismatic and Pentecostal are differentiated based on membership in uniformly Pentecostal denominations (Assemblies of God, Church of God, etc.) Charismatics are members of non-Pentecostal denominations or independent congregations.

Pentecostal, one Presbyterian and one Evangelical.[26] This reflects a good spectrum of Filipino churches.

Insights of Converts

Respondents were asked a number of questions designed to identify basic themes and specific techniques they felt would be most effective in reaching Iglesia ni Cristo members.

All twelve respondents identified using the Bible as important. This included giving them Bibles, reading and studying the Bible with them, inviting them to a Bible study (a discussion, not a debate), having a lunchtime Bible study at work, and urging them to read the Bible on their own. Eleven felt it was important to offer friendship. This included being friendly toward them, giving them quality time, doing things together with them, seeing them as real people rather than as potential converts, and taking a genuine interest in them. Six recommended reaching out to youth. This included youth camps and activities, youth nights out, youth clubs, and youth praise and worship times. Five felt displaying a Christian lifestyle was essential. Four mentioned offering testimony. This included talking about one's daily relationship with God, sharing about God's work in one's life and also about one's own conversion. Four suggested inviting them to church services and other activities. This included getting them to experience evangelical worship and fellowship. Two or three also suggested inviting them to participate in sports competitions and other informal gatherings, developing a better understanding of their church's teachings, resisting the urge to dwell on their wrong teachings or question their beliefs, and prayer.

They were asked what aspects of the gospel they thought would appeal most to Iglesia ni Cristo members. Six suggested

---

[26]Lord of Life Christian Fellowship is an Evangelical church under ABCCOP (Alliance of Bible Christian Community of the Phil) and is a joint undertaking of OMF & World Team workers 18 years ago. Antonio Cabellero, email to author, 5 May 2010, Antonio Cabellero is an elder in that church.

salvation. This included that this salvation is given and we only need to accept it, assurance of salvation and that salvation is only through Christ. Three cautiously recommended teaching about Christ, but this must be explained well: both his humanity and his divinity. Two noted cleansing and forgiveness, and one each noted how to become a child of God and serving God, not others.

This was a difficult question for them to answer. Most had not previously thought about intentional approaches, strategies or gospel themes. The author found this surprising given that most still have family members in the Iglesia ni Cristo and expressed their desire to see these family members convert to evangelical Christianity.

When asked what might help whole families to leave the Iglesia ni Cristo, respondents were taken aback. Without exception, they indicated that they had never thought in terms of entire families choosing to convert. This is probably because individual conversion is sought and taught by evangelical churches, with little or no intentional strategy for the conversion of entire households.

Eleven of the twelve felt strongly that debates about doctrine do not help Iglesia ni Cristo members question their beliefs. On the contrary, debates tend to put them on the defensive and make them more entrenched. The one who felt debates do help referred specifically to *Ang Dating Daan* ("The Old Way" or "Old Path"). This is a New Religious Movement started by Eliseo F. Soriano in 1977 as a new group springing from a 1930s offshoot from the Iglesia ni Cristo.[27] *Ang Dating Daan* is well known for its formal debates with representatives of the Iglesia ni Cristo and its aggressive attacks on Iglesia ni Cristo teaching; there is fierce competition and open conflict between the two groups.

When asked who would be more effective in sharing the gospel with members of the Iglesia ni Cristo, six respondents felt strongly

---

[27]For a brief history of the group, see Justyn, "Iglesia Ni YHWH at ni YHWSA HMSYH ('Ang Dating Daan')," The Bereans Apologetics Research Ministry, http://www.thebereans.net/prof-add.shtml (accessed May 7, 2010).

that Filipinos would do better. Two felt Americans would be more effective, since Filipinos would not shame an American by refusing to listen and Filipinos tend to revere American culture. These two were successful businessmen whose English was exceptional. Three felt Filipinos and Americans would do equally well, and one indicated that Filipinos would be more effective with Filipinos but Americans would be more effective with Americans.

Some practical considerations and recommendations stemming from these observations are described in the next chapter.

Chapter 10

RECOMMENDATIONS

I have written much about what evangelicals have been doing wrong, so I want to begin this chapter by acknowledging the kinds of regular evangelical activities which are attractive to Iglesia ni Cristo members and conducive to opening avenues of communication they are willing to hear.

What Some Evangelical Churches Are Doing Right

Testimonies are attractive to many Iglesia ni Cristo members, so churches which encourage and train members to share their testimonies, both during worship services and outside, may be more effective in attracting the group's members. Since Iglesia ni Cristo members are interested in what the Bible teaches, churches whose pastors preach expository sermons and who offer Bible studies looking at whole passages of Scripture and their context will be more effective in provoking interest, questions and encouraging seekers from the Iglesia ni Cristo. Further, those which have pew Bibles or encourage members to bring their Bibles and read along when passages are read will have a greater impact. Churches giving Bibles to inquirers or guests invited to small group Bible studies will encourage Iglesia ni Cristo members who usually do not own Bibles to begin reading the Bible for themselves. Further, Bible studies which allow attendees to ask questions without being criticized by other attendees and which provide a safe environment for group members to begin to take their journey out of the Iglesia ni Cristo.

Churches which offer programs for whole families—such as Christmas pageants, family sports days and music festivals—

provide opportunities for families to see and experience evangelical Christianity in non-threatening ways, in other words, not pulling individuals out from their families. Iglesia ni Cristo members are able to see, experience and be welcomed into true Christian fellowship.

Where to Go from Here: Ideas for Outreach Attitudes and Methodologies

The following recommendations and suggestions build on the insights from the missiological research discussed in the previous chapters and insights from the case studies.

Moving Beyond Name-Calling and Criticism

Those wishing to reach members of the Iglesia ni Cristo must move beyond heresy-rationalist apologetics. First, Iglesia ni Cristo culture is even more relationally based than Philippine culture in general. Second, these and other such confrontational approaches to apologetics tend to set up barriers rather than building bridges between Iglesia ni Cristo group members and evangelicals. They focus on areas of disagreement rather than agreement. Third, these approaches make evangelicals afraid of interaction and involvement with Iglesia ni Cristo members. Our aim should be to evangelize, not to stigmatize.

In both writing and dialogue it is more appropriate to refer to the group by its proper name, "Iglesia ni Cristo," rather than the acronym, "INC," and to use a neutral descriptor such as "New Religious Movement" rather than the derogatory term "cult." Until recently Iglesia ni Cristo publications always used their full name when referring to themselves. Recent issues of *Pasugo* have only used "INC" in reference to one specific event.[1] Evangelicals should refer to the group respectfully and appropriately.

---

[1] *Pasugo* News Bureau, "Chronicles: INC Music Video Festival—Year 3," 5.

It would be useful for evangelical churches to view the *Bridges: Helping Mormons Discover God's Grace* video[2] as a way of preparing for dialogue and reaching out to Iglesia ni Cristo members in ways that are culturally appropriate. While the *Bridges* video is designed to facilitate evangelistic efforts directed at members of the Church of Jesus Christ of Latter-day Saints, by example it suggests what may be useful in facilitating similar efforts directed at members of the Iglesia ni Cristo. For example, the video discusses aspects of Mormon culture including Mormon worldview, theological differences between Mormons and evangelicals, theological terms held in common with evangelicals but given different meanings, and areas of weakness and need that the gospel addresses. The video includes interviews with some former members of the group who discuss why they left Mormonism and the process by which they were converted. It proposes non-confrontational, friendship-based means of reaching individuals and families, and it discusses some of the difficulties Mormons face when transitioning to an evangelical Christian community. The development of a similar video and small-group discussion guide to assist with evangelizing members of the Iglesia ni Cristo would be helpful.

The evangelical community must deepen its understanding of the Iglesia ni Cristo's culture and worldview. This will require a number of steps. First, non-vitriolic materials about the group should be prepared. These should be fact-checked using a variety of sources, including Iglesia ni Cristo publications and former and current members, to ensure accuracy. It is hard for an Iglesia ni Cristo member to take an outsider seriously if the outsider repeats stories like the common claim that Iglesia ni Cristo members expect their chapels to ascend into the air at Christ's return. Though one source remembered a Sunday school teacher thirty years earlier as having mentioned the claim just once, it has never been an official

---

[2]Salt Lake City Theological Seminary, *Bridges: Helping Mormons Discover God's Grace. Training Program: How to Reach Mormons Effectively with the Good News of Christ,* DVD, Salt Lake City, UT: Salt Lake Theological Seminary, 2003.

doctrine of the church. All Iglesia ni Cristo sources, including former members with whom the author has discussed this idea, have scoffed at it and believe it is a fabrication by those trying to defame the Iglesia ni Cristo.

Since one distinctive feature of Iglesia ni Cristo culture is its use of archaic formal Tagalog terminology and unique Tagalog expressions for a number of its customs, a dictionary of these terms and expressions should be prepared. The author has collected some of these (see Appendix A), but a more thorough compilation by a native Tagalog speaker is in order.

Seminary courses should be developed dealing with New Religious Movements including the Iglesia ni Cristo. Rather than focusing on apologetics alone, these courses should encourage the use of missiological tools in understanding these largely unreached groups. Such courses should become a required element of seminary curricula in the Philippines. Similarly, seminars for pastors and church leaders should be organized. Pastors and church leaders should distribute the information in those seminars to their congregations either in seminar format or as a series of Sunday messages designed to encourage appropriate befriending of and outreach to members of the Iglesia ni Cristo.

Beginning with Areas of Agreement

More thought must be given to areas of agreement and bridges that can be used to communicate the gospel. From the author's research the following gospel themes seem most promising as starting points:

- The Bible: being able to read it for themselves.
- Sin: cleansing, forgiveness, freedom from sin.
- Salvation: a gift of grace, not earned by our fulfillment of duties; only through Christ; assurance of salvation.
- The Holy Spirit: divinity, power and accessibility.

- Christ: Lord, Messiah, born of the Virgin Mary, truly human.
- Having a relationship with Christ: not dependent on church membership.

Christ's divinity and the doctrine of the Trinity must be addressed. However, it is important to begin not with those issues but with areas of felt need, particularly regarding sin and salvation. Several of those interviewed, and even articles in *Pasugo*, have mentioned "feeling" the Holy Spirit.[3] Because the Holy Spirit is so attractive to members of the group, the divinity of the Spirit is probably the best point at which to begin teaching on the Trinity.

Iglesia ni Cristo members sometimes have the idea that evangelical Christians do not believe in the humanity of Christ. This means that teaching about his true humanity and virgin birth can serve as a bridge to teaching about his divinity.

Materials utilizing these themes should be developed by sympathetic seminary professors, qualified apologists and pastors. This includes materials intended to equip evangelical church members for sharing with members of the Iglesia ni Cristo as well as tracts and Bible study materials specifically designed to be given to group members.[4]

Hospitality

Hospitality is an important part of outreach to Iglesia ni Cristo members. The biblical basis for this is clear. Hospitality is a matter of both attitude and action. The attitude should be one of openness

---

[3] The Iglesia ni Cristo teaches that the Holy Spirit is not God but a power sent by the Father in the name of Christ to aid his messengers and his church. The "spirit" teaches and is sent to strengthen believers during worship services.

[4] I recommend two good books cited earlier which include Bible studies on doctrinal material refuting Iglesia ni Cristo teachings. Unfortunately they are written from an apologetics rather than an evangelistic perspective. Wilson and Tetley, *Witnessing to the Cults: A Practical Study Guide for Christian Workers*; Platt, *Counterfeit*.

to the stranger, acceptance and expectation of surprises from God. Actions include invitation to shared lives, reception of the stranger into our homes, and table fellowship with them. Just as we understand ourselves to be guests in God's house, we should realize our vocation as one of inviting others to be guests in our own homes—we must welcome members of the Iglesia ni Cristo as our friends.

The evangelical community must aim at befriending those of the Iglesia ni Cristo. We must see them as friends and neighbors, not as enemies or people to be feared. This means taking an interest in them, sharing common interests and activities with them, and allowing our children to become friends with their children. Officemates should reach out to their colleagues who are members of the Iglesia ni Cristo; employers and managers should actively seek to employ Iglesia ni Cristo members and then care for them not just as employees but also as human beings. Friends and employers must offer them practical assistance in times of need.

Non-confrontational lunchtime or even work-time Bible studies should be offered that involve the reading of longer passages from Scripture. Bibles should be given to participants, so they can read the text for themselves. The Iglesia ni Cristo discourages its members from doing this. Evangelical Christians should talk freely about what they have read in their own Bibles day by day and what they are learning from the Bible at church. This may trigger interest, leading Iglesia ni Cristo members to open the Bible for themselves. Evangelicals can ask them what they learned in their chapel on Sunday or Thursday, what verses were cited, and then open the Bible with them and look at larger passages in which those verses appear so they can see the true context.

Those who have contact with Iglesia ni Cristo members should be bold in sharing their testimonies—both the story of why and how they themselves converted, and also how God continues to work in their lives today.

Since many in the Iglesia ni Cristo are poor, churches should consider practical outreach to the *barangay*s where many of their members live. This would include donating clothing and food, offering medical and dental outreaches, providing circumcision and optical services, distributing medicines, and assisting their children by providing school supplies and shoes and covering their educational fees.

As the evangelical church begins to utilize these methods, there must be additional research and reflection about which of them are most effective. There must be continued consideration of culturally-appropriate evangelistic methods—by native Filipinos.

A People Movement?

Given that the Worldwide Church of God changed, embracing orthodox Christianity, might the Iglesia ni Cristo be transformed in the same way? Nothing is impossible with God, so we should certainly pray for this. The appointment of a new leader, Eduardo V. Manalo, might even open the door. As suggested above, evangelical Christian leaders should seek opportunities to rub shoulders with Iglesia ni Cristo leaders and welcome them in friendship. Evangelical seminaries should allow Iglesia ni Cristo members to enroll in their programs and be willing to listen, dialoguing when appropriate but focusing on the task of teaching the Word of God with joy. The next several years will show how open to change the group's new leadership may be. The evangelical community must not only seek and pray for this openness, but welcome any overtures that may come.

Contextualized Evangelistic Efforts

Could whole families and even entire communities of Iglesia ni Cristo members decide to convert to evangelicalism? What might encourage this transformation? Contextual presentation of the gospel and intentional church planting among group members is essential. In this regard, how might church planting among Iglesia ni Cristo members begin?

The first step might be to rent or buy a building which could be transformed into a beautiful sanctuary whose interior would be without crosses and other religious symbols. There would be pews rather than chairs for seating. Another option would be to use an existing church building, but with special worship services designed specifically for Iglesia ni Cristo members. Again, crosses and religious symbols would need to be removed from the sanctuary for those services.

Worship would start and end on time, with a quiet, meditative tone that is intended to promote reverence and awe.[5] The area used for worship would be used only for worship, not for other church activities. There would be no buying or selling in this area. Services could even be held twice a week, on Sundays and Thursdays, as the Iglesia ni Cristo does. It is important that the church building and its surroundings be kept clean and well-maintained as a sign of respect for God. In the Iglesia ni Cristo this is emphasized because God's name and glory are felt to dwell in the building in a special way, so teaching would need to offer a new basis for this—respect for God himself, not because he dwells in the building.

Evangelical Christians involved in this ministry should dress as Iglesia ni Cristo members do for their own services: women in dresses and skirts; men in polo shirts (with collars) or button-down shirts, not in tee-shirts; male and female ushers in formal *barongs* and white dresses. Men and women might sit on opposite sides of the worship area as in Iglesia ni Cristo worship services. As people enter the sanctuary, an organ might play quietly. Instead of guitars

---

[5] As noted earlier as a relevant example, consider the story of the Russian people's turn to Christianity. Prince Vladimir of Kiev sent envoys to the Bulgars, the Germans and the Greeks. It was the awe-inspiring beauty of the latter's churches and services, which led them to recommend Greek Orthodoxy to him. As a result he decided to be baptized and Russia was Christianized. See "The Christianization of Russia (988)," http://dur.ac.uk/a.k.harrington/christin.html (accessed September 27, 2009).

and drums, a choir and organ should provide assistance during worship. Hymnals and songbooks should be used instead of Power Point files and texts projected on a screen. The hymns and songs should be carefully chosen for their strong doctrinal content. Worshipers should stand for prayer and say, "Amen" or "Yes, Lord" at appropriate points as Iglesia ni Cristo members are used to doing. Since Iglesia ni Cristo members do not usually own their own Bibles, there would be Bibles on the seats or pews, and when a Bible passage is read, the people would be asked to follow along. The speaker announcing a text would pause long enough to give them time to find the passage before beginning to read. The service would be conducted entirely in Tagalog. Preachers would be careful to exegete the Word, not merely tell a lot of stories. Application to real life should be stressed.[6]

The pastor and elders leading the worship services should wear suits. In Iglesia ni Cristo services the offering bags are placed in a box in front of the pulpit; there could be such a box in this intentional church plant. Announcements should be reserved for the end of the service, as they are in the Iglesia ni Cristo. People should not talk inside the building, but save their conversations for later outside the worship space. There should be no children in an adult worship service; instead, children should have their own age-appropriate service.

Celebration of Christmas should not include practices such as the use of lights and Christmas trees that are perceived as "pagan" by the Iglesia ni Cristo. The emphasis would be on the story of Christ's incarnation and events surrounding it. At Christmas there might be a special Thanksgiving offering. In the Iglesia ni Cristo this is a significant year-end event that raises funds to pay for construction of new chapels. In this church plant it could also be

---

[6]For a challenge to the church today regarding the content of worship services see Marva J. Dawn, *Reaching Out without Dumbing Down: A Theology of Worship for This Urgent Time* (Grand Rapids, MI: William B. Eerdmans Publishing Company, 1995).

an important celebration, with the money collected used to support missionaries or a church building fund.

Age-specific activities as well as events for whole families should be offered. Among these should be Bible studies and activities with which members of the Iglesia ni Cristo are familiar. Some suggestions follow:

- For adults: weekly cell and prayer groups; seminars on marital relationships, raising children and finances; livelihood seminars on pig-raising, sewing, manicure and pedicure training, and so on; blood collection drives; romantic banquets and field trips.

- For youth: competitions in sports, Bible passage memorization and singing; games; seminars on courtship, personality development, drug addiction, study habits and teenage relationships.

- For whole families: day trips, picnics, games and competitions. Offering activities for the entire family would encourage the conversion of entire families as they decide together to become evangelical Christians.

Some in the evangelical community may react negatively to this bold model of contextualization. However, nothing proposed here is contrary to any commandment of Scripture. What is suggested is merely the alteration of cultural forms in order to make Iglesia ni Cristo members more comfortable and therefore more receptive to the gospel. This is an experimental model designed to facilitate reaching whole families and larger communities. It should be tried, evaluated for effectiveness and then revised as appropriate. A church plant might begin with the arrangement described and then evolve as Iglesia ni Cristo members come to faith and are freed to worship in new ways.

Concentrated Prayer

Evangelical churches must focus their prayer on the Iglesia ni Cristo. Prayer groups should be encouraged to form in locale evangelical congregations in order to pray specifically for their members' Iglesia ni Cristo contacts as well as for the Iglesia ni Cristo in general. Evangelicals should also pray for those making contact with the Iglesia ni Cristo: for wisdom, for opportunities, for appropriate boldness and vulnerability in sharing, for the empowering of the Holy Spirit. If not enough members in one evangelical congregation are interested in this, invitations should be issued to nearby evangelical congregations to join in a prayer group focusing on the Iglesia ni Cristo.

Patience and Process

Evangelicals must learn to be patient. Conversion is a process, and the conversion of those leaving the Iglesia ni Cristo takes time, often two years or more. Pushing them to move faster only leads to hostility, not openness. Even after deciding to be baptized and join an evangelical church, those leaving New Religious Movements like the Iglesia ni Cristo will have problems.

Janis Hutchinson, a former Mormon who has worked closely with other former members of The Church of Jesus Christ of Latter-day Saints, describes some of these problems. Conversion involves more than letting go of old beliefs. Former members:

> go through a death—not only the death of their previous cult structure but also their former self-image, identity, security, support system and roots. It takes time to get over a death. New believers, therefore cling to former doctrines, attitudes, and behaviors like beloved friends, refusing to let go.[7]

---

[7] Janis Hutchinson, *Out of the Cults and into the Church: Understanding and Encouraging Ex-Cultists* (Grand Rapids, MI: Kregel Resources, 1994), 23.

Well-known psychologist and author Margaret Singer notes a number of struggles for those leaving NRMs: depression, loneliness, indecisiveness, fear of their former NRM, feeling that they are living in a fishbowl, resentment at constant requests to explain their conversion, and feeling that they are no longer part of an elite group.[8] Hutchinson notes that converts may hide these problems because they do not want to appear different or are afraid "of being judged incorrectly."[9]

Evangelical churches attended by former Iglesia ni Cristo members must recognize these issues and be prepared to offer assistance and support. Small groups should be formed which will allow former group members to share freely, without fear of being judged, about things in their new church that they dislike and things in their old church that they miss. Culture shock will be a real experience for many.[10]

Recommendations for Further Research and Study

Since the number of former members of the Iglesia ni Cristo interviewed was small, further research is needed. In particular, converts coming from the lower economic classes and the less-educated need to be found and interviewed. This would be better done by a native Tagalog speaker. Are the same messages attractive? What difficulties do former members experience while moving to poorer evangelical churches, which cannot compete with the resources the Iglesia ni Cristo has? How do we make incorporation into our churches less stressful and more helpful? Most importantly, more research and experimentation must address how to reach whole families and kinship networks.

---

[8] Singer, "Coming out of the Cults," 3, 6-8.
[9] Hutchinson, *Out of the Cults*, 11, 27.
[10] *Ibid.*, 35-37.

Additionally, further study is needed into how the Iglesia ni Cristo does exegesis and how Evangelicals might learn from this for contact and dialoging with them. As different strategies are employed, their effectiveness will need to be evaluated and revisions made. It would be useful to hold a conference on outreach to New Religious Movements to hear what is being attempted and what has shown fruit. Sharing of methodologies that are working with other NRMS might provide some useful ideas.

Concluding Statement

In the book of Acts, Luke's account of the expansion of the early church, the Holy Spirit was the force that impelled the messengers and enabled the spread of the gospel. A number of features of the Hellenistic world were uniquely orchestrated by God to facilitate the church's growth. Important among these were the Pax Romana, the common use of the Greek language, the Roman road system, the Jewish diaspora, and the similar diaspora of early Christians due to persecution. Similarly, the world today offers a unique opportunity for outreach to members of the Iglesia ni Cristo. The Filipino worldwide diaspora, the millions of Overseas Filipino Workers, the use of English both internationally and also within the Philippine school system, access of missionary workers to the Philippines, the widespread availability of print media, the Internet, radio and television opening new vistas for tight-knit, clannish communities—these are just a few of the factors contributing to this period of opportunity.

God's desire is that all the nations of the world hear the good news. Members of the Iglesia ni Cristo have not heard because the message has usually been presented using methods they find offensive, rarely in ways that speak to their felt needs.

The evangelical community would do well to develop intentional strategies for reaching members of the Iglesia ni Cristo. This must begin with the recognition that they are not our enemies but sinners, like us, for whom Christ died. Prayer should permeate all that we do. We need the wisdom and power of the Holy Spirit for the task before us.

APPENDIX A

DICTIONARY OF COMMONLY-USED WORDS AND PHRASES OF THE IGLESIA NI CRISTO

Abiding in God's Words—being taught the doctrines of the church and accepting the preaching of God's messenger, Felix Manalo.
Abuloy—regular worship service offering.
Almighty God—God is the Father and creator of all things; He is not three persons.
Ang Bagong Himnario ng Iglesia ni Cristo—the official hymnal of the church; copies are the property of the church and not kept or owned by members.
Angel from the East—another term for *Sugo* or Last Messenger, Felix Y. Manalo is the Angel from the East mentioned in Isaiah 43:5-6 and Revelation 14:14-15.
Ang Iglesia ni Cristo—radio program promoting the teachings of the Iglesia ni Cristo.
Apostasy—following the time of the Apostles, the church founded by Christ moved away from its original teachings by teaching such things as priestly celibacy and the Trinity.
Ate—literally means older sister; used as a title of respect when addressing female members of the Iglesia ni Cristo.
Baptism—baptism by immersion the Iglesia ni Cristo alone is necessary for salvation; children are baptized at approximately the age of 12. Baptism follows the doctrinal lessons and a six-month probationary period.
Bible Missionary Parties—small evangelistic events, which are usually simple get-togethers.
Bible Studies—see Doctrinal Lessons.
Binhi—means "seed," and is a group for baptized church members up to the age of seventeen.
Brother—proper way of addressing a male member of the Iglesia ni Cristo. This also applies to those in authority, even the Chief Executive Minister.
Brotherhood—members of the Iglesia ni Cristo.
Buklod—means "united in marriage" and is a group for married church members.
Central Office—the central administration of the church in Diliman, Quezon City, from which emanate all lessons and decisions.
Certificates of Recognition—awards given to the Ministers, officers, locales and districts who have performed best at evangelism.
Chapel—one of the names for a house of worship.
Chief Executive Minister or CEM—overseer of the church and successor to Felix Y. Manalo. Felix's son, Eraño Manalo, received the laying on of hands from his father in 1962 and served in this capacity until his death August 31, 2009; Eraño's son, Eduardo (Ka Eddie) V. Manalo, assumed the position following Eraño's death.
Children's Worship Service or CWS—see *Pagsamba ng Kabataan*.
The Christian Era—the time period starting with the birth of Christ and ending with His return.
Christian Brotherhood International—college and university groups for Iglesia ni Cristo members.
Christian Family Organizations—*Binhi, Buklod* and *KADIWA* are groups that usually meet monthly. All Iglesia ni Cristo members belong to one of these groups, based on age and marital status.
Church—does not refer to buildings; it refers to the Iglesia ni Cristo as a whole.
Church Administration—begins with the church leadership in the central office in Diliman, Quezon City, and includes district and locale Ministers and Evangelical Workers.
College of Evangelical Ministry (CEM)—seminary preparing men for ministry; the typical program of studies is six years of class work; located in the New Era complex in Diliman, Quezon City, Philippines.
Deacon/Deaconess—males and females who have taken on the special responsibility of overseeing other members and church activities. They serve as ushers at worship services. Females wear white dresses, and males wear white barong tagalogs with dark pants.
Dedication—has two meanings. It may refer to the official service opening a new chapel or an activity usually held during regular worship services when children are offered to the service of the Lord by their parents and through the laying on of hands by the Minister.
Devotional Prayers—special prayers to seek God's guidance or assistance. Often scheduled for a week or held during times of trouble.
Dispensations—the history of God's work with mankind is divided into three time periods or dispensations:
1. The time of the Patriarchs–starting with Adam and ending with Moses;
2. The time of the Prophets–starting with Moses and ending with the birth of the Lord; and
3. The Christian Era—the present period, or the last days, starting with the birth of the Lord and ending with his second coming on Judgment Day.

Distribution Drive—intensive door-to-door distribution of pamphlets or copies of *Pasugo* in a given area, usually done as a precursor to an Evangelical Mission or Grand Evangelical Mission.
District—also called an Ecclesiastical District; an area covering several locales supervised by a District Minister; similar to a Roman Catholic diocese.
Doctrinal Lessons—twenty-four Bible lessons written by Eraño Manalo and taught by Ministers and Evangelical Workers to those desiring to learn more about the church, required as part of the membership process. Three additional lessons on the church's history are added for those living outside the Philippines.
Duties—refers to the required activities necessary for salvation including attending twice-weekly worship services and weekly prayer group meetings and giving offerings.
Ecclesiastical District—see District.
Edification—teaching Bible studies. Ministers excelling in this are recognized and given awards.

Enter Christ—join the Iglesia ni Cristo.
Evangelical Mission—an evangelistic event, usually at the locale level.
Evangelical Worker—a male who has completed the six-year course of study at the CEM but has not yet been ordained.
Expulsion—those who marry outside the church or are not active are removed from the church's rolls and lose their salvation.
Extension—a locale will start an extension in a new area when there are enough members there. Eventually the extension will become a new locale.
Faithful—remaining faithful means continuing to be active in the Iglesia ni Cristo by attending worship services and weekly prayer group meetings.
Four Angels—the church teaches that "the Big Four" who signed the Treaty of Versailles following World War I were the four angels described in Revelation 7: France, Great Britain, Italy and Germany.
Four Winds of the Earth—World War I.
FYM Medallion—a medallion given to a church officer in recognition for length of service in the church.
Gentile Lands—refers to the registration of the church in Athens, Greece.
Grand Evangelical Mission—a district-wide evangelistic event usually advertised by banners across major roads.
Handog—a member who was dedicated at birth in the Iglesia ni Cristo. This means his or her parents were members. Literally means "an offering." Also the name for the annual Thanksgiving offering.
Holy City—refers to Jerusalem, God's real residence, the place where the saved will live with God forever.
Holy Array—proper attire for worship services meaning that clothing should be clean and formal. Women must wear skirts or dresses, men suits or shirts with collars.
Holy Spirit—is not God but a power sent by the Father in the name of Christ to aid his messengers and his church.
Holy Supper—a ceremony of sharing unleavened bread and diluted wine or juice offered during February and March and required to be taken once a year for the washing away of sins. Also called *Santa Cena*.
Houses of Worship—one of the names for the buildings in which the church holds worship services. It is believed that God's name and glory dwell in these buildings, and that they are exclusively designed by God to offer Him praises. They are the only places in which true worship may be offered. Also called "His temple" or a "chapel."
Housing Settlement—housing projects built for retired workers and their families, current workers or as resettlement projects for those who have experienced disasters.
Iglesia ni Cristo—means "Church of Christ" in Tagalog and is the only name by which the true church founded by Christ should be called.
Ilaw ng Kaligtasan—see Light of Salvation.
Jesus Christ—a sinless man sent by God with the mission of creating and saving "one new man."
KADIWA or *Kabataang may Diwang Wagas*—means "young people with pure spirit," a group for unmarried church members age eighteen and older.
Kapitid—literally means brother; is the term of respect used when addressing male members of the Iglesia ni Cristo.
Lagak Slip—a deposit slip used by members to make weekly deposits towards their Thanksgiving offering.
Last Work of Salvation—the Iglesia ni Cristo is God's last work of salvation before Jesus returns.
Lesson—a sermon preached at a worship service. It may involve questions and answers from different Bible translations or statements backed up by Bible verses. It does not involve any personal opinions or stories. Lessons come from the Chief Executive Minister, and the same lesson is taught in all chapels on a given Sunday or weekday service.
Libretta—a kind of savings passbook showing deposits for the annual Thanksgiving offering.
Light of Salvation—a group, which meets at the locale level, providing training in evangelism. Its members are particularly active in evangelism.
Linis Bayan—a clean-up drive in a particular location on a given day.
Lingap sa Mamamayan—means "care for people" and is a mission providing medical, dental or social assistance to a neighborhood or location on a given day or days.
Local or Locale—a congregation; similar to a Roman Catholic parish.
Matusalem Award—given to the oldest member of a church local.
Messengers—Those appointed by God have the authority to correctly interpret God's will and teach from the Bible. In the past these messengers included Noah, Moses, John the Baptist, Christ and the Apostles. The Last Messenger is Felix Y. Manalo.
Mga Leksiyong Ministeryal—see Doctrinal Lessons.
Minister—a male who has completed six years of ministerial studies at the College of Evangelical Ministry, passed five years of probation and been ordained by the laying on of hands by the Chief Executive Minister.
New Era—refers to the central church complex on Commonwealth Avenue in Diliman, Quezon City, Philippines. The complex includes the Central Temple, a Tabernacle, the church's museum and central offices, the housing for the Chief Executive Minister and his family, New Era University, which houses the College of Evangelical Ministry, and New Era Hospital.
New Era Hospital—the church's hospital.
New Era University—the church's college, offering a variety of bachelor's degree programs.
New Jerusalem—the holy city to which Jesus Christ will return and bring members of the Iglesia ni Cristo and live with them forever.
Oath Taking—all Ministers, officers, choir members, teachers and organists take a yearly oath of office promising to fulfill their assigned duties.
Offering—Donations given to the church. *Abuloy* is the weekly offering; *Pagsiimpan* or *pagbubukod* is year-long giving towards the Thanksgiving offering. The offering itself is called *handog*. *Tanging Handugan* are special offerings.
Officers—deacons, deaconesses and those assigned positions in a district, locale or Christian Family Organization. Titles may include secretary, finance officer, president, chair person, etc.
One Flock—refers to the Iglesia ni Cristo; Jesus Christ calls one flock.

One New Man/One True Church—refers to the Iglesia ni Cristo, which was created and saved by Jesus Christ. Jesus Christ is the head and the Iglesia ni Cristo is the body. The group teaches that the true church was originally founded by Christ in Jerusalem through the shedding of his blood. However, that true church fell into apostasy following the time of the apostles because of false prophets who deceived the church. Hence it had disappeared by the time of the Council of Nicea. Felix Manalo's establishment of the Iglesia ni Cristo in 1914 marked the re-emergence of the true church.
One True God—Almighty God or God the Father.
Pagbubukod—setting aside for the Thanksgiving offering. This is done before or after the worship services over the course of the year. Also called *pasalamat*.
Pamamahayag—an evangelistic event to which members are asked to bring guests.
Pananalapi—the person who counts contributions.
Pasalamat—setting aside for the Thanksgiving offering. This is done before or after the worship services over the course of the year. Also called *pagbubukod*.
Pasugo—"God's Message" in Tagalog, the monthly magazine of the Iglesia ni Cristo. *Ang pasugo* means a word or message coming from Almighty God that is being relayed to a person through His Messenger.
PNK—see *Pagsamba ng Kabataan*.
Pagsamba ng Kabataan—Children's Worship Service, which teaches the church's doctrines and practices to children aged four to twelve.
Prayer Committee—formed in a new location as a precursor to starting a locale. This takes the place of regular worship services until enough members join to start a locale.
Prayer Groups—small groups meeting weekly, made up of several families and led by a deacon, deaconess or an overseer in training to be a deacon. All church members are assigned to a group in the area near their home.
Probationary Period—for those desiring to join the church, a six-month period following the Bible Studies. During this time they must have perfect attendance at twice weekly worship services and weekly prayer meetings and have an exemplary lifestyle.
Propagation—evangelism; Ministers, officers, locales and districts excelling at this are recognized and given awards.
Receiving Christ or God—believing the teachings of Felix Y. Manalo.
Registration—the official opening of a new congregation in a given location.
Relationship with Christ—becoming and continuing as a member of the Iglesia ni Cristo.
Remaining Faithful—continuing in active membership in the Iglesia ni Cristo, shown by observing requirements suchas mandatory attendance at church services on Sundays and Thursdays and weekly prayer groups, and avoiding or refraining from certain things such as marrying a non-church member, gambling, drinking, etc.
Resident Minister—the supervising Minister at a given locale.
Santa Cena—see Holy Supper.
Scroll—a document signed by the CEM and other notaries proclaiming the official opening of a new congregation.
Sister—proper way of addressing a female member of the Iglesia ni Cristo.
Seal—the stamp of the promise and verification of God given to His church and Felix Y. Manalo.
Solemnity—refers to the attitude and behavior of members during worship services. There is no smiling, laughing, talking, or looking around and a distinct order to entering, seating, prayer and offering times, and departure.
Sugo—A messenger appointed by God with the authority to correctly interpret God's will and teach from the Bible. In the past these messengers included Noah, Moses, John the Baptist, Christ, and the Apostles. The Last Messenger is Felix Y. Manalo.
Summer Kindergarten Program (SKP)—a summer activity for children to teach spiritual growth, encourage moral values through Bible stories and promote intellectual, physical and language skills.
Supervising Minister—the Minister overseeing a given district.
Tagisan ng Talino—a Bible and *God's Message* Quiz, a competition often involving teams.
Tagubilin—circulars from the Church Administration, which cover everything from instruction about personal behavior and announcements of activities to publication of approved political candidates.
Tanging Handugan—special offerings members make for purposes such as missions, chapel repairs, one-time purchases, and other special needs of the congregation.
Thanksgiving—may refer to the annual year-end Thanksgiving event or to the offering presented during the occasion.
Tribuna—the name for the area in which the choir sits, higher than the pulpit area, which is higher than that of the general congregation.
The True Church—founded by Jesus Christ in the first century, it apostatized and then re-emerged as the Iglesia ni Cristo in 1914.
Tumba—avenging a wrong against another Iglesia ni Cristo member
Unity—obeying the directives of the Church Administration and submitting to its authority. This also refers to having good relations with other members of the church.
The West—the first foreign mission, begun in Hawaii in 1968.

INDEX

adultery, 22, 53
afterlife. *See* eschatology.
alcohol forbidden, 53
Ang Bagong Himnario ng Iglesia ni Cristo. *See* hymnal.
anniversaries, 55, 124-125
anti-Christ, 47
apostasy, 9, 29, 44, 47, 48, 195
Apostles, 44, 47, 59, 148
Armstrong, Herbert W., 140
Athens. *See* Greece.
attendance, 78, 79
authority, 35, 69-71
Azuza Pacific University, 141-142

bahala na, 74-76
baptism, 7, 54, 67, 102-103, 112, 121, 195
barriers, 154-155
barrio fiestas, 6
bata relationship. *See* client-patron relationships.
Bible(s), 35, 85-86, 179, 184, 187, 184, 186, 189
Bible, authority of, 35
Bible, interpretation of, 36-37, 97-98, 174
Bible Missionary Parties, 98, 195
Bible reading and studies, 101-102, 189. *See also* Doctrinal Lessons.
birthday celebrations, 70. *See also* anniversaries.
blood, eating, 6, 58
bridges, 153-154, 182, 184-185
Bridges video, 131, 149, 183. *See also* Church of Jesus Christ of the Latter-day Saints.
Bridges of God, 136
brotherhood, 56, 195

celebrations, 120-125
Central Administration/Office, 51-53, 96, 113-115, 195
chapels, 55, 88-94, 195. *See also* houses of worship.
Chief Executive Minister 57, 85, 86, 91, 93, 113, 195. *See also* Felix Y. Manalo, Eraño Manalo and Eduardo Manalo.
children, 88, 112
Children's Worship Service. *See* PNK.
choir, 84, 87, 93, 97
Christ. *See* Jesus Christ.
Christian Era, 46, 195
Christian Family Organizations, 106-107, 110, 114, 195
Christmas, 119-120, 189
Church Administration, 96, 106, 195. *See also* Central Administration.
Church of Jesus Christ of the Latter-day Saints, 131, 151-152, 183, 191
Church of Christ, 40, 48
Churches of Christ, 21
client-patron relationships, 71
clothing, 81, 84, 103
College of Evangelical Ministry, 28, 29, 195
Colorum sects, 20
Conversion, 156-158. *See also* group conversion.
converts, verbal, 158
converts, total, 158
Council of Nicea, 9, 44, 48

Day of Judgment, 59, 94. *See also* judgment.
deacon(s), deaconess(es), 52, 82, 105, 109, 116, 195
death, 59-60
debt of gratitude. *See utang na loob.*
dedication, 195. *See* infant dedication.
dedication of chapels, 195. *See* houses of worship
Deputy Executive Minister. *See* Eduardo Manalo.
devotional prayers, 159, 160,195. *See also* prayer.

Disciples of Christ. *See* Mision Cristiana.
dinuguan, 6. *See also* blood.
dispensations, 46, 195
distribution drive, 96, 195
District(s), 95, 106, 115, 118-119, 195
divorce, 11
doctrinal lessons, 35, 54, 101-102, 195
dress. *See* clothing.
drugs, illegal, forbidden, 53
duties, 54-55, 56, 78-79, 103, 195

Easter, 120
eating blood,
ecclesiology, 47-58
elections, 30, 50-51
Ellinwood Bible Institute, 21
eschatology, 58-61
Evangelical Workers, 95, 196
evangelism, 94-100, 148. *See also* mission and Grand Evangelical Missions.
expulsion, 74

faith, 41
Father. *See* God.
Feazell, J. Michael, 141
feeling out. *See Pakikiramdam.*
females. *See* women.
fiestas, 6
first fruits, 51
flock, 8
Four winds of the earth, 196. *See* World War I.

galing, 69-71
Gentiles, 47, 196. *See also* Greece.
God, 37-38, 42, 43, 68, 80, 84, 89, 90
God's Message. *See Pasugo.*
Good Samaritan, 146
Grace Communion International, 142. *See also* Worldwide Church of God.
Grand Evangelical Missions, 97-98, 121, 122, 123, 196
Great Apostacy, 29
Greece, 29
group-based thinking, 63-67
group conversion, 135, 178

Halloween, 120
handog, 87, 196
healing, 105. *See also* health.
health, 125
hiya, 73-74
holidays, 119. *See also* celebrations and anniversaries.
holy array, 196. *See* clothing.
Holy City, 196. *See* Holy Land.
Holy Country. *See* Holy Land.
Holy Land, 60-61, 75
Holy Spirit, 48, 50, 51, 147, 148-150, 177, 184, 193, 196
Holy Supper. *See Santa Cena.*
honor. *See dangal.*
hospitality, 143-147, 185-187
hostility toward evangelicals, 3
houses of worship, 104, 196. *See also* chapel(s).
housing settlements, 118, 196
humanity, 38-39
hymnal, 82, 88
hymns, 126, 189

Iglesia ni Cristo day, 122-123
infants, 50, 54, 112
immortality. *See* eschatology.

incarnational ministry, 150-153
infant dedication, 112
insider movements, 137-140

Jerusalem, 29
Jesus Christ, 40, 42, 45, 49, 56, 59, 60, 68-69, 85, 86, 196
judgment, 39, 59-60. *See also* Day of Judgment.

Kapatid. See brotherhood.
kinship, 63-67

lake of fire. *See* eschatology.
language. *See* terminology.
Last Messenger, 9
Lausanne reports, 13-14, 77, 129, 131-132
Lent, 120
Lesson, 85-86, 200. *See also* doctrinal lessons.
Lingap sa Mamamayan, 98-100, 196
Linis Bayan, 100, 196
Locals, 115-116, 118-119, 196
Lofland-Stark Model of Conversion, 11-12
Lord's Supper. *See Santa Cena*.

Manalo, Cristina Villanueva, 28
Manalo, Eduardo V., 31, 33, 70, 91, 108, 113, 114, 143
Manalo, Eraño G., 27, 28, 30-31, 33, 35, 52, 70, 91, 113, 142
Manalo, Felix Y., 7, 18, 19-23, 24-25, 27, 30, 33, 37, 45, 46-47, 50, 51, 61, 70, 85, 113, 121-122, 142, 155 birthday, 120-121
Manila Bible College, 21
marriage, 29, 58, 110-111
media, 95-96
membership, 66-67
men and women separated, 82
Messenger of God. *See* Felix Y. Manalo.
Messenger(s), 46, 196
Methodist Episcopal Church, 21
Mga Leksiyong Ministeryal. See Doctrinal Lessons.
Minister(s), 52, 70, 85, 94, 95, 116-118, 196
Mision Cristiana, 7, 21, 24
mission, 56. *See also* evangelism.
Mission to the West, 29
missional Spiral, 134
Mormon(s). *See* Church of Jesus Christ of the Latter-day Saints.
music, 83. *See also* hymnal and hymns.

nametags, 79-80, 92
New Era complex. *See* Central Administration.
New Jerusalem. *See* Holy Land.

oaths of office, 110, 196
offerings, 1, 55-56, 86-87, 92, 93, 123-124, 126, 196. See also *handog*.
officers, 108-110, 113, 196
one flock, 49, 196
one new man/one true church, 41, 48, 49, 197
optimistic fatalism. *See bahala na*.
Ora rebellion, 25
ordination. *See* Ministers.
organist, 83
original sin, 39

Pagsamba ng Kabataan. See PNK.
pakikipagkapwa, 69-71
pakikisama. See harmony.
panata. See devotional prayer.
parenting, 111-112
pasalamat. See Thanksgiving Day.

Pasugo, 8, 29, 35, 74, 78, 95, 96, 103, 112, 119, 121, 122, 123, 124, 154, 197
patience. *See bahala na*.
people movements, 136-137, 187. *See also* group conversion.
persecution, 58-59, 61, 75, 85, 125
perseverance, 74-76
PNK, 88, 107, 201
prayer, 50, 55, 56, 84-85, 86, 103-104, 149, 189, 191. *See also* weekly prayer groups and devotional prayers.
predestination disputed, 51
probation, 54, 102, 103, 197
proof-texting, 10
propagation. *See* evangelism.
prophecy, 36
proof-texting, 10
punctuality, 83

radio, 28, 95
relationship with Christ, 45, 197
Resident Minister(s). See Ministers.
resiliency, 74-76
resignation. *See bahala na*.
respect, 69-71
restoration myth, 9
resurrection(s), 59-60
Rome, 29

salvation, 39-42, 53, 178, 184
Santa Cena, 7, 21
Satan, 39
SCAN, 108
Scripture(s). *See* Bible.
seal(ing), 50, 51, 197
Second Coming, 59
Second Death, 60
sermons, 29. *See also* lesson.
Seventh-day Adventists, 7, 22-23
shame see *Hiya*
sickness, 105. *See also* health.
sin, 39, 44, 58, 68, 84, 111, 184
social assistance. *See Lingap sa Mamamayan*.
suffering, 59, 75
Sugo. See Messenger.
Sunday school see *PNK*

table fellowship, 146. *See also* hospitality.
tanding handugan. See offerings.
television, 28, 95
terminology, 126. *See also* vocabulary.
testimonies, 152-153, 181, 186
Thanksgiving Day, 87, 92, 123, 197. *See also* offerings.
Tkach, Joseph W., Sr., 141
Trinity, 9, 37, 185
true church, 9-10, 197
TV. *See* television.

ulat, 170
unions, 30
unity, 56, 74, 197
utang na loob, 72-73, 76

Valentine's Day, 120
vocabulary, 195-197. *See also* terminology.

weekly prayer groups, 55, 70, 105, 193
women, 81, 82, 110-111, 117
World War I, 49
World War II, 36
Worldwide Church of God, 135, 140-143
worship services, 54-55, 78-89

REFERENCE CITED

Abella, Gene N.
    1999   "San Jose Plays Host to Significant Events." *Pasugo* 51(4):32-33.
    2000   "San Jose Couples End 1999 with Great Zeal." *Pasugo* 52(3):25.
    2001   "Northern California Celebrates Church's 87th Anniversary." *Pasugo* 53(10):3-35.
    2004   "Northern California Showcases *Tagisan ng Talino*." *Pasugo* 56(2):5.

Adams, Michael Peter
    2004   "How My Life Turned Out for the Better." *Pasugo* 56(4):27-28.

Agag, Arthur P.
    1999   "Building a Happy Home." *Pasugo* 51(12):6-7.

Agular, Pamela, and Aliw Pablo
    1999   "Northern California Fosters Brotherhood." *Pasugo* 51(9):25-26.

Alcid, Ferdinand
    1998   "The Rightful Preachers of God's Word." *Pasugo* 50(8):8-12.

Allen, Don, et al., eds.
    2009   "Fruitful Practices: A Descriptive List." *International Journal of Frontier Missiology* 26(3):111-122.

Alliance Biblical Seminary students
    1995   Conversations with the author, Quezon City, October.

Alonzo, Manuel, Jr.
    1959   *A Historico-Critical Study on the Iglesia ni Cristo*. Manila: UST Press.

Ando, Hirofumi
    1969   "A Study of the Iglesia ni Cristo: A Politico-Religious Sect in the Philippines." *Pacific Affairs* 42:334-345.

Andres, Tomas Quintin D. and Pilar Corazon B. Alada-Andres
    1986   *Making Filipino Values Work for You*. Manila: St. Paul Publications.

Ang, Charles
    2004   "Iglesia ni Cristo." Unpublished manuscript. Graduate paper for course on New Religious Movements taught by Anne C. Harper and Michael McDowell, Asian Theological Seminary, Quezon City, Philippines.
    2004   "Iglesia ni Cristo Research Paper." Unpublished manuscript. Graduate paper for course on New Religious Movements taught by Anne C. Harper and Michael McDowell, Asian Theological Seminary, Quezon City, Philippines.

Apostal, Adorado A.
    1997   "A Brief History of the Congregation of Israel." *Pasugo* 49(7):54-57. Special issue.

Aquino, Leslie Ann G.
    2009   "Our Brother Eraño G. Manalo Has Been Laid to Rest – INC." *Manila Bulletin*, September 1. On line. Internet. (Available from http://www.mb.com.ph/articles/218672/inc-s-era-o-manalo-passes-away.) Accessed September 2, 2009.

Araneta, Sandy
    2009   "Mammoth Crowds Gather for Iglesia ni Cristo Day." *Philippine Star*, July 28, pp. 1-3. On line. Internet. (Available from http://philstar.com/Article.aspx?articleID=490894&publicatoinsSubCategoryID=63.) Accessed July 28, 2009.

Aromin, Reuben D.
    2002   "No Other Way." *Pasugo* 54(12):6-7.
    2003a   "The Heirs of God." *Pasugo* 55(4):16-18.
    2003b   "The Wonder of God's Words." *Pasugo* 55(10):4-5, 12.
    2004   "Being United with the Church Administration." *Pasugo* 56(1):13-16.
    2006   "True Brothers and Sisters." *Pasugo* 58(11):11-13.

Baldonade, Dahlia, Bella Agustin, and Danilo Ramos
    1999   "Kowloon Launches 'Operation FYM 50.'" *Pasugo* 51(1):26-27.

Banawa, Joanne Dianne S.
    2003   "A Story of a Locksmith Unlocked." *Pasugo* 55(1):28-29.

Barrientos, Gary P.
    2001a   "The Angel Who Ascended from the East." *Pasugo* 53(5):8-9, 32.
    2001b   "Helping People in Times of Need." *Pasugo* 53(7):10, 12.
    2002   "To the Law and the Testimony." *Pasugo* 54(3):6-8.

Beckford, James A., ed.
    1986   New *Religious Movements and Rapid Social Change*. London: Sage Publications/UNESCO.

Bocobo, Antonio E.
    2003   "The People Whom God Recognizes." *Pasugo* 55(8):8-9.

Bocobo, Antonio E., and Melissa C. Frani
    2002   "EVM Officiates Imus, Cavite Dedication." *Pasugo* 54(3):27.

Bouilang, Aileen
    2003   "Metro Manila North Holds *Musikapisanan*." *Pasugo* 55(3):28.

Bourne, Phil
    2009   "Summary of the Contextualization Debate." *St. Francis Magazine* 5(5):58-80. On line. Internet. (Available from http://www.stfrancismagzine.info/ja/images/pdf/6PhilBourneSFM5-5-pdf.) Accessed April 20, 2010.

Bridges, Clarence F., Jr.
    2000   "I Found the True Church." *Pasugo* 52(2):24-25.

Bringas-Tuazon, Jennifer
    2000   "Church Youth Leader and Organizations Recognized." *Pasugo* 52(6):23.

Bromley, David G.
    2007   "Teaching New Religious Movements/Learning from New Religious Movements. In *Teaching New Religious Movements*. David G. Bromley, ed. Pp. 3-26. Oxford: Oxford University Press.

Brown, Peter
    1982   *The Cult of the Saints: Its Rise and Function in Latin Christianity*. Chicago, IL: University of Chicago Press.

Brown, Rick, et al.
 2009 "Movements and Contextualization: Is There Really a Correlation?" *International Journal of Frontier Missiology* 26(1):21-13.
Buckser, Andrew and Stephen D. Glazier, eds.
 2003 *The Anthropology of Religious Conversion*. London: Rowman and Littlefield Publishers, Inc.
Buelva, El P.
 1999a "Metro Manila South Enlists 1,000 PNK Officers." *Pasugo* 51(2):30-31.
 1999b "NEU Conducts Outreach Program for the Aged." *Pasugo* 51(4):31.
 1999c "Church Extends *Lingap* to Muslims in QC." *Pasugo* 51(5):25.
Bulatao, Jaime
 1966 "The 'HIYA' System in Filipino Culture." In *Filipino Cultural Heritage: Filipino Social Structure and Value Orientation*. F. Landa Jocano, ed. Pp. 27-40. Manila: The Philippine Women's University.
Bunag, Franklin T.
 2005 "The House of Worship: Its Importance to God and His People." *Pasugo* 57(1):10-14.
Burrows, Ray
 2001 "I Run This Race to Victory." *Pasugo* 53(5):27.
Busséll, Harold L.
 1983 *Unholy Devotion*. Grand Rapids, MI: Zondervan.
CA
 2010 Personal interview with author. Digital recording. Quezon City, February 5.
 2010 Email to the author. May 5.
 2001 "NEU Perks Up Elderly in Dasmarinas." *Pasugo* 53(6):25.
Cantor, Marlex C.
 2001 "Enhancing Spiritual Life." *Pasugo* 53(6):4-6.
 2002 "Worshipping God in the Proper and Orderly Way." *Pasugo* 54(5):8-10.
 2003 "With Thanksgiving to God Comes the Offering of Sacrifices." *Pasugo* 55(12):7.
 2004a "Survival of the Eldest: Pampanga District Revisited." *Pasugo* 56(1):36-40.
 2004b "Districts Worldwide Open 2004 with Fruitful Missions." *Pasugo* 56(3):4-5.
 2004c "Worldwide GEM Caps Church's 90th Anniversary Commemoration." *Pasugo* 56(9):8-9.
 2004d "How Their Lives Have Changed." *Pasugo* 56(11):9-14.
 2005 "Making Our Parents Proud." *Pasugo* 57(1):29-31.
Capuno, Henry, and Alex Tolentino
 2003 "EVM Visits Enliven Laguna." *Pasugo* 55(10):33.
Cariag, Astrophel, P., Rosemarie O. Carlos, and Villamore S. Quebral
 2000 "330,000 Receive Gospel." *Pasugo* 52(6):26.
Cariaso, Elsa P.
 1999 "Hurdling God's Crucial Test." *Pasugo* 51(9):20-21.
Carlos, Rosemarie O.
 1999 "Cavite Greets 1999 with Renewed Inspiration and Devotion." *Pasugo* 51(3):26.
Castigo, Margie
 2003 "Kuala Lumpur Promotes Health, Reaches Out to Children." *Pasugo* 55(8):30.
Castro, Lloyd I.
 2001a "Can Faith without Good Works Save?" *Pasugo* 53(2):8-10.
 2001b "Those Given to Know the Mystery of God." *Pasugo* 53(5):6-7, 26.
 2001c "God's Planting and Its Right to Serve." *Pasugo* 53(7):26-27.
 2001d "What Makes Up a Blessed Home?" *Pasugo* 53(8):10-12.
 2002 "Salvation, Justice, and the Church." *Pasugo* 54(4):8-9.
Catañgay, Tomas C.
 2001a "Is Serving God a Waste of Time?" *Pasugo* 53(1):26-27.
 2001b "Salvation is God's Gift." *Pasugo* 53(3):4-5,8.
 2001c "A Reminder to Parents." *Pasugo* 53(7):12-13.
 2001d "I Know My Shepherd and Am Known by My Own." *Pasugo* 53(10);4-5.
Catayay, Alma L.
 1999 "DNM Launches Annual Website Contest." *Pasugo* 51(3):26-27.
 2002 "In Love, They Will Always Be." *Pasugo* 54(1):28-29.
Cayabyab, Ronald
 1999 "Western Syndey Gives Officers a Treat." *Pasugo* 51(1):27.
CC
 2010 Interview with Roger Abe. Transcript. Saipan, Northern Mariana Islands, April 29.
Celajes, Abner M.
 2001 "The People of God in these Last Days." *Pasugo* 53(2):28-29.
Centeno, Ramon C.
 2004 "To Dwell in the New Jerusalem." *Pasugo* 56(2):15-16.
Chico, Cristino V.
 1999 "Nueva Ecija Marks 9th Year." *Pasugo* 51(3):27.
Christian Brotherhood International
 n.d. "Constitution." On line. Internet. (Available from http://www.freewebs.com/cbi_bacolod/.) Accessed June 30, 2007.
Christian, William A., Jr.
 1981 *Local Religion in Sixteenth Century Spain*. Princeton, NJ: Princeton University Press.
Chryssides, George D.
 1999 *Exploring New Religions*. London: Cassell.
Chryssides, George D., and Margaret Z. Ashcraft, eds.
 2006 *A Reader in New Religious Movements*. London: Continuum.

Clymer, Kenton J.
    1986   *Protestant Missionaries in the Philippines 1898-1916: An Inquiry into the American Colonial Mentality.* Chicago, IL: University of Illinois Press.

Construction Project Manager for Union Church of Manila
    2000   Conversation with the author, Makati, July.

Cora
    1998   Personal interview with Kevin Alamang. Quezon City, Philippines, October.

Correa, Cromwell S.
    1999   "Pasay Celebrates 43rd Year." *Pasugo* 51(2):36.
    2001   "Pampanga Baptizes 1,013 Converts, Adds 1,015 Officers." *Pasugo* 53(1):33.

CR
    2010   Interview with the author. Saipan, Northern Mariana Islands, April 29.

Crisostomo, Isabelo T.
    1986   "Remembering the Last Messenger of God, Felix Y. Manalo and the Iglesia ni Cristo." *Pasugo* Special Issue 38(3):5-23.
    2001   "Felix Manalo and His Mission." *The Philippine Star*, July 27, Section A, 13.

Crisostomo, Joji S.
    2001   "Hong Kong West Turns 18: Brethren Foster Harmonious Relations." *Pasugo* 53(7):36.

Dabu, Marilou
    2001   "Mississauga Dedicates House of Worship." *Pasugo* 53(7):34.

Daleno, Gaynor Duat-ol
    2009   "Celebrating 40 Years." *Pacific Sunday News*, March 15. On line. Internet. (Available from http://www./guamdn.com/article/20090315/LIFESTYLE/903150319/1014.) Accessed April 15, 2009.

Dancel, Francis
    2005   "*Utang na Loob* [Debt of Good Will]: A Philosophical Analysis." In *Filipino Cultural Traits*. Roland M. Gripaldo, ed. Pp. 109-128. Claro R. Ceniza Lectures, Cultural Heritage and Contemporary Change Series IIID, Southeast Asia, vol. 4 Washington, D.C.: The Council for Research in Values and Philosophy.

Danganan, Amelie L.
    2006   "A Picture of Unwavering Faith." *Pasugo* 58(11):28-29.

Dautrey, Daniel
    1999   "The Dawn of Eternal Life." *Pasugo* 51(2):24-25.

David, Glenn, Bienvenido Magtuto, Jr., and Filomena Alcon
    1999   "Australia Holds First Summer Class, Senior Citizens Day." *Pasugo* 51(5):23-24.

Dawes, David F.
    1997   "Iglesia ni Cristo: 'The True Church' Denies Christ's Diety." *Christian Info News*, August. On line. Internet. (Available from http://www.canadianchristianity.com/cgi-bin/bc.cgi?bc/bccn/0897/iglesia.) Accessed April 15, 2009.

Dawn, Marva J.
    1995   *Reaching Out without Dumbing Down: A Theology of Worship for this Urgent Time.* Grand Rapids, MI: Eerdmans.

Dawson, Lorne L.
    1998   *Comprehending the Cults: The Sociology of New Religious Movements.* Oxford: Oxford University Press.

DE
    2010   Personal interview with author. Digital recording. Alabang, Muntinlupa City, Philippines, January 28.

De Castro, Leonard D.
    1998   "Debts of Good Will and Interpersonal Justice." Paper presented at the Twentieth World Congress on Philosophy, held at Boston, MA, August 10-15, 1998. On line. Intenet. (Available from http://www.bu.edu/wcp/MainAsia.htm.) Accessed April 7, 2008.

de Los Reyes, Benjie
    1999a   "Ministers, Church Workers Take Oath of Office." *Pasugo* 51(4):30.
    1999b   "Metro Manila Districts Baptize More than 2,000." *Pasugo* 51(10):33.
    2000a   "Church Commends Ministers." *Pasugo* 52(5):31.
    2000b   "118 Ministers Ordained." *Pasugo* 52(6):25.
    2000c   "19 Ministers Sworn into Office." *Pasugo* 52(10):33.
    2001   "42 Ministers Take Oath during 8th Ministerial Conference." *Pasugo* 53(4):32.
    2003   "Church Ordains 52 Ministers." *Pasugo* 55(5):33.

De Manila, Quijanode
    1963   "The Empire of the Iglesia." *Philippine Free Press*, April 27:46.

De Neui, Paul H., ed.
    2010   *Family and Faith in Asia: the Missional Impact of Social Networks.* Pasadena, CA: William Carey Library.

Deen, Steven Michael
    2002   "My Dream to Find Fulfillment Came True." *Pasugo* 54(2):8, 27.

Diverte, Benito D., III.
    2006   "Understanding the Christology of the Iglesia ni Cristo for a Better Dialogue." In *Naming the Unknown God*. Abelard O. Gorospe, ed. Pp. 182-197. Manila: OMF Literature, Inc.

DP
    2010   Personal interview with author. Digital recording. Katipunan, Quezon City, January 29.

DR
    1998   Conversation with author. Cainta, Rizal, Philippines, October 6.
    1999   "Monterey Joins Marina Cleanup Drive." *Pasugo* 51(7):25.
    2003   "A Deaconess Makes Her Mark." *Pasugo* 55(11):33.
    2004   "Highlights of the Church's Achievement: A Year After." *Pasugo* 56(4):8-9.
    2005   "Church Keeps Up Construction Boom." *Pasugo* 57(1):8.
    2007a   "Construction, Renovation of Houses of Worship, Infrastructure Projects Continued." *Pasugo* 59(2):5-7.
    2007b   "Renovation of Houses of Worship, Infrastructure Projects Continue." *Pasugo* 59(2):5.

Dy, Manual B.
   1994   "Outline of a Project of Pilipino Values." In Values in Philippine Culture and Education. Manual B. Dy, ed. Pp. 17-22. Manila: Office of Research and Publications, Philippine Philosophical Studies.

Dy, Manual B., ed.
   1994   *Values in Philippine Culture and Education*. Manila: Office of Research and Publications, Philippine Philosophical Studies.

Editor
   2001   "Editorial: To Have and to Hold." *Pasugo* 53(5):3.
   2002a   "Editorial: Lest We Forget Him." *Pasugo* 54(5):3.
   2002b   "Editorial: Blessed Are Those Who Persevere." *Pasugo* 54(11);3, 11.
   2003a   "Editorial: Onward to Spiritual Maturity and Perfect Unity." *Pasugo* 55(1):3.
   2003b   "Editorial: The Work of Salvation." *Pasugo* 55(3):3, 7.
   2003c   "Editorial: Sent to Preach." *Pasugo* 55(5):3, 9.

Editor, Letters to
   1999a   "On Marrying Unbelievers and Youngest Victims of Murder." *Pasugo* 51(6):2.
   1999b   "Overcoming Persecution." *Pasugo* 51(11):2.
   2000a   "Saying Our Amens." *Pasugo* 52(6):2.
   2000b   "On Smoking and Drinking Alcoholic Beverages." *Pasugo* 52(9):2
   2001a   "The Name of the True Church." *Pasugo* 53(3):2.
   2001b   "Not a Stubborn Fact." *Pasugo* 53(6):2.
   2002a   "Christ Is Not Man?" *Pasugo* 54(4):2
   2002b   "God Is Everywhere." *Pasugo* 54(6):2.
   2002c   "On the Giving of Tithes." *Pasugo* 54(7):2.
   2002d   "Are Christ and Jehovah One and the Same God?" *Pasugo* 54(12):2.
   2003a   "Are Infants Baptized in the Church?" *Pasugo* 55(1):2.
   2003b   "On Valentine's Day." *Pasugo* 55(2):2.
   2003c   "Jesus Christ and the Prince of Tyre." *Pasugo* 55(8):2,9.
   2003d   "Is He Unfair?" *Pasugo* 55(9):2, 9.
   2003e   "Letters." *Pasugo* 55(12):2, 7.
   2004   "Mailbox." *Pasugo* 56(5):3-4.

Eggan, Frank
   1971   "Philippine Social Structure." In *Six Perspectives on the Philippines*. George M. Guthrie, ed. Pp. 1-48. Manila: Bookmark.

Elesterio, Fernando O.
   1988   *The Iglesia ni Kristo: Its Christology and Ecclesiology*. Manila: Cardinal Bea Institute, Loyola School of Theology, Ateneo de Manila University.

Enriquez, Virgilio
   1994   *From Colonial to Liberation Psychology: The Philippine Experience*. Manila: De La Salle University Press.

Estopito, Samuel
   2000   "Bago Bantay Holds Parent-Child Communications Seminar." *Pasugo* 52(11):33.

Eudela, Dennis P.
   2001   "Virginia Beach Joins Worldwide Activity." *Pasugo* 53(1):36.

Eudela, Dennis P., and Evangeline G. Galvez
   2000   "Southeastern Seaboard Sets Pace for 2000." *Pasugo* 52(4):32.

Feazell, J. Michael
   2003   *The Liberation of the Worldwide Church of God*. Grand Rapids, MI: Zondervan Publishing House.

Fisher, John
   1874   "The Why and How of Reaching Jehovah's Witnesses." *Evangelical Missions Quarterly* 12(4):227-238.

FL
   2010   Personal interview with author. Digital recording. Fairview, Quezon City, Philippines, January 27.

Flores, Rebecca J.
   2000   "Tinian Dedicates House of Worship." *Pasugo* 52(5):32.

Flores, Rebecca J., Normal Royeca, Marites Miranda, and Edna Domingo
   2001   "Locales Propel Propagational [sic] Activities." *Pasugo* 53(1):35.

FM
   2010   Personal interview with author. Digital recording. Scout, Quezon City, Philippines, January 28.

Fomocod, Y. and S. Gollayan
   2004   "Anaheim Hosts First US 'Digital Video Bootcamp.'" *Pasugo* 56(5):5.

Forro, R.M., Jr., J.B. Silva, and N.C. Caritativo
   2004   "Iloilo North Conducts Choir Day." *Pasugo* 56(1):8.

Frani, Melissa C.
   2002a   "*KADIWA* Celebrates 28th Year through Music Writing." *Pasugo* 54(1):34-35.
   2002b   "Church Member Ranks 8th in Bar Exams." *Pasugo* 54(12):23.

Fuentes, Feljun B.
   1999a   "Editorial: Let Us Sing Praises to the Lord." *Pasugo* 51(4):3.
   1999b   "Editorial: More Than an Expression of Compassion." *Pasugo* 51(8):3.
   1999c   "Editorial: CEM 25 Sterling Years." *Pasugo* 51(10):3.
   2000a   "Editorial: Esteeming Them Highly in Love." *Pasugo* 51(1):3.
   2000b   "Editorial: Spreading the Good News to the World." *Pasugo* 51(2):3.
   2001a   "Editorial: Strengthening the Christian Family Organizations." *Pasugo* 53(1):3.
   2001b   "Editorial: A Heritage from the Lord." *Pasugo* 53(6):3.
   2001c   "From the Managing Editor: Anniversary Greetings, et. al." *Pasugo* 53(7):2.
   2001d   "Editorial: Preserving Christian Values." *Pasugo* 53(10):3.
   2002a   "Editorial: Keeping Us Strong in the Faith." *Pasugo* 54(1):3.
   2002b   "Editorial: Let Us Give Them a Better Future." *Pasugo* 54(2):3.

    2002c   "Editorial: Lest We Forget Him." *Pasugo* 54(5):3.
    2002d   "Editorial: The Church under a Centralized Administration." *Pasugo* 54(7):3.
    2002e   "In the Face of Suffering." *Pasugo* 54(11):4-5.
    2002f   "Dedicating Our Children in the Service of the Lord." *Pasugo* 54(12):5-6.
    2003a   "Editorial: Our Fellowship with the Central Administration." *Pasugo* 55(1):4-5.
    2003b   "Learning How to Pray." *Pasugo* 55(2):4-5.
    2003c   "Milestones in the History of the Church." *Pasugo* 55(4):6-8.
    2003d   "Why We Call Him the Last Messenger." *Pasugo* 55(5): 4-5.
    2003e   "His Enemies No More." *Pasugo* 55(6):4-5.
    2003f   "Where His Glory Dwells." *Pasugo* 55(7):4-5.
Gaddi, G.C.
    2004   "So. California Launches Kindergarten Program, Livens Up Missionary Efforts." *Pasugo* 56(1):4.
Garcia, Delores
    1964   "Felix Manalo: The Man and His Mission." In *50th Anibersaryo, 1914-1964*. Iglesia ni Cristo. Pp. 179-183. Manila: Iglesia ni Cristo.
Garcia, Gino Rinaldo A.
    2002   "Ethnographic Research Paper." Unpublished manuscript. Graduate paper for course on New Religious Movements taught by Anne C. Harper and Michael McDowell at Asian Theological Seminary, Quezon City, Philppines.
God's Message News Bureau
    2004a   "Chronicles: INC Music Video Festival—Year 3." *Pasugo* 56(9):5.
    2004b   "Chronicles: Four New Chapels and Still Counting." *Pasugo* 56(8):7.
Gollayan, Siegfried
    2001   "HK Brethren on the Go." *Pasugo* 53(5):36.
    2003a   "Southern Europe Steps Up Activities." *Pasugo* 55(5):30-31.
    2003b   "Locales in Asia Press Forward." *Pasugo* 55(6):27.
    2004a   "Districts Intensify Missionary Activities." *Pasugo* 56(8):6-7.
    2004b   "More Districts Reap Bountiful Harvest." *Pasugo* 56(9):4-5.
Gonzales, Ronnie C., Bella Q. Agustin, and Maylene D. Zapatero
    1999   "Singapore Celebrates 20th Year; Kowloon Moves Forward." *Pasugo* 51(12):31.
Gonzales, Ronnie Cadiz
    2001   "Church Supports National Family Week." *Pasugo* 53(10):30-31.
    2003   "Northern, Southern Europe Commemorate May 10." *Pasugo* 55(7):32-33.
    2005   "Port of Call: The Ecclesiastical District of the Pacific Northwest in Retrospect." *Pasugo* 57(1):34-40.
Gonzales, Ronnie Cadiz, and Sesina G. Besa
    1999   "Church Sends Relief to Calamity Victims." *Pasugo* 51(5):24.
Gorospe, Vitaliano R.
    1966   *Christian Renewal of Filipino Values*. Quezon City: Ateneo de Manila University.
Grace Communion International
    1998   "Global Lessons from the Worldwide Church of God." On line. Internet. (Available from http://www.wcg.org/lit/aboutus/media/global.htm.) Accessed October 22, 2009.
    c.2004   "Tranformed by Christ." On line. Internet. (Available from http://www.gci.org/aboutus/history.) Accessed April 21, 2010.
    2009   "Worldwide Church of God Announces Name Change." News release April 16. On line. Internet. (Available from http://www.wcg.org/). Accessed October 26, 2009.
    2011   Email to the author. February 8.
Gray, Andrea, and Leith Gray
    2009   "Paradigms and Praxis Part I: Social Networks and Fruitfulness in Church Planting." *International Journal of Frontier Missiology* 26(1):19-28.
Gray, Leith, and Andrea Gray
    2009   "Paradigms and Praxis Part II: Why Are Some Workers Changing Paradigms?" *International Journal of Frontier Missiology* 26(2):63-73.
Green, Michael
    2004   *Evangelism in the Early Church*. Revised edition. Grand Rapids, MI: Eerdmans.
Gripaldo, Rolando M.
    2005   "Introduction." In *Filipino Cultural Traits*. Rolando M. Gripaldo, ed. Pp. 1-6. Clara R. Lectures. Cultural Heritage and Contemporary Change Series IIID, Southeast Asia, Vol. 4, George F. McLean, ed. Washington, D.C.: The Council for Research in Values and Philosophy.
Gripaldo, Rolando M., ed.
    2005   *Filipino Cultural Traits*. Claro R. Lectures. Cultural Heritage and Contemporary Change Series IIID, Southeast Asia, Vol. 4, George F. McLean, ed. Washington, D.C.: The Council for Research in Values and Philosophy.
Guampdn.com
    2009   "Celebrating 40 Years." On line. Internet. (Available from http://guamdn.com/article/20030315/LIFESTYLE/903150319/1024.) Accessed April 15, 2009.
Guingab, Edwin, Rebecca Flores, and Rolando Zepeda
    2001   "Hawaii-Pacific Inducts 300 New Officers." *Pasugo* 53(4):34.
Guiting, Lizerne, and Jennifer Pineda-Dayrit
    2007   "Southern California Sets Annual Volleyball Tourney." *Pasugo* 59(2):11.
Guthrie, George M.
    1971   "The Philippine Temperament." In *Six Perspectives on the Philippines*. George M. Guthrie, ed. Pp. 49-84. Quezon City: Bookmark.
Haack, Gary
    2002   "My True Wealth." *Pasugo* 54(1):30.
Harper, Anne C.
    2001a   "A Filipino Church at 80 Years: The Iglesia ni Cristo at the Turn of the Century." In *Sketches in Philippine Church History*. Anne Kwantes, ed. Pp. 429-450. Manila: OMF Publishers.

2001b	"The Iglesia ni Cristo and Evangelical Christianity." *Journal of Asian Mission* 3(2):101-119.
2008	"New Religious Movements, Part Two: An Analysis of One Movement: The Iglesia ni Cristo of the Philippines." *Journal of Asian Mission* 10(1-2):75-108.
2011	"The Iglesia ni Cristo: A Study of a New Religious Movement and Exploration of Culturally Appropriate Outreach Metholodogies." Dissertation presented to Asia Graduate School of Theology, Quezon City, Philippines, on February 7.

Hershberger, Michele
  1999   *A Christian View of Hospitality: Expecting Surprises*. Scottsdale, PA: Herald Press.

Hesselgrave, David J.
  1991   *Communicating Christ Cross-Culturally: An Introduction to Missionary Communication*. Revised Ed. Grand Rapids, MI: Zondervan Publishing House.

Hexham, Irving, and Karla Poewe
  1986   *Understanding Cults and New Religions*. Grand Rapids, MI: William B. Eerdmans Publishing Company.

Hexham, Irving, Stephen Rost and John W. Morehead, III, eds.
  2004   *Encountering New Religious Movements: A Holistic Evangelical Approach*. Grand Rapids, MI: Kregel.

Hiebert, Paul
  1994   *Anthropological Reflections on Missiological Issues*. Grand Rapids, MI: Baker Books.

Ho, David Y.F.
  1976   "On the Concept of Face." *American Journal of Sociology* 81:867-884.

Hollnsteiner, Mary
  1968   *The Dynamics of Power in a Philippine Municipality*. Quezon City: University of the Philippines.

Hutchinson, Janis
  1994   *Out of the Cults and into the Church: Understanding and Encouraging Ex-Cultists*. Grand Rapids, MI: Kregel Resources.

Iglesia ni Cristo
  1981   *Ang Bagong Himnario ng Iglesia ni Cristo (The New Hymns of the Iglesia ni Cristo)*. Translated by V. Santiago. Quezon City: Iglesia ni Cristo.
  2007   "The Iglesia ni Cristo and the Bible. What God Expects of All Parents and Children. On line. Internet video file produced by the Department of Evangelism, Office of TV Evangelism. (Available from http://www.iglesianicristo.ws.) Accessed April 6, 2009.
  2007   "The Iglesia ni Cristo and the Bible. Worshipping God in an Acceptable Manner." On line. Interent video file produced by the Department of Evangelism, Office of TV Evangelism. (Available from http://wwiglesianicristo.ws.) Accessed April 6, 2009.
  2008   "The Iglesia ni Cristo and the Bible. Divine Rules for Marriage." On line. Internet video file produced by the Department of Evangelism, Office of TV Evangelism. (Available from http://www.iglesianicristo.ws.) Accessed April 6, 2009.
  2009   "Worship Service Schedule." On line. Internet. (Available from http://incsacramento.org/service_schedules.html.) Accessed April 15, 2009.
  n.d.   "Iglesia ni Cristo" On line. Internet. (Available from http://wwwabsoluteastronomyu.com/topics/Iglesia_ni_Cristo.) Accessed April 15, 2009.

Ilan, Noel I.
  2001a   "Overpowering Death." *Pasugo* 53(3):8-10.
  2001b   "Keeping the Spiritual Fervor." *Pasugo* 53(4):6-7.
  2001c   "Who Are Guilty of Rejecting God?" *Pasugo* 53(7):8-9, 30.
  2001d   "The Origin of the Doctrine of Christ's Alleged Deity." *Pasugo* 53(12):4-7.
  2002a   "The Gift of Understanding the Words of God." *Pasugo* 54(1):9.
  2002b   "The Freedom that the Bible Teaches." *Pasugo* 54(10):8-9.
  2003   "Are You Patient Enough?" *Pasugo* 55(1):10-11.

INC-Pasugo.org
  2007   "Places of Worship." On line. Internet. (Available from http://inc-pasugo.org.) Accessed June 15, 2007.

INCWorld
  n.d.   "Manual for New Members." On line. Internet. (Available from http://incworld.faithweb.com/info.htm.) Accessed June 29, 2007.

Inquirer News Service
  2001   "Iglesia to Mark 87th Year Sans Fanfare." *Newsbreak Magazine*, July 24. On line. Internet. (Available from http://archive.inq7.net/archive/2001-p/2001/jul/25/nat_15-1-p.htm.) Accessed February 2, 2003.

Jinco-Flores, Rebecca
  2001   "Saipan Fosters Family Solidarity." *Pasugo* 53(7):33.

Jocano, F. Landa
  1966a   "Filipino Social Structure and Value System." In *Filipino Cultural Heritage: Filipino Social Structure and Value Orientation*. F. Landa Jocano, ed. Pp. 1-26. Manila: The Philippine Women's University.
  1997   *Filipino Value System: A Cultural Definition*. Manila: Punlad Research House.
  1998   *Filipino Social Organization: Traditional Kinship and Family Organization*. Manila: Punlad Research House.

Johnson, Philip S.
  2002   "Apologetics, Mission and New Religious Movements: A Holistic Approach." *Sacred Tribes Journal* 1(1):5-220. On line. Internet. (Available from http://sacredtribesjournal.org/images/Articles/Vol_1/Fall2002/Apol_Johnsonpdf.) Accessed November 9, 2002 and September 10, 2009.
  2004   "Reaching the Christadelphians." In *Encountering New Religious Movements: A Holistic Evangelical Approach*. Irving Hexham, Stephen Rost, and John W. Morehead, III, eds. Pp. 175-192. Grand Rapids, MI: Kregel.

Johnson, Philip, Anne C. Harper and John W. Morehead, eds
  2004   *Religious and Non-Religious Spirituality in the Western World ("New Age")*. Lausanne Occasional Paper no. 45. Sydney: Lausanne Committee and Morling Press.

Johnson, Philip and John Smulo
    2004   "Reaching Wiccans and Mother Goddess Devotees." In *Encountering New Religious Movements: A Holistic Evangelical Approach*. Irving Hexham, Stephen Rost, and John W. Morehead, III, eds. Pp. 209-226. Grand Rapids, MI: Kregel.

Jones, Arthur W., II.
    2004   "No Longer Confused." *Pasugo* 56(8):16-17.

Justyn
    2004   "Iglesia ni YHWH at ni YHWSA HMSYH ('Ang Dating Daan'). The Bereans Apologetics Research Ministry. On line. Internet. (Available from http://www.thebereans.net/prof-add.shtml.) Accessed May 7, 2010.

Kaut, Charles
    1966   "*Utang na Loob*: A System of Contractual Obligation among Tagalogs." In *Filipino Cultural Heritage*. Jocano F. Landa, ed. Pp. 41-63. Manila: Philippine Women's University.

Kavanaugh, Joseph J.
    1955   "The Iglesia ni Cristo." *Philippine Studies* 3(1):19-42.
    1955   "The Stars that Fall—and Mr. Manalo." *Philippine Studies* 3(3):289-296.
    1961   "Survey: the Voice of the Iglesia ni Cristo 1951-1961." *Philippine Studies* 9(4):651-655.

Kenya Church Growth Bulletin
    1997   "Case Studies—God Is Still at Work, Revealing Himself and His Truth to Those Who Sincerely Seek Him." January 1. On line. Internet. (Available from http://strategicnetwork.org/index.php?loc=kb&view=v&id=9900-&fto=9&.) Accessed November 3, 2009.

Khual, Nang Khan
    2002   "My Observations on a Regular Worship Service of the Iglesia ni Christo [*sic*]." Unpublished manuscript. Graduate research paper for course on New Religious Movements taught by Anne C. Harper and Michael McDowell at Asian Theological Seminary.

Kim, Hyoung Beck (Peter)
    2004   "Ethnographic Research Paper." Unpublished manuscript. Graduate research paper for course on New Religious Movements by Anne C. Harper and Michael McDowell at Asian Theological Seminary, Quezon City, Philippines.

Kimura, Erlinda L.
    2000   "Tokyo Launches English Class for Children." *Pasugo* 52(9):24.

Knight, Clayton M., Jr.
    1999   "The Iglesia ni Cristo Enriched My Life." *Pasugo* 51(12):24-25.

Koenig, John
    1985   *New Testament Hospitality: Partnership with Strangers as Promise and Mission*. Eugene, OR: Wipf and Stock Publishers.

Kraft, Charles H.
    1979   *Christianity in Culture: Dynamic Biblical Theologizing in Cross-Cultural Perspective*. Maryknoll, NY: Orbis Books.

Kroll, Steven V.
    2002   "What the Bible Teaches about Death." *Pasugo* 54(11):8-9, 24-25.

Kwantes, Anne C.
    1989   *Presbyterian Missionaries in the Philippines: Conduits of Social Change (1899-1910)*. Quezon City: New Day Publishers.

Lausanne Committee for World Evangelization
    1974   "Lausanne Covenant." On line. Internet. (Available from http://www.lausanne.org/covenant.) Accessed May 2, 2010.
    1980   "Christian Witness to New Religious Movements." Lausanne Occasional Paper 11, mini-consultation of Reaching Mystics and Cultists, held at Pattaya, Thailand, June 1980. On line. Internet. (Available from http://www.lausanne.org/all-documents/lop-11.html.) Accessed April 18, 2010.

Leffel, Jim
    c.1997   "Contextualization: Building Bridges to the Muslim Community." On line. Internet. (Available from http://www.xenos.org/ministries/crossroads/OnlineJournal/issue1/contextu.htm.) Accessed May 17, 2010.

Leoncini, Dante Luis
    2005   "A Conceptual Analysis of Pakikisama [Getting along Well with People]." In *Filipino Cultural Traits*. Rolando M. Gripaldo, ed. Pp. 157-184. Claro R. Ceniza Lectures, Cultural Heritage and Contemporary Change Series, IIID, Southeast Asia, vol. 4. Washington, D.C.: The Council for Research in Values and Philosophy.

Lewis, Gordon R.
    1998   "Our Mission Responsibility to New Religious Movements." *International Journal of Frontier Missions* 15(3):115-123.

Lewis, Rebecca
    2007   "Promoting Movements to Christ within Natural Communities." *International Journal of Frontier Missions* 24(2):75-76.
    2009   "Insider Movements: Honoring God-Given Identity and Community." *International Journal of Frontier Missiology* 26(1):16-19.

Llana-Dela Cruz, Imelda
    1999   "A Woman's Faith in Spirit and Practice." *Pasugo* 51(11):18-19.
    2000   "Portrait of a Fruitful Church Member." *Pasugo* 52(8):9,23.
    2001   "Unwavering Dedication to the Lord's Service." *Pasugo* 53(11):10-11.

Lofland, John, and Normand Skonovd
    1981   "Conversion Motifs." *Journal for the Scientific Study of Religion* 20(4):373-385.

Lofland, John, and Rodney Stark
    1965   "Becoming a World Saver: A Theory of Conversion to a Deviant Perspective." *American Sociological Review* 30(4):862-875.

Lovendino, Dennis C.
    2001   "Remembering the Messenger of God in these Last Days." *Pasugo* 53(5):10-11.

2002a	"Science vs. the Bible." *Pasugo* 54(1):6-8.
2002b	"Worshiping the Creature Rather than the Creator." *Pasugo* 54(8):6-8, 13.

Lynch, Frank
- 1963   "Social Acceptance." In *Four Readings on Philippine Values*. Frank Lynch, ed. Pp. 1-21. Quezon City: Ateneo de Manila University.
- 1984a   "Big and Little People: Social Class in the Philippines." In *Philippine Society and the Individual: Selected Essays of Frank Lynch, 1949-1976*. Aram A. Yengoyan and Perla Q. Makil, eds. Pp. 93-99. Ann Arbor, MI: Center for South and Southeast Asian Studies, The University of Michigan.
- 1984b   "Town Fiesta: An Anthropologist's View." In *Philippine Society and the Individual: Selected Essays of Frank Lynch, 1949-1976*. Aram A. Yengoyan and Perla Q. Makil, eds. Pp. 209-223. Ann Arbor, MI: Center for South and Southeast Asian Studies, The University of Michigan.

Maggay, Melba Padilla
- 2000   *Understanding Ambiguity in Filipino Communication Patterns*. Quezon City: Institute of Studies in Asian Church and Culture.

Malherbe, Abraham J.
- 1983   *Social Aspects of Early Christianity*. Philadelphia, PA: Fortress Press.

Manalo, Eraño
- 1989   *Mga Leksiyong Ministeryal* ("Doctrinal Lessons for Ministers"). Translated by V. Santiago. Quezon City: Iglesia ni Cristo.

Manglicmot, Dexter T.
- 2003   "Why We Need the Church of Christ." *Pasugo* 55(3):8-9.

Manila Bulletin. Daily newspaper
- 2009   "Happy Birthday to Iglesia ni Cristo Executive Minister Eduardo V. Manalo." *Manila Bulletin*, October 30. On line. Internet. (Available from http://www.mb.com.ph/articles/227162/happy-birthday-iglesia-ni-cristo-executive-minister-eduardo-v-manalo.) Accessed December 1, 2009.

Martin, Johnny J.
- 2002   "God's Promise of Eternal Blessing." *Pasugo* 54(2):4-5..

Martin, Walter; Hank Hanegraaff, ed.
- 1997   *The Kingdom of the Cults*. 30th Anniversary Edition. Minneapolis, MN: Bethany House Publishers.

Mayers, Marvin K.
- 1980   *A Look at Filipino Lifestyles*. Dallas, TX: SIL Museum of Anthropology.

McGavran, Donald Anderson
- 2005   *The Bridges of God: A Study in the Strategy of Missions*. Eugene, OR: Wipf & Stock Publishers. (First edition, World Dominion Press, 1955.)

Meimban, Adriel O.
- 1987   "The 73rd Year of the Iglesia ni Cristo." *Pasugo* 39(3):9-15.
- 2004   "The Spiritual Graces Received during Worship Services." *Pasugo* 57(9):8-10.

Melville-Laborde, David
- 2002   "I Found the True Meaning of Happiness." *Pasugo* 54(7):31.

Melton, J. Gordon
- 1991   "Introduction: When Prophets Die: The Succession Crisis in New Religions." In *When Prophets Die: The Postcharismatic Fate of New Religious Movements*. Timothy Miller, ed. Pp. 1-2. Albany, NY: State University of New York Press.
- 2000   "Emerging Religious Movements in North America: Some Missiological Reflections." *Missiology* 28(1):85-98.
- 2004   "Towards a Definition of 'New Religion.'" *Nova Religio* 8(1):73-87.
- 2007   "Introducing and Defining the Concept of a New Religion." In *Teaching New Religious Movements*. David Y. Bromley, ed. Pp. 29-40. Oxford: Oxford University Press.

Mendez, Christina
- 1999   "President Apologizes to Iglesia ni Cristo for Task Force Fiasco." *Philippine Star*, February 2, Metro 1, 4. (Available from http://www.manilatimes.net/national/2003/may1/metro/200305/met1.html.) Accessed May 7, 2004.

Mendoza, Rizza G.
- 2004a   "Scan Int'l Conducts Environmental Activities." *Pasugo* 56(1):6.
- 2004b   "Inside God's Holy Temple." *Pasugo* 56(1):12.

Mercado, Leonardo N.
- 1976   *Elements of Filipino Philosophy*. Manila: Divine Word Publications.

Mercado, Leonardo N., ed.
- 1997   *Filipino Religious Psychology*. Tacloban City, Leyte, Philippines: Divine Word University Publications.

MI
- 2010   Personal interview with author. Digital recording. Imus, Cavite, February 6.

Miller, Timothy
- 1991   *When Prophets Die: The Postcharismatic Fate of New Religious Movements*. Albany, NY: University of New York Press.

Montiel, Cristina J.
- 1994   "Filipino Culture, Religious Symbols and Liberation Policies." In *Values in Philippine Culture and Education*. Manual B. Dy, Jr., ed. Pp. 103-107. Cultural Heritage and Contemporary Change Series III, Asia, vol. 7. Washington, D.C.: Office of Research and Publications and the Council for Research in Values and Philosophy.

Morehead, John W.
- n.d.   "Blog." On line. Internet. (Available from http://johnmorehead.blogspot.com.) Accessed September 10, 2009.
- 2002   "Transforming Evangelical Responses to New Religions: Missions and Countercult in Partnership." Paper presented at the annual meeting of the Evangelical Missiological Society, held in Orlando, FL, October 3-5, 2002. On line. Internet. (Available from http://www.emnr.org/papers/Transforming_Evangelical.pdf.) Accessed December 3, 2002.

	2003	"Ministry to Alternative Spiritualities in Religiously Plural America. Moving Beyond Confronting 'Cults.'" *Occasional Bulletin*, 16(3):3-5. On line. Internet. (Available from http://www.neighboringfaiths.org/Articles.html.) Accessed November 3, 2009.
	2004	"Where Do We Go from Here?" In *Encountering New Religious Movements: A Holistic Evangelical Approach*. Irving Hexham, Stephen Rost, and John W. Morehead, III, eds. Pp. 279-304. Grand Rapids, MI: Kregel.
	2005a	"A Fresh Agenda for Apologetics in the 21st Century." On line. Internet. (Available from http://neighboringfaiths.org/Articles.html.) Accessed November 3, 2009.
	2005b	"Can You Hear Me Now? Insights from Communications and Missions for New Religions." On line. Internet. (Available from http://theooze.com/articles/artilce.cfm?id=1097&page=1). Accessed September 10, 2009.
	2005c	"Reflections on the Divide in LDS Evangelism in Utah: Why I Practice an Incarnational Missions Strategy." On line. Internet. (Available from http://www.neighboringfaiths.org/html.) Accessed May 21, 2008.
	2007	"Amos Young Interview: Pneumatology, Hospitality and Religious Pluralism." Morehead's Musings, February 2. On line. Internet. (Available from http://johnmoreheard.blogspot.com/2007/02/Amos-yong-interview-pneumatology.htm.) Accessed April 23, 2010.
	2009	"From 'Cults' to Cultures: *Bridges* as a Case Study in a New Evangelical Paradigm on New Religions." Paper presented at the conference on New Religions held at the Center for Studies on New Religions, Salt Lake City, UT, June 13, 2009.
Mulholland, Kenneth		
	2004	"Bridging the Divide: Cross-Cultural Missions to Latter-day Saints." In *Encountering New Religious Movements: A Holistic Evangelical Approach*. Irving Hexham, Stephen Rost, and John W. Morehead, III. eds. Pp. 159-174. Grand Rapids, MI: Kregel.
National Statistics Office, Republic of the Philippines		
	2000	"Philippine Census 2000." On line. Internet. (Available from http://www.census.gov.ph/census2000/p000000html.) Accessed June 12 and 13, 2007.
	2002	"Philippines: Population Expected to Reach 100 Million Filipinos in 14 Years." On line. Internet. (Available from http://www.census.gov.ph/data/pressrelease/2002/pr02178tx.html.) Accessed May 12, 2010.
	2010	*Philippines in Figures 2010*. On line. Internet. (Available from http://www.census.gov.ph/data/publications/2010PIF.pdf.) Accessed May 5, 2010.
Nepomuceno, Sylvia E.		
	1993	"Holy Supper in Southeast Asia." *Pasugo* 45(5):34-35.
Netland, Harold		
	1988	"Toward Contextualized Apologetics." *Missiology* 16(3):289-303.
Neumann, Mikel		
	2004	"The Incarnational Ministry of Jesus: An Alternative to Traditional Apologetic Approaches." In *Encountering New Religious Movements: A Holistic Evangelical Approach*. Irving Hexham, Stephen Rost, and John W. Morehead, III, eds. Pp. 25-42. Grand Rapids, MI: Kregel.
Nida, Eugene A.		
	1954	*Customs and Cultures: Anthropology for Christian Missions*. Pasadena, CA: William Carey Library.
NN		
	2010	Personal interview with author. Digital recording. Katipunan, Quezon City, Philippines, February 8.
Nouwen, Henri J.M.		
	1975	*Reaching Out*. London: Fount.
OA		
	2010	Personal interview with author. Digital recording. Katipunan, Quezon City, January 31.
Onishi, Norimitsu		
	2001	"Marcos Seeks to Restore Philippine Dynasty." *New York Times*, May 8. On line. Internet. (Available from http://www.nytimes.com/2010/05/08/world/asia/09marcos.html?emc=etal.) Accessed May 8, 2010.
Palmer, Susan and David Bromley		
	2007	"Deliberate Heresies: New Religions, Myths and Rituals as Critiques." In *Teaching New Religious Movements*. David G. Bromley, ed. Pp. 135-158. Oxford: Oxford University Press.
Park, Joon-Sik		
	2002	"Hospitality as Context for Evangelism." *Missiology* 30(3):385-395.
Pascual, Pamela B.		
	2000	"A Vow of Love Remembered." *Pasugo* 52(10):30-32.
		Pasugo. Magazine of the Iglesia ni Cristo.
	n.d.	"A Brief Profile of the Church." On line. Internet. (Available from http://www.geocities.com/truthfinder_inc/eprofile.htm.) Accessed April 15, 2009.
	2000a	"Converts: I Could Ask for Nothing More." 52(7):24-25.
	2000b	"Converts: The Path to Peace and Salvation." 52(5):11.
	2001a	"Not Good Enough." 53(1):centerfold pamphlet.
	2001b	"Serving God in Truth." 53(10):centerfold pamphlet.
	2001c	"Victory over Death." 53(11):centerfold pamphlet.
	2001d	"The Life Worth Living." 53(12):centerfold pamphlet.
	2002a	"Not a Numbers Game." 54(3):centerfold pamphlet.
	2002b	"Before Time Runs Out." 54(6):centerfold pamphlet.
	2002c	"Attaining Salvation and Eternal Life." 54(7):centerfold pamphlet.
	2002d	"What We Should Know and Understand." 54(8):centerfold pamphlet.
	2002e	"The Choices We Have to Make." 54(9):centerfold pamphlet.
	2003a	"Frequently Asked Questions about the Iglesia ni Cristo." 55(4):9-11.
	2003b	"Facts & Figures: A Brief Profile of the Church." 55(4):13.
	2003c	"Have You Ever Asked Why? #4." 55(5):centerfold pamphlet.
	2004	"Messages." 56(7):2-7.
Pasugo News Bureau		
	1999a	"Miscellany in the Districts: Zamboanga Central Pulsates Youth, Community Projects." *Pasugo* 51(1):29-30.
	1999b	"Miscellany in the Districts: Officers Recognized for Long Years of Service." *Pasugo* 51(2):34-35.
	1999c	"Miscellany in the Districts: Districts Promote Literacy for the Less Fortunate." *Pasugo* 51(3):29-30.

	1999d	"Miscellany in the Districts: Minister Receives Plaque of Appreciation." *Pasugo* 51(5):28-30.
	1999e	"Miscellany in the Districts: Summer Kindergarten Program Graduates 9,224." *Pasugo* 51(8):34-37.
	1999f	"Miscellany in the Districts: Arayat, Gumaca Locales Celebrate Diamond Year." *Pasugo* 51(9):28-30.
	2000a	"Miscellany in the Districts: *KADIWA*'s 26th Year Remembered." *Pasugo* 52(2):33-37.
	2000b	"Miscellany in the Districts: Education Program Produces Graduates in Three Districts." *Pasugo* 52(3):26-29.
	2000c	"Miscellany in the Districts: Districts Intensify Edification Program." *Pasugo* 5(4):35-37.
	2000d	"Miscellany in the Districts: Muslim Community Benefits from *Lingap*." *Pasugo* 52(5):34-39.
	2000e	"Miscellany in the Districts: Tarlac Receives Award." *Pasugo* 52(6):27-30.
	2000f	"Miscellany in the Districts: *KADIWA* Promotes Fellowship through Healthy Competition." *Pasugo* 52(7):34-39.
	2000g	"Miscellany in the Districts: Church Serves Payatas Tragedy Victims." *Pasugo* 52(9):28-29.
	2000h	"Miscellany in the Districts: Metro Manila North Strengthens Family." *Pasugo* 52(10):37-39.
	2001a	"Miscellany in the Districts: *Lingap* Missions Held in Mindanao." *Pasugo* 53(1):37.
	2001b	"Miscellany in the Districts: Youth Captures National Title." *Pasugo* 53(2):37-39.
	2001c	"Recently Conducted Blood Drives." *Pasugo* 53(2):39.
	2001d	"Miscellany in the Districts: Religious Program Gives Birth to New Locale." *Pasugo* 53(3):30-31.
	2001e	"Miscellany in the Districts: Oldest District Commemorates 77th Year." *Pasugo* 53(4):36-39.
	2001f	"Miscellany in the Districts: Districts Boost Officer Leadership; Swear in 10,600 Officers." *Pasugo* 53(5):37-39.
	2001g	"Miscellany in the Districts: Districts Join Worldwide Missionary Campaign." *Pasugo* 53(10):37-39.
	2002a	"Miscellany in the Districts: Students in Benguet Receive Words of Wisdom." *Pasugo* 54(1):37-39.
	2002b	"Miscellany in the Districts: Metro Manila North PNK Inducts New Officers." *Pasugo* 54(3):28-31.
	2002c	"Miscellany in the Districts: Districts Focus on Family Activities." *Pasugo* 54(11):34-37.
	2003a	"Miscellany in the Districts: Samar South Pushes Forward." *Pasugo* 55(2):35-37.
	2003b	"Miscellany in the Districts: SCAN Launches '*Bantay Lansangan* 2003.'" *Pasugo* 55(6):28-31.
	2003c	"Miscellany in the Districts: Districts Commemorate FYM's 117th Anniversary." *Pasugo* 55(7):34-37.
	2003d	"Miscellany in the Districts: Rizal GEM Draws Over 25,000; Pangasinan West Dedicates New House of Worship." *Pasugo* 55(11):35-37.
	2004	"Chronicles: INC Music Video Workshop—Year 3." *Pasugo* 56(9):5.
Pellien, Robert F.		
	2002	"The Lord Gave Me Another Chance." *Pasugo* 54(6):8, 26.
Peña, Ricardo		
	1985	*Major Religions in the Philippines*. Pasig, Rizal, Philippines: Alliance Publishers.
Phelan, John L.		
	1959	*The Hispanization of the Philippines: Spanish Aims and Filipino Responses 1565-1700*. Madison, WI: University of Wisconsin Press.
Philippine Star. Daily newspaper		
	2003	"Why Pinoys Behave the Way They Do." May 11, 2003, Section I:6.
Pineda, Perlino, and Filomena Alcon		
	1999	"Melbourne Joins Conservation Project, Cleanup Drive." *Pasugo* 51(2):33.
Pinnoch, Donald		
	1999	"The Charismatic Movement." *Pasugo* 51(10:5-8.
Platt, Donald		
	1981	*Counterfeit*. Manila: OMF Literature.
Pohl, Christine D.		
	1999	*Making Room: Recovering Hospitality as a Christian Tradition*. Grand Rapids, MI: Eerdmans.
Pumar, Rudy, and Amy Simon		
	2001	"Northeastern Seaboard Renews Vigor for 2001." *Pasugo* 53(2):36-37.
PW		
	2010	Personal interview with author. Digital recording. Imus, Cavite, February 6.
QL		
	2010	Personal interview with author. Digital recording. San Juan, Metro Manila, January 23.
	2010	E-mail to the author. March 7, 2010.
Quilang, Aileen B.		
	2003	"Metro Manila North Holds '*Musikapisanan*.'" *Pasugo* 55(3):28.
Quito, Ermita S.		
	1994	"The Ambivalence of Filipino Traits and Values." In *Values in Philippine Culture and Education*. Manual B. Dy, Jr. Pp. 51-54. Cultural Heritage and Contemporary Change Series III, Asia, Vol. 7. Washington, D.C.: Office of Research and Publications and the Council for Research in Values and Philosophy.
Rafols, Richard R.		
	2002	"King William's Town Focuses on the Family." *Pasugo* 54(1):35.
Rambo, Lewis R.		
	1993	*Understanding Religious Conversion*. New Haven, CT: Yale University Press.
Reed, Robert R.		
	1990	"Migration as Mission: The Expansion of the Iglesia ni Cristo Outside the Philippines." In *Patterns of Migration in Southeast Asia*. Robert R. Reed, ed. Pp. 153-181. Occasional Paper Series, No. 16 Berkeley, CA: Centers for South and Southeast Asia Studies International and Area Studies, University of California at Berkeley.
	2001	"The Iglesia ni Cristo, 1914-2000 from Obscure Philippine Faith to Global Belief System." *Bijdragen tot de Taal-, Land- en Volkenkunde, Journal of the Humanities and Social Sciences of Southeast Asia and Oceania* 157(3):561-608.
Reiter, Rudoph Konrad		
	2001	"A Life of Spiritual Purpose." *Pasugo* 53(20:30-31.
Reototar, Lailo N.		
	2001	"Light Has Shone on Me at Last." *Pasugo* 53(6):10-11.

Richardson, Don
    1975   *Peace Child*. Ventura, CA: Regal Books.
    1984   *Eternity in Their Hearts*. Ventura, CA: Regal Books.
Rosquites, Jeffrey V.
    2003   "Iglesia ni Cristo Children's Choir Featured in Grand Evangelical Mission." *Pasugo* 55(6):10-11.
    2004   "EVM Officiates Brixtonville Thanksgiving, Dedicates New House of Worship." *Pasugo* 56(2):7.
Rost, Stephen
    2004   "Paul's Areopagus Speech in Acts 17." In *Encountering New Religious Movements: A Holistic Evangelical Approach*. Irving Hexham, Stephen Rost, and John W. Morehead, III, eds. Pp. 113-136. Grand Rapids, MI: Kregel.
Royeca, Norma O.
    2000   "Pacific Northwest Symposium Focuses on the Family." *Pasugo* 52(12):26.
Royeca, Norma O. and Janette Matugas
    2002   "Pacific Northwest Beats the Cold Weather." Pasugo 54(4):32.

Royeca, Norma O. and Rhodora D. Rigor
    2003   "Pacific Northwest Builds on Family Quality Time." *Pasugo* 55(8):31.
Ruivivar, Tino C.
    2005   *The Absurd Claims and Biggest Mistakes of the Iglesia ni Cristo*. Quezon City: Evangelical Life Publications.
Ruiz, Marie
    1999   "Highway Hills: Rising above the Odds." *Pasugo* 51(1):24-25.
    2000a   "The Methuselah of Anaheim." *Pasugo* 52(2):22-23.
    2000b   "Never Remiss in Serving the Lord." *Pasugo* 52(40:24-25.
    2000c   "Celebrating 25 Years of CLASS: Honoring the Newly Appointed Secretary of Justice." *Pasugo* 52(8):32.
    2001a   "A Family Bequeaths a Priceless Heirloom." *Pasugo* 53(1):10-12.
    2001b   "Paragons of Benevolence." *Pasugo* 53(3):26.
    2001c   "Cradle of Love." *Pasugo* 53(5):30-32.
    2003   "A Promise Fulfilled." *Pasugo* 55(11):8-9.
Ruiz, Marie, Ronald Acob, and Glenn David
    2004   "Metro Manila South Sings Praises in One Voice." *Pasugo* 56(2):9.
Sahagun, Tranquilino, and Lorenzo Mauel
    2001   "Bagong Buhay Brethren Brave Odds to Spread Gospel Truth." *Pasugo* 53(10):32-33.
Salazar, Jose P.
    2003   "The Worthy and Acceptable Worship Service." *Pasugo* 55(9):24-25.
Saliba, John A.
    1995   *Understanding New Religious Movements*. Grand Rapids, MI: Eerdmans.
Salt Lake Theological Seminary
    2003   *Bridges: Helping Mormons Discover God's Grace*. Training Program: How to Reach Mormons Effectively with the Good News of Jesus Christ. DVD. Salt Lake City, UT: Salt Lake Theological Seminary.
San Pedro, Joel V.
    1998   "The Church of Christ Triumphant." *Pasugo* 50(8): 12.
    1999   "The CEM: Continuing the Work of the Messenger." *Pasugo* 51(10):4-7.
    2000   "10 Tips for Helping Your Child Grow Spiritually." *Pasugo* 52(9):9-10.
    2001a   "The 'Jesus' that Does Not Save." *Pasugo* 53(7):23-24.
    2001b   "Remembering God's Promises." *Pasugo* 53(11):4.
San Pedro, Rommel V.
    2001a   "The Stewards of God's Mysteries." *Pasugo* 53(4):10-11.
    2001b   "The Father Alone Is God." *Pasugo* 53(6):8-9, 11.
    2001c   "Refuting Christ's Alleged Deity in Romans 9:5." *Pasugo* 53(7):24-25, 31.
    2001d   "Scripture Twisting to Their Own Destruction." *Pasugo* 53(11):7,12.
    2002   "Is There Such a Thing as God's Chosen People?" *Pasugo* 54(7):10-12.
    2003   "Will Jesus Christ Save You?" *Pasugo* 55(7):27-28.
Sanders, Albert J.
    1962   "Iglesia ni Cristo: Factors Contributing to Its Growth and Future." *South East Asia Journal of Theology* 4(1):43-56.
    1969   "An Appraisal of the Iglesia ni Cristo." In *Studies in Philippine Church History*. Gerald H. Anderson, ed. Pp. 350-365. Ithaca, NY: Cornell University Press.
Santiago, Benildo C.
    2003   "The Proper Way of Worshipping God." *Pasugo* 55(7):8-9.
Santiago, Bien
    2005   "Iglesia ni Cristo." Blog April 27. On line. Internet. (Available from http://aboutiglesianicristo.blogspot.com/.) Accessed April 15, 2009.
Santiago, Bienvenido C.
    2001   "Editorial: the Church Administration Ministering to a Global Flock." *Pasugo* 56(1):2-3.
    2002a   "Editorial: Blessed Are Those Who Persevere." *Pasugo* 54(11):3, 11.
    2002b   "Editorial: Worshipping the Lord from the Days of Youth." *Pasugo* 54(12):3.
    2003a   "Editorial: Onward to Spiritual Maturity and Perfect Unity." *Pasugo* 55(1):3,11.
    2003b   "Editorial: Four Decades of Reminiscence." *Pasugo* 55(4):3-5.
    2003c   "Editorial: Making Friends." *Pasugo* 55(6):3, 7.
    2003d   "Editorial: Building Houses of Worship for God's Glory." *Pasugo* 55(7):7.
    2003e   "Getting the Good News Across." *Pasugo* 55(10):3, 7.
    2003f   "Editorial: Thanksgiving to God: Our Solemn Vow." *Pasugo* 55(12):3.
    2004a   "Editorial: Preserving and Strengthening the Family." *Pasugo* 56(2):2-3.
    2004b   "Editorial: Reflections on the Man Who Spoke God's Words to Us." *Pasugo* 56(5):2-3.
    2004c   "Editorial: Called to Declare Praises for God." *Pasugo* 56(8):2-3.

Santiago, Myrna V.
    2001   "Haifa, Israel Becomes New Locale." *Pasugo* 53(3):27.
Santos, Wilfredo B.
    2002   "For Whom Is God's Salvation?" *Pasugo* 54(1):10-11, 31.
Sarol-Valdez, Michelle
    1999   "I Found the Way to God's Kingdom." *Pasugo* 51(10):26-27.
See, Alyssa
    1999   "Europe Celebrates 25th Year." *Pasugo* 51(1):28.
Serrano, Ricardo U.
    1964   "Brothers of Faith and Courage." *50th Anibersaryo 1914-1964*. Iglesia ni Cristo. 184-206. Quezon City: Iglesia ni Cristo.
Singer, Margaret T.
    1979   "Coming out of the Cults." On line. Internet. (Available from http://www.factnet.org/Margaret_Thaler_Singer/Coming_out_of_the_Cults.html.) Accessed December 14, 2009.
Sledge, Benjamin S.
    2001   "My Guide to Eternal Life." *Pasugo* 53(3):12.
Smith, Gordon
    2010   *Transforming Conversion: Rethinking the Language and Contours of Christian Initiation*. Grand Rapids, MI: Baker Academic.
Small, Larry
    2003   "God's Message Piqued My Curiosity." *Pasugo* 55(12):9.
Smith, Stephen Kent
    2001   "A New Beginning for All of Us." *Pasugo* 53(1):28-29.
Smulo, John
    n.d.   "Missional Apologetics" and "A Missional Apologetic Manifesto." On line. Internet. (Available from http://missionalapologetics.com.) Accessed September 15, 2007 and September 10, 2009.
Snee, Colin
    1999   "New Religious Movements and the Churches." In *New Religious Movements: Challenge and Response*. Bryan Wilson and Jamie Cresswell, eds. Pp. 169-180. New York, NY: Routledge.
Sta. Romana, Julita Reyes
    1955   "The Iglesia ni Cristo: A Study." *Journal of East Asiatic Studies* 4(3):329-430.
    1959   "The Iglesia ni Cristo." *The Sower* 1(3):36-42.
Stark, Rodney, and William Sims Bainbridge
    1987   *A Theory of Religion*. New Brunswick, NJ: Rutgers University Press..
Suarez, E.T.
    2002   "Officials Greet INC on 88th Year Today." *The Manila Bulletin*, July 26. On line. Internet. (Available from http://mb.com.ph/news.php?search=yes&sect=1&fname=MAIN/202-07/MN020726172615989o.text.) Accessed February 5, 2003.
Tam, M.
    2004   "Washington, D.C. Turns a Decade Old." *Pasugo* 56(1):5.
Tapales, Robert
    2002   "He Led Me to Truth." *Pasugo* 54(10):32-33.
Taylor, Harold
    2004   "Contextualized Mission in Church History." In *Encountering New Religious Movements: A Holistic Evangelical Approach*. Irving Hexham, Stephen Rost, and John W. Morehead, III, eds. Pp. 43-62. Grand Rapids, MI: Kregel.
Tennent, Timothy C.
    2007   *Theology in the Context of World Christianity*. Grand Rapids, MI: Zondervan.
Thawn, Sing Khaw
    2004   "Ethnographic Research Paper." Unpublished manuscript. Graduate paper for course on New Religious Movements taught by Anne Harper and Michael McDowell. Asian Theological Seminary, Quezon City, Philippines.
"The Christianization of Russia (988)"
    n.d.   On line. Internet. (Available from http://www.dur.ac.uk/a.k.harrington/christin.html.) Accessed September 27, 2009.
The Sunday Times
    2003   "INC Files Libel Charges against Ang Dating Daan's Eli Soriano. May 11. On line. Internet. (Available from http://manilatimes.net/national/may/2003/may/11/metro/20030511met1.html.) Accessed April 28, 2004.
Tiangco, Joseph Anthony Narcisco
    2005   "Understanding the Filipino Philosophy of Resilience: *Katatagang-Loob* [Emotional Strenght {sic}/Resiliency] and Its Phenomenological Considerations." In *Filipino Cultural Traits*. Rolando M. Gripaldo, ed. Pp. 57-57. Carlo R. Ceniza Lectures, Cultural Heritage and Contemporary Change Series, Southeast Asia, vol. 4. Washington, D.C.: The Council for Research in Values and Philosophy.
Tippett, Alan R.
    1977   "Conversion as a Dynamic Process in Christian Mission." *Missiology* 5(2):203-221.
Tkach, Joseph
    1997   *Transformed by the Truth*. Colorado Springs, CO: Multnomah Books.
Travis, John
    1999a   "The C1 to C6 Spectrum." In *Perspectives on the World Christian Movement*. Ralph D. Winter and Steven C. Hawthorne, eds. Pp. 658-659. Pasadena, CA: William Carey Library.
    1999b   "Must All Muslims Leave 'Islam' to Follow Jesus?" In *Perspectives on the World Christian Movement*. Ralph D. Winter and Steven C. Hawthorne, eds. Pp. 660-663. Pasadena, CA: William Carey Library.
Tuggy, Arthur Leonard
    1971   *The Philippine Church: Growth in a Changing Society*. Grand Rapids, MI: Eerdmans.

	1976	*The Iglesia ni Cristo: A Study in Independent Church Dynamics.* Quezon City: Conservative Baptist Publishing, Inc.
	1978	"Iglesia ni Cristo: An Angel and His Church." In *Dynamic Religious Movements.* David J. Hesselgrave, ed. Pp. 85-101. Grand Rapids, MI: Baker Book House.

Tuggy, Arthur Leonard and Ralph Toliver
    1972   *Seeing the Church in the Philippines.* Manila: OMF Publishers.

Turner, Harold W.
    1985   "New Mission Task: Worldwide and Waiting." *Missiology* 13(1):5-21.

Tzu, Lao
    c.600-531 BC   "Go to the People." In *Tao Te Ching (The Book of the Way).* On line. Internet. (Available from http://thinkexist.com/quotation/go-to-the-people-live-with-them-learn-from-them/348565.html.) Accessed April 26, 2010.

Uk, Lal
    2002   "A Research Paper on the Iglesia ni Cristo Worship Service." Unpublished manuscript. Graduate paper for course on New Religious Movements taught by Anne Harper and Michael McDowell. Asian Theological Seminary, Quezon City.

Van Rheenan, Gailyn
    2003   "Monthly Missiological Reflection #25: From Theology to Practice: The Helix Metaphor." On line. Internet. (Available from http://missiology.org/mmr/mmr25.htm.) Accessed May 2, 2009.
    2004   "Foreward." In *Encountering New Religious Movements: A Holistic Evangelical Approach.* Irving Hexham, Stephen Rost, and John W. Morehead, III, eds. Pp. 17-24. Grand Rapids, MI: Kregel.
    2006a   "Monthly Missiological Reflection #26: From Theology to Practice: The Helix Metaphor." On line. Internet. (Available from http://missiology.org/mmr/mmr26.htm.) Accessed May 2, 2009.
    2006b   "Monthly Missiological Reflection #34: From Theology to Practice: The Helix Metaphor." On line. Internet. (Available from http://missiology.org/mmr/mmr34.htm.) Accessed November 1, 2009.
    c.2007   "Monthly Missiological Reflection #39: From Theology to Practice: The Helix Metaphor." On line. Internet. (Available from http://missiology.org/mmr/mmr39.htm.) Accessed November 1, 2009.

Velasco, Eva, Gabriel Cabasada, and Anne Marie Sandoval
    2003   "Southern California Youths Take Lead." *Pasugo* 55(5):32.

Velasco, Eva, and Rosette C. Dawson
    2002   "Southern California Shares the Faith." *Pasugo* 54(11):32.

Villaneuva, Marichu and Christina Mendez
    1999   "President Apologizes to INC for Task Force Fiasco." *Philippine Star*, February 2, 1, 4.

VJ
    2003a   Personal interview with author. Transcript. Taytay, Rizal, Philippines, January 21.
    2003b   Personal interview with author. Transcript. Antipolo, Rizal, Philippines, April 1.
    2004a   Personal interview with author. Transcript. Taytay, Rizal, Philippines, February 4.
    2004b   Personal interview with author. Transcript. Cainta, Rizal, Philippines, May 20.

Wilson, Alex, and Christine Tetley
    1985   *Witnessing to the Cults: A Practical Study Guide for Christian Workers.* Parañaque City, Luzon, Philippines: Church Strengthening Ministry of Foreign Mission Board, SBC, Inc.

Winter, Ralph and Steven C. Hawthorne, eds.
    1999   *Perspectives on the World Christian Movement.* Third Edition. Pasadena, CA: William Carey Library.

Woodbury, Dudley J.
    1989   "Contextualization among Muslims: Reusing Common Pillars." In *The Word among Us: Contextualizing Theology for Mission Today.* Dean S. Gilliland, ed. Pp. 282-312. Dallas, TX: Word.

Yong, Amos
    2007   "The Spirit of Hospitality: Pentecostal Perspectives toward a Performative Theology of Interreligious Encounter." *Missiology* 35(1):55-73.

Zuñiga, Larni E.
    2002   "Ethnographic Research Paper." Unpublished manuscript. Graduate paper for course on New Religious Movements taught by Anne Harper and Michael McDowell. Asian Theological Seminary, Quezon City, Philippines.

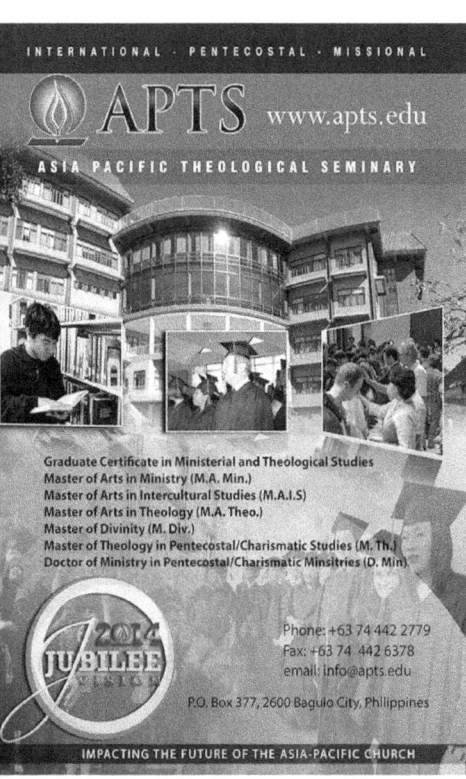

APTS Press Monograph Series Books 1 and 2

Theology in Context

In this book, Dave Johnson discusses a biblical response to Folk Catholicism in the Philippines. Specific topics include what the Bible says about:
- All Saint's Day and the dead returning to their gravesites
- How Filipinos have been transformed by the power of God within their own cultural setting
- Praying to Mary and the saints
- Demon Possession
- Town Fiestas
- Sickness and Healing
- And much more!

About the Author

Dave Johnson, D-Miss, has been an Assemblies of God (USA) missionary to the Philippines since 1994 and has conducted extensive research on lowland Filipino culture. He is also the author of Led by the Spirit: The History of the American Assemblies of God Missionaries in the Philippines and is the managing editor of the Asian Journal of Pentecostal Studies, the theological journal of the Asia Pacific Theological Seminary in Baguio City, Philippines. He can be contacted at www.apts.edu or through his own website, www.daveanddebbiejohnson.com.

Now available at:

ICI Ministries
2909 Raffles Corp. Center
Emerald Ave., Ortigas Center
Pasig City
Tel. (632) 914 9800

ICI Distribution Center, Valenzuela
BBC Compound, Gov. I Santiago St.
Malinta, Valenzuela City
Tel. (632) 292-8509/
294-6137/444-9139

APTS Bookstore
444 Ambuklao Road
Baguio City

For other locations please contact us at www.apts.edu.

NEW FROM APTS PRESS

LEAVE A LEGACY
Increasing Missionary Longevity

Russ Turney

In this second volume of the new APTS Press Monograph Series, Dr. Russ Turney presents a compelling case study of why some missionaries leave the field far too soon. Normal attrition occurs because of health problems, retirement, or the obvious call of God to go elsewhere. However, Turney notes that far too often missionaries leave due to interpersonal conflicts with their colleagues or nationals, problems with authority and other issues, that, Turney contends, could be significantly reduced. He then presents an excellent strategy for dealing with these and other issues, enabling missionaries to continue in their calling long term and finish well.

This strategy will help equip not only missionaries and mission leaders from both the West and the Majority World, but also pastors and church members who love and support missionaries and who want to learn how to strengthen them better through prayer and action. Anyone who shares the warm hearted conviction that missionaries can and should leave a legacy will benefit from this book.

Now available at:
APTS BOOKSTORE
444 Ambuklao Road Baguio City

Jet Bookstore
Porto Vaga, Session Road
Baguio City

ICI Bookstore
BBC Compound,
Malinta, Valenzuela City

Asia Graduate School of Theology Philippines (AGST)

Preparing Scholars and Leaders for the Church in Asia, the Pacific, and beyond.

Programs

Doctor of Ministry (D.Min.) in Peace Studies
Doctor of Missiology (D.Miss.)
Doctor of Education (Ed.D.) in Christian Counseling
Master of Theology - Doctor of Philosophy (Th.M.-Ph.D) in
  Theological Studies, Church History, and Biblical Studies (OT & NT)
Doctor of Philosophy (Ph.D.) in :
  - Intercultural Studies
  - Transformational Learning (Education)
  - Transformational Development
  - Holistic Child Development (HCD)
  - Peace Studies

Asia Graduate School of Theology (AGST) is a consortium of evangelical seminaries in the Philippines established by Asia Theological Association (ATA) in 1984:

Asia-Pacific Nazarene Theological Seminary
Asia Pacific Theological Seminary
Asian Seminary for Christian Ministries
Asian Theological Seminary
Biblical Seminary of the Philippines
Int'l Graduate School of Leadership
Koinonia Theological Seminary Foundation, Inc.
PTS College & Advanced Studies

54 Scout Madrinan St. Quezon City 1103, Philippines | Telefax: (63-2) 410-0312 | Email: agstphil@gmail.com | www.agstphil.org

www.ingramcontent.com/pod-product-compliance
Lightning Source LLC
Chambersburg PA
CBHW070315230426
43663CB00011B/2136